Religion, Intergroup Relations and Social Change in South Africa

Religion, Intergroup Relations and Social Change in South Africa

G.C. Oosthuizen
J.K. Coetzee
J.W. de Gruchy
J.H. Hofmeyr
B.C. Lategan

Work Committee: Religion
HSRC Investigation into Intergroup Relations

Pretoria
Human Sciences Research Council
1985

This report has been prepared by the Work Committee: Religion which was appointed on 30 November 1981 by the Main Committee of the HSRC Investigation into Intergroup Relations.

The report contains the joint findings, opinions and recommendations of the Work Committee: Religion, and in some instances, of individuals and groups on the Work Committee which dealt with matters about which there might be differences of opinion. The five authors are responsible for the report in its final form. The findings contained in this report do not necessarily reflect the opinions of either the HSRC or the Main Committee of the Investigation into Intergroup Relations, or of any official body. This report is regarded by the Main Committee of the HSRC Investigation into Intergroup Relations as a submission by the Work Committee. The viewpoints and recommendations of the Main Committee are contained in the final report prepared by the Main Committee.

HN
39
.S6
H77
1985

Work Committee: Religion
HSRC Investigation into Intergroup Relations

Director: Dr H.C. Marais

ISBN 0 7969 0256 9

First print: July 1985
Second print: April 1986
Printed by J.C. Instoprint

PREFACE

This report is the result of a scientific investigation into the many contentious issues which affect the lives of millions in this country. Those involved in its writing were concerned that such a document could easily deteriorate into detached analyses. This awareness, however, motivated them not to concentrate in the first place on what churches and theologians have said about intergroup relations, but on those who are most affected in the present circumstances. Much of the theological and church discussion that has taken place in the past has been far removed from the actual situation and these very discussions form part of the problem.

Those involved in the drawing up of the report were deeply disturbed by recent events in the country. These were a vivid and tragic confirmation of how real many of the issues which are discussed are. The report is therefore presented in the hope that it will contribute, in however small a way, towards a clearer understanding of the forces involved and towards a better future in this troubled land.

We would like to thank all those who made this report possible, especially the following:
● The researchers who undertook the research for the different projects in the field of religion
● The members of the Work Committee: Religion for their invaluable advice and support
● The Main Committee, and particularly the director, Dr H.C. Marais and his staff for their untiring efforts and encouragement throughout the project.

The Authors
March 1985

PREFACE TO THE SECOND IMPRESSION

The public interest in the findings of the Main Report of the HSRC Investigation into Intergroup Relations and its subreports (released in July 1985) was such that it necessitated the reprinting of this subreport on religion after six months. We are grateful to share the results of this research with a wider audience.

Apart from minor typographical corrections, the first impression is reproduced here unchanged.

The Authors
February 1986

TABLE OF CONTENTS

ii

CHAPTER 1

INTRODUCTION

THE AIM OF THE REPORT

This report on the significance and role of religion with regard to intergroup relations in South Africa today is not an attempt to provide a comprehensive account of the religious situation. Its terms of reference were provided by the HSRC Investigation into Intergroup Relations of which it is a part. Nevertheless, because religion is such a central factor in human and intergroup relations, not least in contemporary South Africa, this limitation has allowed immense scope for research and reflection. For several reasons listed below the report cannot claim to be exhaustive or to be based upon research which has covered the total field of enquiry. At the same time however, it does claim to provide an introduction and insight to the main issues and concerns which are central to the problem of religion and intergroup relations in South Africa. Its point of departure is that of the science of religion. It is not written to justify any particular religious or theological viewpoint, but simply to lay evidence on the table and to come to an understanding of the role and significance of religion in human relations. In order to understand better both the contribution and the limitations of the report, we begin with a brief history of its inception and development.

A BRIEF HISTORY OF THE REPORT

In many ways the history of the report reflects the extremely complex nature of group relations in South Africa, revealing both the difficulties and challenges of the situation. In line with the general approach of the HSRC Investigation into Intergroup Relations, an "open" approach was adopted from the outset. By this is meant that even at the basic level of the demarcation of possible research areas and themes, the aim was to be as non-directive as possible. To prepare the ground for the project, the Director, Dr H.C. Marais of the HSRC, invited a core group of representatives from the universities and the various churches

1

to join in a round of informal discussions during 1981. The main task entrusted to the group was to make a preliminary survey of the problem areas related to intergroup relations in the field of religion and to suggest possible people to serve on a Work Committee: Religion. Subsequently, the following persons accepted the invitation to form the work committee, and to take responsibility for initiating and supervising research for this part of the project:

Prof. G.C. Oosthuizen (Chairman (UD-W); Prof. C.J. Alant (UNISA); Prof. D.J. Bosch (UNISA); Prof. G.D. Cloete (UWC); Prof. C.W. Cook (RhU); Prof. J.W. de Gruchy (UCT); Prof. J.J.F. Durand (UWC); Dr F. Edwards (RhU); Dr B. Goba (UNISA); Rabbi I. Goss; Prof. J.A. Heyns (UP); Prof. M.P. Krishna (UD-W); Prof. B.C. Lategan (Co-ordinator) (US); Prof. S.S. Maimela (UNISA); The Rev. Jan Mettler, Dutch Reformed Mission Church; Prof. B. Spoelstra, Hammanskraal Theological School; Prof. T.D. Verryn (UNISA).

The committee met for the first time on June 21, 1982 and compiled the following list of possible research themes:

1. Religiosity in South Africa

This theme can be researched on at least three levels:

a. The function of religion in general.
b. Description of the present situation in terms of religion and religious communities.
c. Trends and statistics.

1.01 Empirical studies on the distribution of religious communities in South Africa.
1.02 The concept of civil religion.
1.03 The effect of social structures on ecumenical co-operation and *vice versa*.
1.04 The role of the church in mobilising groups — an historical and contemporary perspective.
1.05 The religious community as pressure group within society and *vice versa*.

2. The function of religious communities in South Africa

2.01 The dynamics of interaction within and between religious communities, with special reference to e.g. confessional differences, intolerance, prejudice, etc.
2.02 Tension between the need for contextualisation and the danger of loss of identity as religious group.

3. Pluralism as religious phenomenon

3.01 Pluralism as religious phenomenon on both intergroup and intragroup level. e.g. with regard to race, generation, denomination, class, caste, etc.

3.02 Challenges to established religious authority — the phenomenon of dissent.
3.03 Discrepancy between the self-perception of a specific religious community and the group interests of its membership.

4. Relationship between church and state (confer theme 1 and note b)

4.01 Various models of church and state relations.
4.02 Communication between church and state.
4.03 Religion and politics.
4.04 Attitudes of religious communities towards involvement in the greater South African predicament.

5. Ideology and religion in South Africa

5.01 Marxism and religion.
5.02 Nationalism and religion.
5.03 The relationship between ideology and religion.

6. Religion and economic aspects

6.01 Economic justice from a religious perspective.
6.02 Religion as an agent of development.
6.03 The relationship between economic conditions and forms of religiosity in society.

7. The role of religion in motivating socio-political action e.g. attitudes towards violence, passive resistance and civil responsibilities

8. Concepts of man in South Africa

8.01 Human rights.
8.02 Race.
8.03 Personal identity (self-perception).

9. Methodology of the study of religion

9.01 Various analyses of society, for example marxist, nationalist, etc.
9.02 The relationship between a normative and a descriptive approach.

10. Religion and change

10.01 Religion and rapid social change in South Africa.
10.02 The impact of the oikumene (the world) on South Africa.

The committee took sole responsibility for identifying these themes. At no stage did the HSRC or any other body prescribe certain topics or eliminate others. There were only two provisos. First, the research had to contribute to the description or explanation of the nature and processes of intergroup relations in contemporary South Africa. Second, the methodological approach to be followed in each individual project had to be stated clearly and the research had to comply with accepted scientific standards. It was explicitly stated that the list of themes was not meant to be exhaustive and researchers were invited to submit additional proposals. Information concerning the project was distributed to the research community in the form of a brochure and every attempt was made to reach all potential researchers.

Thirteen major research tenders were submitted and by March 1983 the following ten had been approved by the committee:

Prof. D. Crafford (UP)	Pluralisme as religieuse verskynsel: Die onafhanklike Swart kerke en bewegings in Suid-Afrika en groepverhoudinge.
Prof. J.S. Cumpsty (UCT) Dr J.H. Hofmeyr	The role of religion in motivating or inhibiting socio-political action in the lower socio-economic group and ensuing counter influences upon the religious group.
Dr D.A. Du Toit (US)	Menseregte: 'n empiriese en teoretiese ondersoek vanuit teologies-etiese perspektief.
Miss J. Grobbelaar (UNISA)	Die verband tussen kerk en identiteit met betrekking tot die ''Kleurling-Griekwa'' bevolking in Griekwaland-oos.
Dr J.J. Kritzinger (UP)	'n Statistiese beskrywing van die godsdienstige verspreiding van die bevolking van Suid-Afrika.
Prof. B.A. Müller (US)	Die openbare verkondiging van die Kerk as medium van verbetering en verandering van tussengroepverhoudinge.
Dr L.M. Muntingh (US)	'n Ondersoek van die religieuse Joodse en die Moslem-gemeenskappe binne 'n oorwegend Christelike gemeenskap in Suid-Afrika insoverre dit tussengroepverhoudinge bepaal.

Dr K. Nürnberger (UNISA)	The interaction between economic power relations and patterns of conviction in the South African society seen in the light of a Christian ethic.
Prof. G.C. Oosthuizen (UD-W)	a. Religion and inter- and intragroup relations in a pluralistic religious context of a South African city b. The effects of South African Chinese religious trends in a puralistic society.
Prof. P.J. Robinson (UWC)	Die gemeenskapsrol van die NG Sendingkerk met spesiale verwysing na tussengroepverhoudinge.

It was one of the specific aims of the committee to promote research within an intergroup context. By this is meant the ideal, wherever possible, of engaging researchers from different backgrounds and with different perceptions of the South African situation to work together on the same project. In two cases, that of Oosthuizen and Müller, it was possible to make use of such a team. In this way, the basic research itself became an exercise in intergroup relations. The work of these two projects benefitted greatly from the reciprocal control inherent in such an approach and it is highly recommended for future work in this field. However, the work committee did not succeed in being as fully representative as it would have liked. During the course of the investigation, Profs Cloete, Maimela, and Dr Goba resigned from the committee, while Prof. Verryn's untimely death was also a great loss. Towards the end of the project Prof. J.K. Coetzee (UOFS) and Dr J. H. Hofmeyr (UCT) were invited to join the committee.

A deadline for submitting completed research was set for August 31, 1984. The individual reports were subsequently evaluated by members of the committee, with requests for alterations and additions where necessary. An editorial committee consisting of Profs Coetzee, De Gruchy, Lategan, Oosthuizen, and Dr Hofmeyr was established to oversee the collation and organization of material for the compilation of this report.

The majority of the projects focused on specific situations (e.g. in Durban and the Cape Flats), which did not necessarily reflect trends in the country as a whole. In order to obtain data on a county-wide scale, the HSRC conducted a multipurpose survey during August 1983, in which 4 000 respondents from all different groups participated (cf Main Report). In this survey a substantial number of questions relating to religion were included. The data collected from this source formed the basis of a report by Prof. J.K. Coetzee (Religie as inisieerder, begeleier en inhibeerder van sosiale verandering) and was used substantially in the compilation of this report.

One fact which became clear during the early stages of the investigation was that there are virtually unlimited opportunities for research in the field of religion. When the original list of themes is compared with the completed research, it is obvious that only some aspects of a vast field have been covered. This report should therefore be seen partially as an exploratory venture, pointing to areas in urgent need of further research. The work committee supplemented the original reports with material drawn from other existing sources. At best, it hopes to have highlighted the forces at work in the field of religion which influence intergroup relations most directly and to have pointed out the dangers and opportunities inherent in the situation.

Devising a framework for this report was a difficult task because of the methodological variety and breadth of scope of the commissioned material. On the one hand it was felt that the integrity of the original research should remain intact, yet on the other it was necessary to select and condense from this material in order to give the final report co-herence. In the end the following approach was settled on:

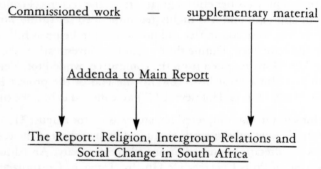

The addenda provide a ready reference to the more important findings of the major commissioned survey-based research. The value of the original work is that it includes much detail which could not be included in the final report. We therefore refer the reader to the original material to evaluate and check on the use that has been made of it in this report.

FURTHER LIMITATIONS OF THE REPORT

While the report is based on research which we regard as more than adequate for the conclusions at which we have arrived, as the history of the report has indicated we were unable to muster all the resources which would have been needed for an exhaustive study. We were, for example, dependant upon the participation, interests and research of those who volunteered to assist us. As a result there are important gaps in the research done for the report. For example, there is a predominance of research on the role of religion in urban areas and comparatively little in rural areas. Yet, the urban areas are clearly crucial for the purposes of this study and we were greatly aided by the fact that a research team led by Prof. G.C. Oosthuizen (UD-W) focussed on the Durban metropolis with its intensely varied religious composition, while another led by Prof. J.C. Cumpsty (UCT) focussed on the situation within the Coloured community in Athlone, Cape Town.

The committees' awareness of the research gaps led it to look beyond some of the research specifically commissioned for its work. This was felt to be necessary otherwise the report would have lacked the comprehension it has now managed to achieve. The criteria for consulting and including the results of other research were strictly determined by the most evident gaps, by the scientific reliability of the material, and by its appropriateness for the overall concerns of the report.

Certain other limitations should be noted. Chief among these is the composition of the work committee, as well as the research teams and individual researchers. With regard to the latter, no persons representing what might be called the very conservative or very radical wings were willing or able to participate. And, despite considerable effort to include people of diverse backgrounds and even radically opposed positions within the work committee, in the end it was composed of members who were in a large measure of agreement on both the issues to be studied and on the conclusions to be drawn from the research reports. This has undoubtedly influenced the shaping of the final report. Nevertheless the committee is of the opinion that while the report is not the work of a group which is fully representative of the South African reality, it is sufficiently broadly based to represent a significant consensus on the issues at stake.

Of course, it might well be asked whether it is at all possible given the present situation in South Africa to muster a team of research workers and a committee which would be fully representative. It might also be asked whether such a group could function. Indeed, the seriousness of the HSRC project on Intergroup Relations is highlighted by this very fact, and it is exacerbated by the divisive and even conflictual nature of much religious commitment. To a certain degree then, the report itself is indicative of the problem to which it addresses itself.

The last mentioned problem is an indication of the fact that however much the committee may have striven for objectivity, and that has certainly been an important element in its work and that of the researchers involved, there is ultimately no neutral position on the kind of issues with which the report deals. On the contrary, each of those involved, however much they have sought to be objective, has a particular perspective and position on the questions at hand.

The overall perpective of the work committee emerges most clearly in the section where we discuss the social role and significance of religion within the South African context. In anticipation, let it be said that there was consensus within the committee that the present intergroup situation in South Africa is critical, and that unless such relations are dramatically improved even more tension and conflict will result. There was also consensus that sound or healthy religion should promote good interpersonal and intergroup relations. In this latter role religion may often be critical of society, since one of the most important functions of religion is to uphold ideal standards and values. However, though it produces social tension in its critical function, the rationale for religion is the healing of social relations.

From a scientific point of view perhaps the most serious problem with which the committee has had to deal is that of methodology. All those familiar with the contemporary state of social scientific research will be aware of the intense debate on method which has dominated the discipline during the past few decades. The committee itself was deeply conscious of the issues involved when both setting the project in motion and in evaluating and collating the various research reports. It is inevitable that a diverse group of researchers, including theologians, sociologists and others involved in the scientific study of religion, should differ in some respects in their approach to their task. Theologians, for example, generally work from the perspective of a faith commitment whereas for many social scientists who have such a commitment it is by no means necessarily normative for their research. Moreover, there are various schools of social science, each with its own methodological approach. The committee kept all this in mind in evaluating each research project and in incorporating its findings in this report, aware that in doing so it was itself taking a particular stance on the work submitted.

In terms of what we have set out to do, limitations such as these we have mentioned, most of them inevitable in a research project of this kind, do not detract from the research which has been done and the conclusions to which this work has led us. On the contrary, we believe that by highlighting certain key issues and religious forces at work in our context the overall intergroup situation has been clarified, and tendencies which both facilitate and hinder group relations have been identified. Because of the nature of religious affiliation in South Africa, and the powerful though ambivalent social role which religion in its various dimensions plays, it is a vital aspect in group relations as a whole.

RELIGION: ITS SOCIAL ROLE AND SIGNIFICANCE

It is notoriously difficult to provide a comprehensive and satisfactory definition of religion. Yet, a working definition is clearly needed if we are to have a common basis for discussing its role in intergroup relations. Fortunately, a broadly common understanding of what religion ought to be seems to have emerged in the research done for this report. While not a definition, it provides a basic framework from within which the nature and actual functions of religion in South Africa can be understood.

SOME ESSENTIAL ELEMENTS AND FUNCTIONS OF RELIGION

Religion is most clearly recognizable as one among many other institutions in society. It may even be argued that there is no such thing as religion in general, but only particular religions and religious groups as exemplified in the religious institutions. Yet, when we survey the various forms of religion there appears to be a factor which, in a broad sense, runs through all of them. Briefly, religion is supposed to be that which places life as a whole into some sort of perspective: it gives ''meaning'' to life. History suggests that the attempt to achieve a general orientation to life flows spontaneously out of human nature. This being so, the elements of religion can be defined to be simply that in any society upon which people draw in the attempt to develop a sense of what life or reality are about. A religious group is then one in which people share in and actively express such a sense of reality. When such a group forms, we have institutionalized religion.

Clearly, in the above view the viability of any particular religion will depend on its being adapted to life's circumstances. No matter how abstract the formulations of a religious system might be, it will only have relevance to its adherents if they feel it to be congruent with their general experience of life. There is therefore, an inextricable process of interaction between the elements of religion on the one hand and the life-experiences of religious people on the other. A constant interplay takes place as each is shaped by and adjusted to the other.

For our purposes there are three among the many elements of a religion which it is important to highlight. They are:

- The beliefs (or perhaps even only vaguely articulate feelings) about what reality/creation is like. In most of the great historical religious traditions this manifests in part in beliefs about some sort of ultimate and perhaps transcendant being.

- The behaviours which stand as an attempt to express an adequate response to the above-mentioned sense of reality. These may be directly expressed in ritual forms of worship, but also indirectly in terms of the general "pattern" according to which life is lived.

- The symbols which give concrete expression to the convictions and attitudes embodied in the above two elements. As such, religious symbols combine a truth value component with a motivational component. They both symbolize reality and motivate responses to it.

Because religion is such a dynamic phenomenon it is sometimes difficult to recognize what its elements are in any particular society. To the early missionaries, for example, it was not always obvious what counted as religion in Africa, nor is it always obvious where religion is to be found today in the developed societies of the West. Yet, if being religious is natural then this difficulty has more to do with our preconceptions concerning what ought to be part of a religious system than with the actual lack of it. Usually, it is our familiarity with the existing and recognizable religious institutions which blinds us to the existence of new or alternative ones.

Ideally, the institutional religions ought to be the source of the elements of religion. When they are, they provide an easily identifiable social context in which people appropriate what the religion has to offer. When they fail however, people draw on whatever else may be available as the means to express their religiosity. It is precisely the latter process which lies behind much of the dynamic history of religion. It is a history which has seen the great religions undergoing constant adaptation and change in their concrete expression. New religious movements have emerged and existing religions have faltered and died out, sometimes after being dominant in a culture for hundreds of years. This dynamic can be a primary cause of the difficulty of recognizing where religion is in a particular social and historical setting. It is in fact the history of religion which stands as the clearest evidence that the forms of a religion must be related to the life-experiences of those it serves.

ASPECTS OF THE RELATION OF RELIGION TO SOCIETY

In theory, it is important to recognize that the lack of a clear definition of religion sometimes makes religion difficult to measure or observe. When institutional religion fails to be the motivator it ought to be, then measures of religiosity based on it will fail to provide a true gauge of religious activity. Yet, for practical reasons, it is the existing and recognizable religious groups which have to form the starting point when we study the social role of religion.

In terms of the ideal functions of religion, institutional religions ought to be the main guide as to the social values which determine any society's structure. Their teachings ought to be the influence according to which people in that society place themselves in a social context and from that position, relate to everything else. In terms of their actual functions however, institutional religious groups seldom conform to the above standards. They cannot avoid being affected by the socio-historical context in which they are situated. Even the forms by which they identify and express themselves are related to and drawn from the environment of which they are a part. Instead of being the independant motivators of human activity they are supposed to be, they often fall subject to or become determined by the forces which surround them. For these reasons among others, the social role of religion has often been understood in a reductionistic way. Yet, to reduce the activity of religion to a function of its environment is to oversimplify what is in fact a highly complex and dynamic relationship. Religion is both shaped by and a shaper of society and its social role cannot be understood unless attention is paid to the full dynamics of this interrelation.

Religious symbols are a vital element in religiously motivated activity. When they are at work their importance lies in their dual function. On the one hand, they express the understanding or feeling that people have about reality as a whole. As such, they represent religious truth, albeit in a highly concentrated form. On the other hand, they come to be associated via their use, with powerful motivational feelings. In this way they represent, in just as concentrated a form, religious values. These two functions, when wrapped together in the effective religious symbol, constitute an extremely potent combination. Arguments as to whether religion or the environment are primary are irrelevant under these conditions. Understanding the concentration of motivational power in the religious symbol, its ability to move the group, and the consequences for society at large are far more important. It is for this very reason that the exercise of religion can have profound consequences on intergroup relations in a heterogenous society. Moreover, it is for this reason that a proper understanding of the functions of religion is so central to understanding intergroup relations in South Africa.

THE AMBIVALENCE OF RELIGION IN ITS SOCIAL CONSEQUENCES

Religious symbolism play an important role in the successful institutional religion.

11

At best, religious symbols can become a binding factor in society, creating a common focal point for defining social values and objectives. Within the framework of values they establish it can become possible for social debate to take place in a constructive way, using the religious matrix as a touchstone for conciliation. This "utopian" situation seldom occurs however. Though religion can provide a rallying point for the members of a society, it can also be profoundly divisive. At this point it begins to make sense to speak of religion, not in purely abstract terms as one set of mechanisms or one kind of phenomenon among others in society, but in terms of its value to society. In the history of all the great religious traditions periods are to be seen in which religion has played a profoundly destructive role. It makes sense therefore to speak of religion as healthy or sick and to attend seriously to the factors which lie behind its going bad or promote its going well.

In a heterogeneous society like that of South Africa there is almost an inevitability about religion functioning in a divisive and destructive way. Because of its claims to ultimacy and the strength of commitment which accompanies it, religion contains the seeds of division. There are fundamental differences between the beliefs and values of the great religious traditions. Even within the great traditions severe differences of understanding can occur. When these differences are coupled to the intense feelings which go with real religious commitment, serious schisms and divisions develop in the society and it may fall apart. Thus, while religion ought to provide general values around which a society can unite, unfortunately it often has the opposite effect. At worst, religion can become the fundamental motivation behind open and violent intergroup conflict.

In view of its potentially divisive character, it may well be argued that religion is antithetical to good human relations, especially in a multi-religious society. In a basic way the mere attempt to win converts for a particular religion can prove to be severly destructive of social life. The logical conclusion to this argument is that if we are to promote good human relations in South Africa we should either get rid of religion or force everyone to belong to the same religion. Perhaps we ought to hope that the potential atrophy of institutional religion described above actually takes place. A fourth alternative would be the development of a "civil religion" which binds everyone together irrespective of their traditional religious differences. One of the indications that South Africa has reached a critical phase in intergroup relations however, is the fact that research shows none of these options to be immediately viable or perhaps even possible (See Chapter 3).

One of the most destructive forms that religion can take in is that in which it becomes allied to the interests of a particular group to the exclusion of others. Then it may be misused to legitimate injustice and the abuse of power, leading to the dehumanization of individuals and groups. As the research reflected in this report will show, this has already happened to a significant degree in South Africa. Yet, even here there is an inevitability about the way in which this undesirable phenomenon is built into the nature of religion itself. Because religion finds expression in the context of life's experiences, it undergoes inevitable adaptation to reflect the particular life-circumstances of the social group or class for whom it is functioning to provide meaning. In this way, a common religious tradition with a common pool of symbols can receive expression in fundamentally different and even incommensurate ways when adapted to the circumstances and needs of the different groups it serves in a society. This is especially true of a society whose structure is as highly stratified as is that of South Africa. Coetzee has drawn attention to the way in which this process can then result in religion being used by those in positions of privilege to legitimate their position while for those for whom the society is seen to be unjust religion legitimates the need for change (Addendum I:6). In fact, the mobilization of religion by opposing groups in this way is one of the most fundamental ways in which religion can come to be an initiator of social change for some while being a way of resisting social change for others.

The harmful potentials described above and often seen in the functions of institutional religion are not, we believe, of the essence of religion. Nevertheless the history of the role that religious groups have actually played in different societies and at different times alerts us to its ambivalences. One of the basic tasks of this report is the attempt to understand these processes better and to suggest how they might be contained.

CRITICAL ISSUES

Thus far we have dealt in general terms with the nature and associated problems of religion and intergroup relations with only a few indications as to the situation in South Africa. It is essential now that we become more specific and introduce the major critical issues with which the report deals. Though each of these is dealt with in detail in the body of the report, a brief introduction at this stage is appropriate in order to provide an overview that will enable the reader more easily to see the report in its entirety. The fact of the matter is that each of the issues is related to the others, so that while they may be described apart they really need to be seen as parts of a whole.

CONFLICTING PERSPECTIVES

South African society is in a state of flux. There are conflicting trends, for example, greater polarization between blacks and whites coupled with well-meaning attempts to bridge the gaps between the conflicting groups. As the largest religion in South Africa, it is inevitable that Christians and therefore the churches and their members will be deeply involved, whether they like it or not, in the unfolding social drama. To a considerable extent, the drama is being played out within the church itself. The mainstream western churches have come to play an increasingly significant role in the articulation by many Blacks of the struggle for justice. Among white Christians, significant numbers are using the church in both trying to change and to maintain the *status quo*. Yet a third group, including many among the fast growing Black Indigenous churches, appear to have set aside the attempt to give active expression to their religious ideals in terms of conventional political activity.

Traditionally South African society has been very divided between different groups of people. This means that present divisions run deep in the social history of the country. These divisions have almost invariably been justified or exacerbated by religious claims and commitments, a phenomenon which remains true today. Consider, for example, the fact that there are many within the church in South Africa today who, in affirming obedience to God, advocate disobedience to certain laws of the land which they regard as unChristian. Yet there are many others who believe that Christians should obey the state absolutely and without question. Similarly there are those Christians who support revolutionary forces, those who believe that the state is an exemplary guardian of Christian civilization, and many shades of opinion between these extremes. All the religious groupings in South Africa and especially Christians are often radically divided in their perception and analysis of the social situation. In the public eye this has been most clearly demonstrated in the controversy surrounding the declaration by some churches that apartheid is a heresy.

If human and social relations deteriorate further in South Africa it is conceivable that the growing escalation of conflict between groups could eventually result in something akin to civil war. Given the social composition of South Africa such a development would mean that Christians would be at war with one another. This is precisely the situation which obtains in Northern Ireland and the Middle East where religion and group interests have become coterminous. Thus, when we speak about the role of religion in human relations in South Africa we are dealing with a vital issue in which the stakes are high. In view of this it is imperative that the use of religion in general and Christianity in particular to defend group interests be transcended. As has been indicated above this will be no easy task. However, a difference has to be established between the normative claims of a religion and the use that is often made of it to legitimate specific group interests. In this sense it has become a fundamental task in South Africa to de-ideologize and de-absolutize religion in the way that it is interpreted by any one group. Such an exercise need in no way impinge on the universalistic claims of the various religions, for it involves simply the attempt to free religion from a too narrow association with the particular life context and needs of any one group.

RELIGION AND SOCIAL JUSTICE

At the centre of intergroup conflict is the perception by groups that they are being unjustly treated. While such a perception may be wrong or distorted, that does not make the sense of being wrongfully treated any less real for those involved. Thus, in addressing the problem of social justice it is essential that a proper analysis be made of the social situation in order to ascertain who is being unjustly treated and in what way. This is not a straightforward task as there are significant differences of opinion as to what constitutes social justice. How justice is defined is often dependent upon who defines it. In a situation in which those in power have a different perception of what constitutes justice by contrast with those without power this becomes highly problematical. For the latter a fundamental shift in the existing power relations is often seen to be the minimum requirement in the move to justice.

While we are fully aware of the immense difficulties involved, and of the gap between religious ideals and reality, it is nonetheless true that the major religious traditions do provide important and fundamental resources for determining what justice means and what it should entail. For example, all the major religious traditions teach a social ethic that transcends particular group interests. According to the Judeo-Christian tradition, social righteousness or justice is inseperably bound up with faith in God and is regarded as essential for the health and well-being of society.

For the purposes of this report we have pinpointed three inter-related issues regarding social justice in South Africa which are of particular urgency at this time and of central importance for intergroup relations. These are: (i) Human rights, (ii) Economic justice, (iii) The problem of violence. Each of these is dealt with in the report in Chapter 4, but it is important that their relevance for the report and their interconnection be stressed at this point.

On the basis of the evidence which we have, it is clear that there are serious flaws within the present social structure of South Africa with regard to both human rights and economic justice. At the heart of the problem are the tensions generated by racial, class, and other group differences and prejudices. For too long specific group interests, especially those of the Whites, have determined the shape of human rights and the distribution of wealth. As long as this continues to be the case, intergroup relations in South Africa will continue to be conflictual rather than constructive. Moreover, the more such injustice prevails the more it engenders polarization, frustration, and a desperation which results in violence. Many Blacks in South Africa regard the present social structures as themselves inherently violent, so that many would regard a violent response as entirely legitimate. Such a view is particularly strong among young Blacks, but it is not confined to them. We are firmly committed to the view then, that without a new dispensation of social and economic justice which is not based on race, intergroup relations in South Africa will continue to deteriorate and become increasingly violent.

RELIGION AND SOCIAL CHANGE

In South Africa religion functions both to promote and resist change. Particularly within the White community it functions to legitimate resistance to social change while for many Blacks it is used to sanction opposition to the *status quo*. From a Judeo-Christian perspective as well as that of other religious traditions, just social change in unjust situations is concomitant with basic religious values and with a concern for social justice. Clearly, the particular way in which religion might be used to promote a more just social order must be adapted to the particular concerns, hopes, and fears of the various groups in South Africa. Its role will therefore vary according to the particular circumstances and needs of each community. Unless this is taken into account even the most well-meaning attempts to promote justice may go seriously wrong. In conclusion, the following points are of particular importance:

● Just as religion is so often tied up with particular group interests, it also has the potential to enable groups to transcend those interests for the sake of the common good of the whole society. Fundamental to this process is the need to de-absolutize the religious legitimation of particular group interests.

● Through their teaching and preaching as well as their communal life, religious institutions are able to provide social cohesion and hope for those who are underprivileged and relatively powerless so that they are not only able to retain their dignity as human beings but also able to find the strength to work for change. Similarly, religious institutions should be able to help those who fear change to see both the need for just change and its relation to that which gives meaning to life and hope for the future.

● Given the predominance of Christianity in South Africa, it has an important role to play in providing a common vision for a new and more just society. While such an ideal may always be beyond realisation in practice, it can at least provide norms by which change can be guided. In this process, the non-Christian groups and those whose position is unknown like the Black Indigenous churches ought to play a significant role. Religious leaders of all kinds have a special responsibility to contribute to the improvement of human relations in South Africa. In the ultimate analysis however, intergroup relations are intimately connected with the desire for and access to power of those involved (Addendum I:1). To the extent that those in positions of power are Christian therefore, the Christian tradition in particular has a responsibility to ensure that South Africa becomes a more just society in which conflict can be overcome.

CHAPTER 2

THE PATTERNS OF RELIGIOUS AFFILIATION AND EXPECTATION IN SOUTH AFRICA

INTRODUCTION

As the empirical point of departure for this report on the role of religion in intergroup relations we turn to the patterns of religious affiliation and expectation in South Africa. With regard to religious affiliation, an important source of information is that of the national census conducted in 1980. A project to investigate this material was funded by the Work Committee: Religion and the results reported in Kritzinger, 1984. The pattern of expectations emerged in two nation-wide multi-purpose surveys conducted by the HSRC during 1983. Many of the questions dealt with the role that South Africans expected religious movements to play in South Africa. They were analysed and formed the basis of an extensive report (See Addendum I). In this chapter we summarize the more important findings.

RELIGIOUS AFFILIATION IN SOUTH AFRICA

The 1980 national census divided South Africa into seventy-one statistical regions. Three "independant states", namely Transkei, Bophuthatswana and Venda were included as separate geographical units. In certain respects, the census is a crude measure of religious affiliation. For example, in some cases it is clear that respondents gave incorrect information. In others, there were insufficient categories of response to allow for a proper differentiation of religious affiliation. Nevertheless, it provides a global overview of religious affiliation in South Africa.

A regional breakdown of religious affiliation across South Africa is given in table 2.1. Four features of these statistics stand out. First, 77,0 % of South Africans claim at least nominally to be Christian. Second, the largest single

Table 2.1
Religious composition of the total population (percentages and numbers in thousands)

Religion	Cape %	Natal %	OFS %	Transvaal %	Ciskei %	Gazankulu %	KaNgwane %	KwaNdebele %	KwaZulu %	Lebowa %	Qwaqwa %	Transkei %	Bophuthatswana %	Venda %	Total Duisende	Total %
Dutch Ref.	26,1	4,7	30,6	14,8	3,8	1,6	1,9	5,8	1,0	4,0	24,1	1,8	9,2	2,6	3 676	12,5
Ref.	0,3	0,9	0,7	1,1								0,2	0,5	1,4	146	0,5
Herv.	0,2	0,4	0,6	2,6								0,1	0,1		249	0,8
Angl.	11,0	7,1	5,2	6,2	5,3	0,4	0,6	1,9	5,0	1,5	5,7	12,3	6,8	0,6	2 040	6,9
Meth.	10,3	8,1	13,9	7,7	26,8	0,4	2,5	1,3	6,8	1,5	8,9	25,8	12,4	0,3	2 978	10,1
Presb.	2,0	2,3	2,5	1,6	6,2	2,5			1,8	1,0	4,4	5,4	0,8	0,3	646	2,2
Congr.	4,1	0,3	0,3	0,6	4,3	0,6	0,6	1,9	1,5	0,2		1,0	3,9	0,9	467	1,6
Luth.	2,0	2,6	1,1	3,6	1,0	0,6	0,6	1,9	4,9	7,1		1,4	12,4	7,2	1 045	3,6
R.-Cath.	7,5	12,0	10,4	9,0	4,7	3,3	3,7	5,1	14,4	7,4	9,5	7,7	8,9	2,3	2 701	9,2
A.F.Miss.	1,1	0,2	1,6	0,7	0,6	0,6		1,3	0,3	0,2		0,4	0,3	0,3	191	0,7
Other Apost.	0,4	0,3	0,6	1,0								0,1	0,2		132	0,4
Independent Black	9,7	14,7	17,1	22,2	23,3	20,2	55,3	53,2	31,9	24,7	16,4	11,4	28,6	15,4	5 857	19,9
Other	12,1	7,6	4,9	9,6	7,5	10,7	9,9	12,2	4,4	4,6	9,5	7,3	10,7	6,4	2 475	8,4
Total Christian — N	4 419	1 635	1 728	6 744	567	207	121	132	2 467	913	139	1 968	1 432	130	22 603	
Total Christian — %	86,8	61,1	89,4	80,8	83,6	40,3	75,2	84,6	72,1	52,3	88,0	75,0	94,8	37,7		77,0
Jewish	0,7	0,3	0,1	0,9											119	0,4
Hindu	0,1	17,5		0,4											512	1,7
Islam	3,1	3,4		0,8					0,1						319	1,1
Other	0,8	1,2	0,3	0,6	0,3	0,6			0,6	0,8	0,6	11,2	1,9	8,4	522	1,8
Unknown (including Black Traditional)	8,5	16,7	10,2	16,5	16,1	59,1	23,6	15,4	27,2	46,8	9,5	13,8	3,2	53,6	5 285	18,0
Total Non-christian — N	672	1 041	204	1 607	111	307	40	24	955	834	19	655	79	215	6 762	
Total Non-christian — %	13,2	38,9	10,6	19,2	16,4	59,7	24,8	15,4	27,9	47,7	12,0	25,0	5,2	62,3		23,0
TOTAL — N	5 091	2 676	1 932	8 351	678	514	161	156	3 422	1 747	158	2 623	1 511	345	29 365	
TOTAL — %	100,0	100,0	100,0	100,0	100,0	100,0	100,0	100,0	100,0	100,0	100,0	100,0	100,0	100,0		100,0

Source: Kritzinger, 1984:9.

religious groupings are those of the Black Indigenous churches (19,9 %) and a large "unknown" one (18,0 %). Third, 51,4 % of South Africa's population does not belong to any one of the mainstream western Christian churches. Finally, even though the numbers in some cases are small, most of the world's great historical traditions are represented.

The largest conventional western church grouping in Southern Africa is that of the Dutch Reformed (NGK) tradition which represents 12,5 % of the population. Methodism follows with a proportion of 10,1 %. Neither of these groupings is unified however, the first being divided on racial lines and the second, a multi-racial church but divided by the Transkei break-away in the late 1970s. The largest multi-racial and unified church in South Africa is therefore the Roman Catholic Church (9,2 %).

A further breakdown of religious affiliation in racial terms is useful as an aid to interpreting the results (See table 2.2). Christianity dominates in most of the racial groups with proportions in excess of 74 %. Among the Indians, Hinduism predominates (62,4 %) with Islam second (18,8 %). The largest proportion of the "unknown" group is that among Blacks. This suggests that what we have in this group are mostly people who identify more closely with Black African traditions than with conventional Christianity.

Certain regional features of table 2.1 are worth noting. First, the only general grouping relatively well-represented in all the regions is that of the Black Indigenous churches. In certain areas, KaNgwane (55,3 %) and KwaNdebele (53,2 %), this grouping constitutes an outright majority. Another religious grouping with a significant following is that of the Black Traditional group. In Venda they constitute a large portion of the 53,6 % of the "Unknown" category as well as in the case of Gazankulu's 59,1 %.

It is important when considering these statistics to bear in mind that the Black Indigenous and Traditional groupings do not constitute united religious bodies. Nevertheless, in terms of their features it makes empirical sense to combine them loosely into a whole which differs significantly from the rest. In certain sociological respects they are like groupings.

CHURCH AFFILIATION AMONG THE BLACK ETHNIC GROUPS AND GROUP AFFILIATION WITHIN THE CHURCHES

In table 2.3 the distribution of church affiliation across the conventional Black ethnic groups is given while in table 2.4 the population distribution is given within each of the major churches. When census data are presented in this more

Table 2.2

Religious composition of the main population groups (percentages and numbers in thousands)

Religion	Whites	Coloureds	Indians	Blacks
Dutch Ref.	37,4	26,0	0,5	6,5
Ref.	2,8			
Herv.	5,4			
Angl.	10,1	13,5	1,1	4,7
Meth.	9,1	5,4	0,5	9,2
Presb.	2,8		0,2	2,1
Congr.		6,5		1,2
Luth.		3,7	0,1	4,1
R-Cath.	8,7	10,1	2,6	9,9
A.F. Miss.	2,8	1,9		0,7
Other Apost.			2,8	
Independent Black		4,5		29,3
Others	12,5	15,6	4,7	6,3
Total Christian	91,8	87,0	12,5	74,1
Jewish	2,6			
Hindu			62,4	
Islam		6,3	18,8	
Other	0,6	1,2	1,5	0,6
Unknown (including Black Traditional)	5,0	5,5	4,9	25,3
Total Non-christian	8,2	13,0	87,5	25,9
TOTAL (N)	4 528	2 613	821	16 924

Source: Kritzinger, 1984:22

detailed way, errors of measurement become important. Mainly, the census failed to distinguish between essentially different denominations which share the same name. Thus, the group portrayed as Presbyterian actually represent at least four different churches. There are similar problems involved in the inclusion of Methodists, Lutherans, and Baptists under single headings. Nevertheless, certain conclusions can be drawn.

Table 2.3

Religious composition of the Black ethnic groups (percentages and numbers in thousands)

Religion		Xhosa	Zulu	Swazi	South Ndebele	Nguni group	North Ndebele	North Sotho	South Sotho	Tswana	Sotho group	Shangaan Tsonga	Venda	Other	Sub-Total	Total
Dutch Ref.	N	223	126	35	26	409	20	113	359	346	838	28	17	8	53	1 300
	%	4,0	2,2	4,1	6,6	3,3	7,7	4,8	20,6	12,1	11,6	2,8	3,1	7,6	3,2	6,1
Angl.	N	522	249	19	11	801	9	52	116	224	401	12	6	5	22	1 224
	%	9,3	4,4	2,3	2,8	6,4	3,3	2,2	6,7	7,8	5,6	1,2	1,1	4,2	1,3	5,7
Meth.	N	1 314	409	43	12	1 778	9	49	206	352	616	15	4	6	26	2 419
	%	23,4	7,2	5,0	3,1	14,2	3,4	2,1	11,8	12,3	8,5	1,5	0,8	5,7	1,6	11,3
Presb.	N	283	104	4	2	392	1	27	49	23	99	20	2	3	25	516
	%	5,0	1,8	0,4	0,5	3,1	0,3	1,1	2,8	0,8	1,4	2,0	0,4	2,5	1,5	2,4
Congr.	N	97	80	10	5	192	1	7	7	85	99	2	3	1	6	297
	%	1,7	1,4	1,1	1,4	1,5	0,5	0,2	0,4	3,0	1,4	0,2	0,6	0,9	0,4	1,4
Luth.	N	61	262	20	11	354	9	193	16	319	537	17	38	1	57	948
	%	1,1	4,6	2,3	2,8	2,8	3,5	8,2	0,9	11,1	7,4	1,7	7,1	1,3	3,5	4,4
R.-Cath.	N	374	739	60	22	1 195	19	185	272	243	720	70	19	18	107	2 022
	%	6,7	13,0	7,0	5,6	9,5	7,3	7,9	15,6	8,5	10,0	7,0	3,6	16,3	6,5	9,4
A.F.Miss.	N	36	27	8	7	77	11	11	24	19	57	4	2	7	7	141
	%	0,6	0,5	0,9	1,8	0,6	1,2	0,5	1,4	0,7	0,8	0,4	0,3	0,6	0,4	0,7
Independent Black	N	1 039	1 903	411	184	3 537	86	617	390	851	1 944	230	104	28	361	5 842
	%	18,5	33,5	48,1	46,9	28,2	32,4	26,3	22,4	29,7	26,9	23,1	19,3	25,4	22,0	27,3
Other	N	416	283	82	49	830	19	112	95	164	390	105	36	6	147	1 367
	%	7,4	5,0	9,6	12,4	6,6	7,2	4,8	5,5	5,7	5,4	10,5	6,8	5,3	9,0	6,4
Total Christian	N	4 365	4 182	692	329	9 565	176	1 364	1 534	2 626	5 701	503	231	77	811	16 076
	%	77,8	73,6	81,0	83,8	76,3	66,4	58,1	88,0	91,6	78,9	50,5	43,2	70,6	49,5	75,1
Other religions	N	15	36	7	2	59	3	17	7	9	36	7	2	5	13	108
	%	0,3	0,6	0,8	0,5	0,5	1,0	0,7	0,4	0,3	0,5	0,7	0,3	4,2	0,8	0,5
Unknown (including Black Traditional)	N	1 232	1 464	156	62	2 914	86	967	202	232	1 486	487	302	28	817	5 218
	%	22,0	25,8	18,3	15,8	23,2	32,3	41,2	11,6	8,1	20,6	48,9	56,5	25,6	49,8	24,4
Total Non-christian	N	1 247	1 500	163	64	2 973	89	984	209	241	1 522	494	304	33	830	5 326
	%	22,2	26,4	19,0	16,2	23,7	33,6	41,9	12,0	8,4	21,1	49,5	56,8	30,4	50,5	24,9
TOTAL	N	5 610	5 683	854	392	12 539	265	2 348	1 742	2 868	7 223	996	535	109	1 640	21 402
	%	100,0	100,0	100,0	100,0	100,0	100,0	100,0	100,0	100,0	100,0	100,0	100,0	100,0	100,0	100,0

NOTE: For the purposes of this table the total populations of Transkei, Bophuthatswana and Venda are considered as respectively Xhosas, Tswanas and Vendas
Source: Kritzinger, 1984 : 24

Table 2.4

Population components of the main religious groups (percentages and numbers in thousands)

Religion		Whites	Coloureds	Indians	Blacks	Total N	Total %
Dutch Ref.		48,7	19,5	0,1	31,7	3 478	100,0
Ref.		63,5	3,9	0,3	32,3	202	100,0
Herv.		89,2	1,0	0,4	9,4	276	100,0
Angl.		28,3	21,8	0,6	49,4	1 613	100,0
Meth.		19,6	6,6	0,2	73,6	2 113	100,0
Presb.		25,8	1,5	0,4	72,3	499	100,0
Congr.		5,8	41,8	1,2	51,2	407	100,0
Luth.		4,7	11,5	0,1	83,7	835	100,0
R.-Cath.		16,7	11,2	0,9	71,2	2 356	100,0
A.F. Miss.		41,5	16,1	0,9	41,5	303	100,0
Bapt.		29,3	6,3	1,2	63,2	255	100,0
Christian	N	4 157	2 273	103	12 541	19 074	
	%	21,8	11,9	0,5	65,7		100,0
Islam	%	0,7	49,8	47,0	2,5	328	100,0
TOTAL	N	4 528	2 613	821	16 924	24 886	
	%	18,2	10,5	3,3	68,0		100,0

Source: Kritzinger, 1984:34

With respect to table 2.3, significant differences are shown between the Black ethnic groups as regards religious affiliation. The Indigenous churches and the Traditional groups are the only ones which are generally well-represented. The Traditional group is particularly strong among the North Sotho while the Indigenous churches are particularly strong among the Zulu and Tswana. Methodism and the NGK in Africa are the only churches beyond the Indigenous churches with a large proportion among any group, the first among the Xhosa and the second among the South Sotho. The Anglican Church is an important proportion of the Xhosa while the Roman Catholic Church is an important proportion of the Zulu and South Sotho.

Turning now to table 2.4 the statistics suggest that Blacks dominate all but the Afrikaans churches in terms of numbers. However, this ignores the fact that many of the churches are divided in a significant way among themselves. For example, Lutherans and Baptists have separate and autonomous synods, one White and the other Black. In one case, that of the Congregationalists, the figures are misleading in that the largest grouping of Congregationalists i.e. the United Congregational Church, contains a majority of Coloureds, not Blacks. The general pattern of affiliation indicates however that the Black constituency in Christianity, whether conventional or unconventional, is by far larger than that of any other group.

URBAN AND RURAL DIFFERENCES

The difference between urban and rural areas is significant with regard to religious affiliation. The rural areas have significantly fewer church affiliated people than the urban population, mainly because of the 3,26 million Blacks in the rural areas who still adhere, more or less, to the traditional religion. Another 0,75 million are found in the "independant states". Thus, 4 of the 10,4 million Black rural inhabitants do not belong to a Christian church.

In the cities five of every six people claim to be associated with a church. All the churches have the majority of their members in the cities. Of the main racial groups, only the Blacks (62 %) are still predominantly rural. However, urbanization is proceeding rapidly among this group which raises the question as to how it will affect trends in their pattern of religious affiliation. The growth of the Indigenous churches in the urban areas has been strong to date. Whether this will continue is an important question.

TRENDS IN AFFILIATION

The most interesting trends are those relating to growth. The proportional membership for 1960 and 1980 of a range of churches relative to the total population of South Africa can be seen in table 2.6. All but three have decreased as a proportion of the total population. The exceptions are:

● The Black Indigenous churches which have become the largest Christian grouping in South Africa.

● The Roman Catholic church which has been growing steadily among all but the Indian groups.

● What the census calls "Other Churches". What exactly these are we cannot say. Their growth suggests a certain measure of disillusionment with the conventional churches.

In all, the statistics present a sobering picture. The religious groups with the highest socio-political profile in South Africa are those of the more conventional churches and more recently Islam (See Muntingh, 1984). Yet they represent the minority of South Africans. Close to 50 % of South Africans have no religious voice in the public domain.

Table 2.5
Religious composition of the total population, as distinguished between urban and rural (percentages and numbers in thousands)

Religion	Whites		Coloureds		Indians		Blacks	
	Urban	Rural	Urban	Rural	Urban	Rural	Urban	Rural
Dutch Ref.	35,4	53,0	18,9	49,4	0,5	0,6	5,8	7,0
Ref.	2,6	4,5						
Herv.	5,0	8,7						
Angl.	10,6	5,9	15,4	7,0	1,1	0,6	7,0	3,3
Meth.	9,6	5,3	5,4	5,2	0,5	0,8	13,0	6,8
Presb.	3,0	1,5			0,2	0,2	2,8	1,7
Congr.			6,6	6,3			1,4	1,1
Luth.			3,0	5,8	0,1	0,3	4,6	3,8
R.-Cath.	9,4	3,5	11,4	5,9	2,7	1,5	11,0	9,2
A.F.Miss.	2,7	3,0	1,8	2,1			0,6	0,8
Other Apost.					2,8	3,1		
Indigenous Black			4,4	5,1			29,8	28,9
Other	12,9	9,9	18,0	7,6	4,6	5,7	7,7	5,4
Total Christian	91,2	95,3	84,9	94,4	12,4	12,7	83,7	68,1
Jewish	3,9	0,2						
Hindu					61,6	70,2		
Islam			8,1	0,1	20,0	7,6		
Other	0,6	0,3	1,4	0,5	1,5	1,1	0,5	0,6
Unknown (including Black Traditional)	5,2	4,1	5,7	5,0	4,5	8,4	15,7	31,2
Total Non-christian	8,8	4,7	15,1	5,6	87,6	87,3	16,3	31,9
TOTAL N	4002	526	2002	610	744	78	6480	10444
%	100,0	100,0	100,0	100,0	100,0	100,0	100,0	100,0

Source: Kritzinger

Table 2.6

Religious composition of the total population, 1960-1980 (percentages and numbers in thousands)

Religion	1960 N	1960 %	1970 N	1970 %	1980 N	1980 %
Dutch Ref.	2 289	14,3	3 006	13,8	3 676	12,5
Ref.	124	0,8	154	0,7	146	0,5
Herv.	217	1,4	258	1,2	249	0,8
Angl.	1 403	8,8	1 716	7,9	2 040	6,9
Meth.	1 707	10,7	2 307	10,6	2 978	10,1
Presb.	321	2,0	578	2,7	646	2,2
Congr.	291	1,8	395	1,8	467	1,6
Luth.	651	4,1	949	4,4	1 045	3,6
R.-Cath.	1 076	6,7	1 898	8,7	2 701	9,2
A.F.Miss.	198	1,2	219	1,0	191	0,7
Other Apost.	299	1,9	712	3,3	132	0,4
Bapt.	152	1,0 .	247	1,1		
Indigenous Black	2 313	14,5	2 716	12,5	5 857	19,9
Other	684	4,3	1 271	5,8	2 475	8,4
Total Christian	11 727	73,3	16 427	75,4	22 603	77,0
Jewish	115	0,7	118	0,5	119	0,4
Hindu	328	2,1	430	2,0	512	1,7
Islam	191	1,2	260	1,2	319	1,1
Other	9	0,1	29	0,1	522	1,8
Unknown (including Black Traditional)	3 617	22,6	4 530	20,8	5 285	18,0
Total Non-christian	4 261	26,7	5 367	24,6	6 762	23,0
TOTAL	15 988	100,0	21 794	100,0	29 365	100,0

THE ROLE OF RELIGION IN SOUTH AFRICA: THE EXPECTATIONS OF SOUTH AFRICANS ACCORDING TO THE MULTI-PURPOSE SURVEY

The multipurpose survey conducted by the HSRC during 1983 tested the opinions of South Africans on a wide variety of topics in relation to religion e.g. its importance, the validity of the involvement of religious movements in socio-political processes, etc. The results of the survey form the most reliable basis that we have for estimating the social role that South Africans themselves think religious movements ought to play. They were analysed in great detail by Coetzee from which the summary below has been taken (See Coetzee, Addendum I).

ESTIMATES OF THE IMPORTANCE OF RELIGION

We have defined religion in a way which indicates that it should be of fundamental importance to everybody. Empirical surveys often show however that religious membership plays little role in the social behaviour of respondents. In order to measure the importance which South Africans themselves assign to religion, the following questions were asked:

● What role does religion (church or synagogue or temple or mosque, etc.) play in your life?

● What role has a religious movement (church, synagogue, temple or mosque, etc.) played to change your opinions or beliefs?

● What is the influence in general of religious movements (church, synagogue, temple or mosque, etc.) on South African society?

A composite result for these questions was computed (Addendum I: Data 2). Of the four race groups, the highest proportion who rate religion as important or very important occurs among the Coloureds (68,6 %). The Indians follow (62,6 %), then the Blacks (59,5 %), and finally the Whites (50,4 %).

An analysis of the responses of the four groups to the specific question about the general influence of religious movements in South African social life highlights certain other factors (Addendum I: Data 1). In contrast with the relatively low precentage of Whites who rate religion as important, a much higher proportion of them rate the influence of religious movements highly (79,5 %). The corresponding percentages for the other groups are: Coloureds (75,9 %), Indians (70,5 %), and Blacks (61,5 %).

The results confirm that religion is seen to be important rather than unimportant. Yet, while a relatively small proportion of Whites rate religion as important on the composite measure, a far larger proportion rate the social influence of religious movements as important. Coetzee explains this by suggesting that the lower measure reflects the low importance that religion is assigned in the personal lives of individual Whites. The higher measure on the other hand reflects the perception of Whites that the structure of South African society is Western and incorporates institutionalized western religions as an integral and therefore influential part. The low proportions of Blacks and Indians who agree that religious movements have social influence may reflect the disjunction between the religious movements of these two groups and South Africa's dominating western environment (Addendum I).

Results obtained in the South African Social Values Survey conducted by Markinor (1982) shed further light on the above figures. In the Markinor survey, large proportions in all the groups indicated that they may be religious in terms of the ideal definition of religion. The majority (85 %) indicated that they ask what we take to be a basic religious question i.e. that as to the meaning of life; and an even larger proportion (90 %) indicated that they practice what we take to be a basic religious activity i.e. that of praying or meditating (Markinor, 1982, p. 51 and 64). These figures do not give a measure of the religious intensity of those who responded. However, they contrast dramatically with the figures obtained for certain of the more conventional measures of institutional religiosity. According to Markinor for example, low proportions among the Black (52 %) and the English-speaking white (48 %) groups agree that the church has adequate answers to the moral problems and needs of the individual. In these two groups the proportions which believe that the church has adequate answers to "man's spiritual needs" are 59 % and 60 % respectively (1982, p. 66). In the latter group, 66 % express the opinion that there is no one true religion (1982, p. 60). In the Black, Coloured and Asian groups, relatively large proportions sometimes or often have the feeling that life may be meaningless (35 %, 41 % and 45 % respectively) (1982, p. 51). The only group in which the proportions consistently favour conventional Christianity are the Afrikaans-speaking White group.

While no one measure is decisive, we take the cumulative results reported above to indicate that though religion is important to most South Africans, for many of them the established conventional religious movements are not fulfilling their ideal functions. The fact that Whites indicated a low importance for religion in their personal lives in the HSRC survey may mean then that conventional religion is unimportant, rather than that religion itself is unimportant. Yet, the measures are not conclusive. It provides a classic example of the importance of measuring religiosity in a way which is not dependant on the conventional measures which institutionalized religion provides.

THE SOCIO-ECONOMIC EFFECTIVENESS OF RELIGION

We have suggested strongly that religion at best is intimately related to the general life-experience and context of the people for whom it provides meaning. Religious movements evoke support when members perceive them to be meeting their needs. This, in turn, is related to members' personal and collective circumstances. Ample illustrations of this exist in the history of religion. The general relation between forms of Christianity and socio-economic levels is but one example.

In the multipurpose survey a range of questions was asked concerning the socio-economic effectiveness of religion. Among the statements for which respondents' opinions were elicited were the following (See Addendum I: Data 3-6):

3. Religious movements mean little if they do not contribute to the basic needs (e.g. food and clothing) of all the people in South Africa.

4. Religious movements can do little to solve general social and economic problems.

5. Various religious movements should co-operate more to change South African society.

6. Theme: Socio-economic effectiveness of religion.

There is a general consensus among all the groups that religion ought to make a contribution to the basic needs of all South Africans though the proportions differ significantly between groups. It is lowest among Whites (52,1 %) and highest among Blacks (69,3 %). As Coetzee suggests (Addendum I), these results indicate the greater likelihood that a respondent who lacks the material goods will believe that one of the functions of religion should be to supply these goods.

It is one thing to believe that religious movements should fulfil a socio-economic function however, and quite another to believe that they are capable of doing so. This contrast is represented in the differences between data 3 and 4. With the exception of the Coloured group, the results indicate a "pessimistic shift". It is marked among the Indians and particularly significant among the Blacks. In the latter group, 63,7 % agree that religious movements can do little to solve social and economic problems. The results indicate that many South Africans, particularly Blacks, do not think that religious movements in general are able to fulfil the social and economic role expected of them.

THE ROLE OF RELIGION IN THE STRUGGLE FOR STRUCTURAL CHANGE AND JUSTICE

There are many aspects of the sociopolitical organization of South Africa which cause considerable hardship and suffering to South Africans, particularly to people who are not White. As was indicated in chapter one, it is our view that religion provides one of the fundamental resources for pinpointing what is wrong with existing social structures. As we also indicated however, religion on this score tends to be ambivalent. Those in positions of privilege tend to understand and express their religion in a way which legitimates existing social structures. It is mostly those who are under-privileged and who feel oppressed who can be expected to agree that religious movements ought to play a role in changing social structures (Addendum I).

The ambivalence of religion has an important consequence for the relationship between the ideas of social change and justice. Those in positions of privilege may well agree that religious movements ought to be involved in the promotion of justice, yet they may not agree that social changes are needed for that purpose. Coetzee points out that religious movements and their leaders can play an influential role in this regard (Addendum I). By specifically connecting the pursuit of human rights and justice to aspects of the social structure, the debate on what justice and human rights mean can be sharpened and brought to public attention. In South Africa this has been done by a wide variety of religious leaders across a broad political spectrum.

In the multipurpose survey a variety of measures were used to test this issue. In order to measure the attitude of South Africans to the role of religious movements in structural change, what Coetzee calls ''structural liberation'', the following statements were grouped (Addendum I: Data 9-16):

9. Religious movements must do everything they can to eliminate discrimination in society.
10. The practising of religion can never be separated from care for the poor of all population groups.
11. The practising of religion can never be separated from the care of the suppressed in all population groups.
12. A religious movement should take a stand against racial discrimination.
13. A religious movement should always act against laws that affect the lives of its members.
14. A religious movement can even condone violence when people's rights and human dignity are restricted.
15. Religious movements should encourage their members to protest peacefully against injustice.
16. Theme: Religion and structural liberation.

Attitudes to the involvement of religious movements in the promotion of social justice, were measured by the following group (Addendum I: Data 17-21):

17. Social justice should be the most important item in the work of religious movements.

18. Religious movements should always oppose all forms of suppression.

19. It is acceptable that religious movements act as advocates for the rights of all people (human rights).

20. Religious movements that continuously keep themselves busy with equal rights for various groups are not busy with their real task.

21. Theme: Religion and social justice.

As Coetzee notes, there are some dramatic differences between the White responses and those of the rest to these items. Only 31,4 % of the Whites agreed that a religious movement ought to make a stand against racial discrimination. The proportions for Blacks, Coloureds and Indians by contrast were 66,9 %, 66,5 %, and 61,8 % respectively. On the question of a religious movement taking action when laws such as the race laws harm the lives of its adherents, the proportions which agreed were as follows: Whites 41,0 %, Blacks 61,4 %, Coloureds 65,8 % and Indians 59,7 %. The most dramatic result is that on the question of the use of force. In both the Black (53,3 %) and the Indian (48,0 %) groups, the largest proportions were those who agreed that a religious movement could approve of violence when human rights were infringed (Addendum I: Data 12-14). This result is supported by further statistics obtained in the multi-purpose survey. In answer to a question as to whether the use of violence was legitimate to achieve political objectives 45,3 % of the Blacks responded that it was (HSRC Surveys, MPS/OV/56-59 and MPS/OV/71-74).

When the statements become more general, the gap between the different groups begins to close. The majority in all of the groups agreed that religious movements ought always to take a standpoint against all forms of oppression: Whites 52,5 %, Blacks 66,5 %, Coloureds 75,8 %, and Indians 66,8 %. Similarly, the majority in all groups agreed that religious movements ought to defend the rights of all people: Whites 53,0 %, Blacks 56,8 %, Coloureds 66,2 %, and Indians 62,7 %. Relatively speaking, the White proportions on these questions are still quite low. But the wide discrepencies observable in relation to questions which have to do with discrimination are not present (Addendum I: Data 19 and 20).

The results illustrate clearly the differences that exist between the perceptions and expectations of those who are under-privileged and those in positions of privilege in South Africa. Each expresses its expectations concerning the role of religious movements according to a fundamentally different pattern. Blacks, Coloureds, and Indians expect religious movements to work for structural liberation and to promote justice. Whites by contrast are not against religious movements promoting justice and opposing oppression, yet they are against religious movements being involved in the elimination of racial structures. The majority of Whites apparently do not see the present social structures of South Africa to be incommensurate with human rights. The importance of these figures is twofold: First, they illustrate the extent to which Whites differ from the rest in their perception of the South African situation. Second, they confirm the way in which the abstract concepts of justice and human rights are given specific meaning in terms of the way that people are orientated within their social setting.

RELIGIOUS MOVEMENTS, SOCIAL CHANGE, AND TRADITION

In South Africa with its highly polarized socio-political character, there is a danger that the full complexity of the relation of desired social structures to the concepts of human rights and justice will not be appreciated. Though only obliquely, two further measures obtained in the multipurpose survey are important in this regard. Respondents were asked for their opinions on the following statements (See Addendum I: Data 7 and 22):

7. A religious movement should help in limiting changes in society.
22. A religious movement should not get itself involved in politics (e.g. apartheid or integration).

Except for the Whites, the majority in all the groups agreed that religious movements ought to help to limit social change: Whites 26,3 %, Blacks 70,1 %, Coloureds 48,5 %, Indians 55,5 %. In response to the second question, the majority in all the groups agreed that a religious movement should not get involved in politics: Whites 79,9 %, Blacks 58,1 %, Coloureds 60,3 %, and Indians 60,8 %. Once again it is important not to minimize the differences between Whites and the rest. Yet, in comparison with the figures obtained for the items on discrimination, these results may seem surprising. Coetzee suggests that responses to the item about social change might reflect the belief in the Black, Coloured, and Indian groups that religious movements ought to uphold traditional values (Addendum I). In other words, the traditional role religion is expected to play in these societies is conservative. For many Whites on the other hand, the way that institutional religion has stood in the way of change in the past has led to its conservative function being partially discredited — hence the White response. Fundamentally therefore, this apparently paradoxical result may reflect the character and importance of contemporary tradition in all four of the groups. In all four, religious movements are expected to conform or to relate to traditional values in a particular way.

In suggesting the above interpretation it is vital to note that we are not imply-
ing that respondents have contradicted themselves. Clearly, the Black, Coloured,
and Indian groups do not see their preference for the conservative function of
religion to be incommensurate with the need for structural liberation. What
is suggested however, is that whatever changes are advocated, traditional values
remain important. In these groups therefore, the promotion of human rights
appears to involve both structural liberation and the preservation of tradition.
The two aspects are not seen to be incompatible.

In spite of the lack of information, it is possible to make certain observations
in regard to responses to the second item about political involvement as well.
The very high percentage of Whites who agree that religious movements should
not be involved in politics indicates a certain sensitivity in this group to the sociopolitical functions of religion. Given the overall pattern of their responses, this
is not a surprising result. On the other hand, the large proportions in the other
groups who are against political involvement on the part of religious movements
suggests that there may be a tension in their expectations of religion. On the
one hand they expect religious movements to oppose race legislation, on the
other they do not agree that religious movements should be involved in politics. This is an issue to which we shall return.

THE ROLE OF RELIGIOUS MOVEMENTS IN UNITING THE POPULATION GROUPS OF SOUTH AFRICA

In the present critical state of intergroup relations in South Africa, the potential
of religion to play a conciliatory role may be a crucial factor. The results discussed above indicate clearly the extent to which Whites are out of step with
the other groups in their perception of the South African situation and expectations of religious movements. As we have indicated however, this is one of the
ways in which religion actually tends to function ambivalently. Its divisive potential appears to be just as great as its conciliatory potential. In a multi-religious
society like that of South Africa this divisiveness is enhanced. In the multipurpose survey, responses to the following two statements indicated how South Africans feel on this issue (See Addendum I: Data 23-25):

23. Organised religious movements should try to bring the different population groups
closer together.
24. Religious movements in South Africa should try harder to bring the various population groups with the same faith closer together.
25. Theme: Religion and reconciliation.

As with most of the other issues, the perception of the role of religion among Whites differs markedly from that of the other groups. According to the composite measure, only 46,4 % of the Whites agree that religious movements ought to a bring the population groups together. This compares with 57,4 % of the Indians, 79,7 % of the Coloureds, and 84,3 % of the Blacks.

The result is perfectly explicable in the light of the policy of separate development. The majority of Whites agree with separate development and for many, particularly the Afrikaner, this extends to seperation in the church. In other words, in this group, bringing the different groups together is not a means by which religious movements can fulfil their consiliatory role! Yet, for the other groups, even though less so for the Indians, the two functions appear to be much more closely interrelated. A further statistic provided by the multipurpose survey lends support to this view. Whereas only 20,1 % of the Whites agreed that South Africans would co-exist in peace if allowed to mix freely, the proportions for the other groups were all in excess of 70 % (HSRC Surveys, MPS/OV/56-59 and MPS/OV/71-74). The result is a stark indication of the intergroup differences that run through South African society. It is difficult to imagine that the majority in all groups would not agree that religious movements ought to play a conciliatory role. Yet, here we see that the population groups differ fundamentally in the way that they expect religious movements to fulfil this function.

CONCLUDING REMARKS

The statistics presented in this chapter provide some vital guidelines for understanding the potential role of religion in South Africa. With respect to the population census the most important phenomenon has been the growth of the Black Indigenous churches. What is most significant about this grouping is that it has no established representation in the social or political arena. Various attempts to "appropriate" the Indigenous churches have been made by people on both sides of the present polar political divide in South Africa. There are indications however that the Indigenous churches themselves are beginning to organize as an independant Christian grouping in Southern Africa. Until that happens, no-one can truly claim to "speak for" them. The absence of religious representation in the sociopolitical arena extends to many other religious groups. The high-profile groups, both pro- and anti-establishment, represent fewer than half of South Africa's population.

Turning to the multipurpose survey, the statistics confirm that the general sense of urgency expressed in chapter one is not unfounded. Deeply entrenched differences of perspective on the situation in South Africa are reflected in the different pattern of expectations among the groups. This is especially true of the way that the Whites differed from the rest. On the whole, the different expectations that each group has of religious movements are explicable in terms of what we know about South Africa. Yet, a curious tension emerged in the expectations that the groups other than White expressed. Whereas most of them agreed that religious movements ought to promote structural liberation, large proportions disagreed with the involvement of religious movements in politics. This apparent anomaly provides a pointer, we believe, beyond the pattern of expectations. For, it is one thing to expect that religious movements should fulfil certain functions, but quite another for the movements concerned to attempt to do so or, in attempting, to succeed. It is also one thing to agree that a religious movement ought to behave in a certain way, but quite another to be prepared to participate in that behaviour. These distinctions are important for they relate to the difference between the ideal and the actual functions of religion. It is now to an attempt to understand the processes by which religion actually appears to be functioning in South Africa that we must direct our attention.

CHAPTER 3

CONFLICTING PERSPECTIVES: RELIGION IN A HETEROGENEOUS SOCIETY

INTRODUCTION

We have seen that South Africans belong, in nominal terms, to a great variety of different religions. We have also seen that they hold a varied and to a certain extent explicable range of opinions about what the role and relevance of religious movements ought to be. However, the significance of these features of the South African religious situation can only be made clear in the context of a more general description of intergroup processes and the actual role of religion in them. As a point of departure we turn to one of the more prominent features of the situation i.e. the use of Christianity to support fundamentally different perspectives on the South African social situation.

THE USE OF RELIGION TO ARGUE CONTRARY SOCIOPOLITICAL POSITIONS IN SOUTH AFRICA

Given the motivational power of the effective religious symbol we need hardly press the point that there is a potential for conflict in any multi-religious society. This potential is exacerbated when religious dividing lines are coupled to others like those of race or class. Then we get a "sectarian" situation where the religion of a group plays an active role in legitimating its particular social and political orientation. The above conditions presently apply to South Africa. Recently a marked shift of religious symbolism to the center of public debate has taken place. Religious argument has featured prominently for example, in the split between the so-called "verlig" and "verkramp" elements among the Afrikaners.

With the election of Dr A. Boesak to the presidency of the World Alliance of Reformed Churches and the declaration of apartheid as a heresy a third faction has been brought to public notice. Involved here are the contrary perspectives of the Black and Afrikaans historical churches. The award of the Nobel Peace Prize to Bishop Tutu has further highlighted this polarity. In combination with the widespread rejection of the New Constitution the above factors have given a high profile to the role of religion in public debate. Religious symbolism, particularly that of Christianity, has become central to the expression by different groups of their hopes and fears for South Africa.

AFRIKANER CIVIL RELIGION

The term "civil religion" refers to a situation in which symbols with a religious power play an essential role in the expression of political positions. These symbols need not derive from a religious tradition. What is important however is that they do the work that religious symbols typically do, that is to say, that they link values to perceptions of reality and that they have motivational power.

In recent studies, the term "Afrikaner civil religion" has gained some currency in the analysis of Afrikaner nationalism (See for example Bosch, 1983). It refers to a situation in which there was a congruence between the religious attitudes encouraged by the NGK on the one hand and Afrikaner nationalism on the other, especially as represented by the Nationalist Party. Afrikaans analysts appear to agree that the foundations for this connection were laid back in the 1870's with the early stirrings of Afrikaner nationalism (Bosch, 1983, p. 16 and 22). Developments during and after the second Anglo-Boer War accelerated this process, especially the treatment of Afrikaans civilians in the British concentration camps and the "anglicization" policies followed by Lord Milner. By the 1940's the process appears to have been complete with the NGK in essential agreement with the policy of apartheid.

There have been elements of Afrikaner Nationalism which have aimed at the political and economic domination of South Africa and the elevation of the Afrikaner to a place above all other groups (See Wilkins, I. and Strydom, H., 1978, p. 349-351). No such oppressive intention appears to have been behind the position of the NGK however. Analysts may show that the NGK position tied in with its specific interests. Yet the fact remains that many of the churchmen allied themselves to Nationalist policy because they believed the demands of Christian responsibility and the facts of the situation warranted it.

Kinghorn has brought together the beliefs and sentiments which lay behind the Afrikaner Churches' best intentions at this time (1984). They are worth repeating here briefly. In 1942 we find local anthropologists expressing the following views:

38

". . .each nation has. . .a separate nature, possibilities and destination. . . The Native can only reach this destination if he receives the correct guidance from the higher-developed White. . . The fact that Whites are, at least spiritually, superior to non-Whites, is universally accepted and verified by scientific research. . . Therefore the Afrikaner nation not only has the right, but also the obligation, to take on the leadership of this country."

(Quoted in Kinghorn, 1984, p. 5)

Earlier in the same piece the writers expressed the view that Afrikaner actions must be led by Christian morality and that the "Christian-national view of life" should serve as the basis for any solution.

Further quotations come from Van der Walt and Viljoen. According to the former ". . .under a dispensation of fully-fledged apartheid, the native can realize himself fully" (Kinghorn, 1984, p. 8). To the latter, the *goal* of apartheid was the ". . .development, advancement, upliftment. . ." and extension of ". . .greater rights and privileges. . ." to the Black (Kinghorn, 1984, p. 9). Both saw the policy of apartheid as the means to provide Blacks with a context in which they could be both free to rule themselves and free from White political and economic domination. Moreover, *both argued this in the context of a Christian critique of the way that Blacks were being treated by Whites.*

There is an unsavoury paternalism in these pieces. Yet, as Kinghorn points out, the basis for these views was the belief in racial superiority and guardianship, a sense of White responsibility to the Black rooted in Christian compassion! The intentions of all those who implemented government policy were almost certainly not as honourable as those of the churchmen. However, the two fell together, forming a potent ideological combination backed by a strong definition of Afrikaner identity. Central to this definition was the notion of the Afrikaner as a nation of God's elect. The detachment that the church needs to remain alert to abuses by the state of its power, disappeared. The process of identity formation involved poets, philosophers and outright ideologues. Religion played a crucial role in it, especially in the way it was used to "mythologize" Afrikaner history. (See Bosch, 1983 for a more detailed analysis of these developments).

In South Africa today we face a fundamental split in Afrikaner nationalism. The more noble religious motivation behind a "hard-line" apartheid can still be found in a document like that of A.P. Treurnicht's *Credo van 'n Afrikaner* (1975). In the reform element the notions of racial superiority and guardianship are no longer so evident. What the present government does claim to stand for however, is the creation of a state based on Christian principles in which justice prevails and the rights of minorities are protected. In the effort to put these ideals together some form of group separation along racial and geographically defined lines continues to play a crucial role. And as the preamble to the New Constitution bears out, the ultimate appeal is still to Christian principles as the foundation.

BLACK CONSCIOUSNESS AND BLACK THEOLOGY

A dramatically different perspective on the sociopolitical reality of South Africa comes from the conventional Black churches. Allan Boesak, President of the World Alliance of Reformed Churches has written of apartheid:

"Whatever grandiloquent ideal this ideology may represent for white people, for blacks it means bad housing, being underpaid, pass laws, influx control, migrant labour, group areas, white bosses and black informers, condescension and paternalism. . ."

(quoted in Maimela, 1984, p. 41)

Black religious protest and with it the development of Black Theology has a long history. In 1884 Tile, reacting against White domination and penetration of the Transkei, broke away from the Methodist Church to form the first so-called Black Indigenous church. He was followed by Mokone in 1892 who broke away to form the Ethiopian Church. In 1912 the Ethiopian Church played an active role in the founding of the South African Native National Congress, later to become the African Nationalist Congress. With the banning of the ANC and the PAC in 1960 there was, as Maimela remarks, a temporary lull which ". . .distorted the dynamics of the South African politics, for it gave the impression that Black Power never existed as a force to be reckoned with in South Africa. . ." (Maimela, 1984, p. 43).

In the 1970's we have seen the re-emergence of a more sophisticated form of Black Power or Consciousness. An essential component of the new Black Consciousness is the belief that Black attitudes themselves constitute a stumbling block to liberation. In this view the years of living in a White dominated system have created an attitude of mental slavery in Blacks which leads them to accept the situation as it is. It has therefore become necessary for the Black to define and express pride in Black identity, a process which echoes that by which Afrikaner nationalism rose to pre-eminence.

The re-emergence of Black Consciousness created, according to Maimela, a "new theological climate" (Maimela, 1984, p. 45). The starting point for the Black theological critique of South Africa is the observation that the entire social structure is oppressive and not the way that God would will it. The structure systematically entrenches White privilege and domination by preventing Black access to resources. The NGK, in its theological backing of apartheid, may not have intended these to be the consequences of apartheid, but that they are is undeniable. Legal enforcement of the system is oppressive and related to clearly intolerable levels of suffering. Its effect on people is dehumanizing, both in the less than human way in which its implementation treats Blacks and in the less than human way in which Whites are forced to act in implementing it. In the view of Black Theology it is inconceivable that the God of the Bible would permit such a situation to continue. All of South Africa needs to be liberated, Blacks from the attitudes which allow the system to be perpetuated and Whites from the attitudes which enforce it.

The biblical appeal of Black Theology is primarily to the God of the exodus and the Christ who stands on the side of the underdog and the down-trodden. For Black theologians the exodus of the Jews from Egypt is proof that God is on the side of the oppressed. Moreover, the biblical God is clearly one who punishes the unjust — this the turbulent history of the Old Testament shows. Maimela argues therefore: ". . .translated into (the South African) situation, it means that the God of the biblical tradition is the God who is likely to side with Blacks against the White power structures. . . Black Theology hopes to convince Blacks that their struggle for freedom from political bondage is not contrary to God's will. . ." (Maimela, 1984, p. 47).

Black Theology has played a prominent role in the South African Council of Churches with its majority Black churches and has been a strong point of debate within the Reformed churches. In 1984 the theme of the annual conference of the SACC was "The God of the Poor". Black Theology features prominently therefore as part of the doctrine of many Christians in South Africa. According to Maimela, it is not racially exclusive for "blackness" is a term which can be applied to anyone who "shares the attitude or awareness" of oppression. "Blackness" is a symbol for a particular sense of identity in the South African situation. Irrespective of skin colour or cultural background, those who identify with the Black struggle for liberation qualify as Black (Maimela, 1984, p. 48).

THE SCOPE OF DEBATE AND DEPTH OF DIVISION

The issue which brought the socio-political standpoint of the conventional churches into sharp public focus was that of the doctrinal status of apartheid. Early in 1982 it was declared a heresy by the World Alliance of Reformed Churches (WARC). As Coetzee points out, this judgement is the most basic and direct way in which the concrete institutional form by which a religious group expresses itself can be rejected by another in the same tradition (Addendum

I). Subsequently in South Africa it became a focal issue at various church conferences. As one of the prime-movers behind the declaration by the WARC the N.G. Sendingkerk took the lead that year in declaring apartheid a heresy. It was also outspokenly against the Group Areas, Mixed Marriages, and Influx Control legislation (Addendum I). Later, the Methodist, Anglican, and United Congregational Churches followed suit. The executive committee of the Anglican Church went as far as declaring the entire social structure of South Africa to be irredeemably racist (Addendum I). The NGK responded to the situation at its synod by postponing the revision of its position for four years, a move which illustrated the depth of indecision in its ranks.

In a report of this length it is not possible to go into the details of the religious and sociopolitical orientations of the above groups. Both what we have called Afrikaner civil religion and Black theology are complex phenomena containing different viewpoints. However, what our analysis does show is that:

• Religion is presently central to the legitimation by major opposing groups in South Africa of their sociopolitical orientations.
• As such it is functioning as an essential ethical resource for those critical and defensive of the South African situation.

The history of Afrikaner nationalism clearly demonstrates the way in which religion, when it is allied to a broad range of the hopes and fears of a group, comes to play a powerful motivating role in the activity of that group. Religion has been central to the creation of a sense of Afrikaner identity and the justification by the Afrikaner of his sociopolitical orientation. In this process the religious mythologization of group experience/history has been a powerful factor. In contemporary Black Theology we are seeing the process repeated. The extent to which even the so-called "reform" element of Afrikaner nationalism is in disagreement with the position of Black Theology is a disquieting element of the situation. For the latter the entire structure of South African society is riddled with injustice and needs changing; for the former however, the demand for such far reaching changes constitute an intolerable threat to identity.

RELIGION AND IDENTITY: WHO SPEAKS FOR WHOM?

In attempting to evaluate the significance of the official church standpoint on any controversial issue we are faced with a basic difficulty, namely, that of knowing to what extent the official view reflects the views of the rank and file. With religion and religious leadership featuring so prominently in the public debate on social and political matters this problem is more pressing. In the discussion above we have highlighted some deep religious divisions that exist in South Africa at the present time. We have seen how religion has been used to define group identities and sociopolitical orientations. The groups concerned stand in opposition to one another and the division between them is receiving prominent media coverage because of the intensity with which the issues are being debated. The situation is further complicated by the extent to which opposition to government policy unites widely disparate and essentially opposing groups. Moreover, media coverage may be distorting the extent to which the public statements of various spokesmen represent group opinions. Many religious groups such as the Black Indigenous churches do not have a voice in the debate. Despite the significance of the debate therefore, there is strong evidence that the *religious concerns* of many South Africans have a different focus.

The Black critique of South African social structures does not sit easily with Whites. This is not simply a matter of the differences between the White Afrikaans churches and Black Christians. It is also a matter of the internal differences that exist between Black and White viewpoints in the conventional "English" churches. The proposed union of the United Congregational and the Presbyterian churches has run into difficulty over such disagreements. Many Whites appear to have difficulty with the *extent* of the Black critique of present social structures. White sensitivity to the use of religion in the critique of the government was clearly illustrated in the multipurpose survey.

To some the above tension may seem to be a predictable function of race and of the way that South African social structures favour Whites at the expense of the rest. Evidence that such an interpretation is an oversimplification comes from a surprising quarter. One of the most notable trends highlighted in the recent national census has been the growth of the Indigenous churches among Blacks. At the forefront of this growth have been the Zionist churches. To judge by the national census, their growth appears to have occurred at the expense of the conventional churches, especially the Methodists and Anglicans.

In terms of intergroup relations the significance of the trend to Indigenous Black churches lies in the social orientation of the majority. Most of them exhibit a disinclination to be involved in conventional political activity. This does not mean that they have no sociopolitical opinions or significance. It does mean however that their sociopolitical role is a complex one which cannot be understood in conventional political terms. Taken with what appear to be some of the White attitudes it means that a significant section of the South African population presently appears not to incorporate a conventional political focus in its religious position. It also means that the present trend among Blacks is away from those church groups whose leaders claim to represent Black interests. This does not mean that they are disillusioned with the leadership. In fact, surveys repeatedly show that the majority of Blacks express sentiments which are generally in line with those of the conventional church leadership. It does suggest however that many Blacks are not satisfied with the way in which the conventional churches are fulfilling their roles. Moreover, it provides an indication of the complexity of the role of religion in individual and social life. Archbishop Hurley has declared the communication gap between church leadership and White church membership to be one of the most pressing problems facing the Roman Catholic Church (Addendum I). If the trend among Blacks is anything to go by however, then this, to a degree at least, is true also of the conventional Black churches.

THE BLACK INDIGENOUS CHURCHES

Typically researchers identify three main types of Black Indigenous church *viz.*: the Ethiopian, Zionist, and Indigenous Apostolic. Of the three the Ethiopian is both the earliest and the only one with any tradition of political involvement. The biggest is the Zionist, started in 1904 by an evangelist from the United States. Initially some organizational integrity was maintained between different groups. Now however it would be most accurate to say that the growth of these churches has assumed a life of its own. Their significance can be gauged by the rapidity of their growth. Between the years 1960 and 1980 membership of these churches increased by almost 300 %. From about 2 million in 1960 they have increased in number to just short of 6 million. As a proportion of the Black population this represents an increase from 20 % to 29 %. They now number 36 % of all Black Christians.

The attitude of the authorities to these churches over the years has been most unaccommodating. Privileges which follow government recognition of a church include the granting of land for building churches and schools, and recognition of marriage officers. Yet, despite the fact that the numbers of such churches must have grown by about 500 in the years between 1925 and 1941, only 2 were recognized by the government (Sundkler, 1961, p. 76). In 1955 the Tomlinson report recommended the freezing of further recognition of churches. Oosthuizen reports little change in the unaccommodating attitude of the government since then (Private communication). The attitude of many in the churches, particularly the Black clergy, has been equally unaccommodating. The growth of the Black Indigenous churches in the face of such general hostility is a tribute to the strength of the underlying social and environmental forces to which they are a response and to the way in which these churches have fulfilled Black religious needs.

Many issues are raised by the growth of these churches. For conventional Christianity, they pose problems of the integrity of the Christian tradition. (See the fears expressed by Crafford, 1984, p. 37). For the social scientist a basic question is that of the cause of their growth. In terms of intergroup relations however, these are secondary issues. Our primary concern here must be to evaluate their role in South African society as one type of religious group amongst and in relation to others. Given the level of sociopolitical rhetoric that exists in the conventional churches the trend towards these apparently non-political churches may seem to be an anomaly. But it alerts us to the complexity of South African social reality with its great variety of groups and group interests. It is also a warning that the assessment of the social role of religion in any society cannot proceed only from a focus on those aspects which enjoy a high public profile, but must pay attention to developments on the ground. Finally, in the way that it contrasts with the use of religion by the Afrikaans and conventional Black churches it draws atttention to the breadth of the functional role of religion in its satisfaction of human needs and aspirations. In the Black Indigenous churches we have yet another significant grouping in South Africa in which religion is playing a powerful motivational role in identity formation and sociopolitical orientation, but one with no obvious conventional political expression.

THE BROAD FUNCTIONAL ROLE OF RELIGION

Though it may seem a distant comparison, the closest parallel to the Black Indigenous churches in the history of European Christianity has been the Pentecostal movement. Like the Pentecostal movement, the Indigenous churches have experienced their greatest growth in the unsettled urban environment that has developed out of rapid urbanization. Government policy has not accommodated this process. Like the Pentecostal movement, the Indigenous churches appear to offer a ''religious haven'' in this hostile environment, one which offers emotional security in a group setting where there are few other alternatives.

It is common to characterize the social orientation of movements of the above sort as dualistic. Members of such movements tend to invest so much emotional energy in their religious group that they appear to have little concern for other forms of social involvement. They may then be described as ''other worldly'' or ''escapist''. Certainly it is true that they exhibit little overt concern in their religious activity to be involved in conventional political activity. However, to see them in this way is to oversimplify the dynamics of the social role of such movements. A broader understanding of the functional role of religion in society is needed to make this clear.

THE HIERARCHICAL NATURE OF RELIGIOUS IDENTITY

Cumpsty, Hofmeyr, and Kruss suggest a simple but effective hierarchical model for understanding the way that religion operates to relate people to their environment (Addendum II). Briefly, if religion is to be that system within society which relates the individual to the rest of society, then there are various "levels of aggregation" for which such relationship has to be defined. The whole can be pictured as follows:

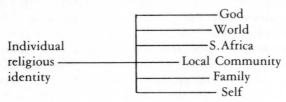

Heterogeneous societies are characterized by the presence in them of many different groups. Some of these may see themselves to be operating at the national level e.g. political parties; some at the local level e.g. sports clubs; and some may span many levels from the local to the international e.g. religious movements. In such societies, an individual's sense of identity comes to be a complex collage formed by the way that she appropriates the beliefs and values of groups representing the various levels. So, for example, someone may identify themselves as a Town Councilor and Dutch Reformed Afrikaans Housewife Transvaal Nationalist South African Female Christian Human Being, etc. A feature of modern life is that some of these components of identity need not have a recognizable institutional form which sponsors it. In the example given above, the image that the individual may have of herself as a housewife may have more to do with advertisements than with her actual activities. In any case, given this great variety, there will be some need to order the varying values and aspirations that each possibility represents if life is not to become too chaotic.

It is fundamental to the self-understanding of religion and of most religious groups that they will provide the ultimate resources for ordering values and aspirations. In the religious person therefore, it is supposed to be the beliefs and values of the religious group which determine this ordering. This has the following consequence: Ideally, religious beliefs and values should be central to the choice by individuals of the other forms by which they might choose to identify with and involve themselves in society.

The process of individual identity formation is clearly complex with many problems of integration. For the individual strongly committed to a religious group the identity gained in association with that group might largely solve the problem. The motivation behind the research conducted by Cumpsty *et al* however, was the perception that many of the more confusing social processes occur precisely when individuals find that the beliefs and values of the groups with which they identify do not integrate (Addendum II). To take the example given above, the "Housewife" component may conflict with the "Town Councilor" component. Then the "Dutch Reformed Christian" component ought to mediate between the two, for it is one of the roles of religion to mediate when such problems of integration arise. In practice however, the religious component may sometimes mediate, but often it does not.

THE FUNCTIONAL ADEQUACY OF THE SOCIAL ORIENTATION OF BLACK INDIGENOUS CHURCHES

Given the broad functional role of religion in the formation of social orientation it is not surprising that there should be forms of religious expression which involve little active conventional political orientation. This we believe is what the Black Indigenous churches represent. They occur under social conditions which offer few possibilities of identification at what Cumpsty *et al* refers to as the mid-levels of social aggregation (Addendum II). For this reason their members manifest an apparently narrow range of social concerns and involvements. However, we now recognize that they represent religion at work in a most effective way. They encourage a social orientation and urban identity which is well-matched to the demands of the circumstances in which they occur.

The range of functions served by the Black Indigenous churches have been analysed many times (See Oosthuizen, 1968, p. 3-19 for instance) but it is worth repeating a few here. That such groups may be small is of no consequence to their members since the belief is that they are connected to "God" or "powers" of ultimacy. Their emotionalism may jar against European sensibilities yet this emotionalism clearly plays a significant role in providing their members with the energy needed to cope with a difficult environment. The "Spirit of God" gives power and vitality. It inspires them to work and inculcates responsibility and self-service. Free play is given to the creative expression of religious identity in these movements, especially in the richness of their ritual expression. We see then that the phenomenological characteristics of the movements are entirely appropriate to the social environment in which they occur. They are, in the best sense of the words, rational responses to extremely difficult life-problems.

It is worth pausing briefly to ask how the general perception of these groups as a social or apolitical might have arisen. Certainly the members of such groups appear to concentrate their lives narrowly on the life of the group. The assump-

tion that an adequate identity must involve a wider group affiliation is errone-
ous however. What these movements represent is the judgement that, taken
as a whole, the beliefs and values of the religious group are the best resource
available and the only one needed to cope adequately with urban life.

In the intergroup context of South Africa the Black Indigenous churches pose
an important problem. Their growth apparently constitutes a challenge to the
authority of the vocal political representatives of Black interests. However, in
spite of their apparent passivity one often hears it said that Black Indigenous
churches have a potential for direct forms of political action (See Villa-Vicencio,
1983, p. 41 for example). The grounds for such assertions are not secure. Yet,
the assertion raises an important question, namely, that as to the hidden potentials for future group action. This is a fundamental problem in the attempt to
estimate the future direction of social developments.

MEASURING POTENTIALS FOR THE FUTURE BEHAVIOUR OF RELIGIOUS GROUPS

Black Indigenous churches constitute a religious grouping whose members' identities appear to focus sharply on that of the particular church to which they belong. Consequently, though they have a strong religious base from which they
participate actively in economic processes, they *appear* to have no political concern and therefore what many might feel is a narrow range of ethical concerns.

The apparently passive political character of groups such as these and the statements of their leaders influence our estimate as to their likely future social role.
History demonstrates clearly however that our best efforts to anticipate the future in terms of the overt character of a group are frequently wide off the mark.
This must have to do in part with hidden potentials and with the failure to measure them. Our task here cannot be to provide a general solution to this problem
for the social sciences. However, research into the motivational role of religion
conducted for this project has offered some insights.

The problem has to do with our tendency to oversimplify our understanding
of the structure of society. We tend to think of social structures in terms of the
recognizable groups they contain. Future developments are then thought of in
terms of the way that those groups might interrelate. What has emerged most
clearly from our research however is the danger of generalizing about groups
in this way. It is individuals who make history and herein lies the difficulty,
for individuals themselves are clearly unaware of the conflicting motivations that
a particular social process may bring to the surface. We have no method for knowing how an individual might integrate the complex of motivations that certain

kinds of social process ignite. However, our research has highlighted some of the potential tensions that do exist and in which religion appears to be playing a role.

RELIGION AND RACE: CONFLICTING COMPONENTS IN IDENTITY

In a large and ambitious survey of metropolitan Durban a research team led by Oosthuizen attempted to measure the role of religion in intergroup attitudes and relations (Addendum III). The questionnaire used surveyed many issues but had a fundamentally simple structure. Its basis was the attempt to measure the attitude of various religious groups to interreligious and interracial contact of various sorts. Groups surveyed included the Black, Indian, Coloured, and Afrikaans and English speaking White Christians, Muslims, Buddhists, Jews and Hindus, Portuguese and Greeks. Sample sizes for each group were small, yet an ubiquitous pattern emerged which illustrated in a fundamental way what we believe to be basic in the process of identity formation. The results offer a clear demonstration of the way that conflicting elements may be incorporated in individual identity without those involved being aware of it.

For our purposes the questions which showed up this tension were those measuring the contrasting strength of religious and racial affiliations for each group. For example, respondents were asked whether they would be prepared to have someone from a *different race group* but of the *same religion* lead their services. The majority in virtually every group including the Afrikaans one, were prepared to do so. A second question asked respondents whether they would be prepared to have someone from the *same race* but of a *different denomination* lead their services and this time the majority answered negatively (Addendum III).

The importance of these questions is that they measure the relative strength of the religious and racial component in each person's identity. The results indicate that for most of those surveyed the religious component was stronger than the racial one in this area of potential intergroup contact. Moreover, for all but the Afrikaners the religious component was stronger by a long way. The levels of multi-racial acceptance suggested then that religion transcended race entirely for most of those interviewed. Given the ideal social function of religion this is perhaps as it should be, for religion is supposed to unite people rather than divide them.

Indications of potential tension came however from a different set of questions. In this case respondents were asked about the acceptability of multi-religious and multi-racial marriage and schooling. On these questions the results were perhaps surprising. A high proportion in many of the groups was against multi-racial marriages and schooling even if they involved people of the same religion (Addendum III). Responses were not as uniform on these questions as they were on multi-racial worship. However, the responses indicated that for many people, notably the Blacks and Afrikaans-speaking Whites, the more important component of identity on this issue was not religion but race. In particular, the majority of the Blacks interviewed were against the idea of multi-racial schooling (Addendum III).

In the acceptance of multi-racial worship but not multi-racial schooling, even when underpinned by religious unity, many respondents indicated a latent tension between the roles of religion and race in overall identity formation. A final question helps to put this into perspective. Respondents were asked their opinion on the preservation of ethnic identity. Large majorities in all the groups were in favour of the preservation of ethnic identity though not by law (Addendum III). This suggested that a general sense of identity and a desire to preserve it was present in all those interviewed. Of the three words "religious", "racial" and "ethnic", it appears that the last was most acceptable as a description of this general sense of identity. The religious and racial components were present as well, but only as contributing factors in the "ethnic" one. Only in the Muslim group was the religious factor so strong that religion and ethnic identity were, to all intents and purposes, the same. In most of the other groups, the religious factor was stronger than the racial one, but with important areas in which a racial factor was also present.

The three measures of identity used in the research of Oosthuizen and his team are quite basic, even crude. Measures made by the multipurpose survey indicated that religion, as one among other measures e.g. language, race, hometown, etc; comes quite low down in the scale when South Africans think of their identity. Nevertheless, what Oosthuizen's research clearly shows, is that religious and racial components are in tension in the general sense of identity of many of those interviewed. Many are probably not aware of this, for the present social structure in South Africa limits contact between groups. If multi-racial schooling and worship were to begin to take place freely however, the intergroup contact that followed would very rapidly bring these tensions to the surface. Since the locus of tension is the individual person, the initial process would not involve tension between groups. As individuals began to express these conflicts publicly however, what began as latent tensions of identity within individuals would become problems of group identity.

RELIGION AND ETHICS: LEVELS OF CONCERN IN TENSION

By the way in which it regulates intergroup contact, the structure of South African society plays a decisive role in the development and expression of group identity. The research conducted by Oosthuizen and his team has drawn attention to the way that this structure inhibits the realization of religious and racial tensions in this process. Further research has demonstrated another aspect of the way that the structure of South African society influences the expression of group values. In this case what it measured was the difficulty of integrating in a harmonious way the ethical demands that the South African situation makes (Addendum II).

In research conducted among Coloured members of various Christian churches in Athlone, Cape Town, a team headed by Cumpsty analysed the role of religion in the articulation of ethical and sociopolitical orientations. Using a variety of measures three basic sociopolitical types were identified. These the researchers called Neutrals (44 % of the total), Pietists (35 % of the total), and Socials (14 % of the total). As the names suggest, the so-called "Neutrals" expressed little interest in active social involvement, whether political or religious. The "Pietists", on the other hand expressed great interest in religious activity, but no interest in political activity. The "Socials" expressed active interest in all forms of activity — political, charitable, and religious (Addendum II).

The factor which connected religious and sociopolitical orientations was found to be ethics. Each group expressed an ethical concern as part of its religiosity which was found to be exactly congruent with its sociopolitical concerns. The "Pietists", for example, displayed an intense but narrow range of concerns while the "Socials" displayed the broadest range. The relationship of each group to society was therefore pictured as follows (an unbroken line indicates a strong commitment to activity at that level, a broken line a weak commitment) (Addendum II).

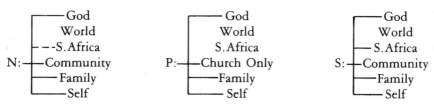

According to this picture the "Socials" are the only type who express confidence in the attempt to articulate religious values at the national level. The other two, like the members of the Black Indigenous churches, appear to have opted out of that level.

The difficulty of integrating ethical values in South Africa emerged with respect to certain tensions present in the responses of all three groups. For example, though the two politically passive groups expressed disinterest in political activity and *scepticism* with respect to its value (Addendum II), many in those groups identified most strongly with the politically more "radical" groups in South Africa. The United Democratic Front and the South African Council of Churches attracted a lot more sympathy than groups like the Labour or Progressive Federal Parties. The results indicate therefore that both the assessment of and willingness to be involved in political activity is at odds with the affective pull of certain high-profile sociopolitical groups. If the "Neutrals" and "Pietists" are disinclined to be involved in the expression of religious concern at the national level, then there are those among them for which this is in conflict with their affective allegiances.

Among the "Socials", the conflict expressed by the "Neutrals" and "Pietists" was not present as they openly supported both socio-political activity at the national level and the groups representing such activity. However, in their case a similar tension at the national level but with respect to a different sort of problem emerged. For them it was not a question about group sympathies, but a question about ethical priorities which revealed the tension. Respondents were asked to rate various characters with varying ethical profiles as "better" or "worse" Christians. The question forced a pay-off between individual, local community, and national levels of ethical concern and therein lies its importance (See Addendum II for a more detailed account). For "Pietists" and to a lesser extent "Neutrals" there was no problem. They approved of conventionally good interpersonal behaviour and disapproved of ethical concern at the national level if it involved sacrificing the interpersonal level. The question forced "Socials" however to choose between two levels of ethical concern to both of which they were positively committed. In a revealing response, the majority assigned the greater priority to the national level (Addendum II). According to the results therefore, the "Socials" appear willing to sacrifice harmony between people and in the local community if they believe that religious concern, expressed in values for the national level, justifies it. Moreover, the results may not be isolated. In a survey conducted by the HSRC in the PWV area (MPS/OV/30/32) a small but significant proportion of Indians and Coloureds agreed that protests in which people might die were necessary for accelerated political change in South Africa.

The research indicates that the expression of religious values at the national level is problematic. A large number of people avoid this tension by opting out of the religious expression of sociopolitical values. However, a latent potential to get involved emerged in the way that many of them identified with groups like the UDF and SACC. For those who were willing to be involved at the national level, a different problem was present. Having a wide range of ethical concerns, they had difficulty integrating every level of concern. It is a feature of rapid social change that it sometimes appears to force a sacrifice of interpersonal values for the sake of "higher" national objectives. This sacrifice many of the so-called "Socials" appeared to be willing to make. In general then, a substantial number of people in this apparently politically passive community indicated a potential to be active even if it would involve disharmony in the local community.

RELIGION FOR THE INDIVIDUAL AND RELIGION FOR SOCIETY: FUNCTIONS IN TENSION

The research conducted by the teams of Oosthuizen and Cumpsty (Addenda II and III) illustrate clearly that the individual and social functions of religion are in tension in South Africa. This, as the research shows, has to do with the difficulty of integrating the pursuit of different group concerns in the present South African social structure. The tensions highlighted by both projects are fundamentally tensions of value. In metropolitan Durban and for a wide range of groups, the values associated with something called "ethnic" identity were discovered to incorporate unresolved elements of religious and racial identity. In Athlone, the expression of religious values at the national level was found to be in tension with its expression at the personal level. In both cases we suggest, the tensions must be seen as endemic to the present social structure of South Africa. Cumpsty *et al* point out that the majority of South Africans have for so long had no way of participating in the national level of decision making that, if anything it functions as a source of "common enemy" symbols for them (Addendum II).

The vocal part of the debate about South Africa's future, in other words, that part which receives the most attention in the media, occurs mostly at the national level of concern. Justice for all is debated in an abstract way which does not spell out in detail what justice would require and ignores the existing suffering or potential for future suffering at local levels. Of course, those participating in the debate score points against each other by highlighting local suffering. However, neither appears to appreciate the full impact that the implementation of their strategies has or would have on *the individual in a community*. Fundamentally, this ignorance is not wilful. It arises out of a combination of intense concern coupled with a certain lack of sociological and psychological sophistication.

53

Ignorant even if intense concern is a description which applies to both sides of the polar divide presently occupying the public eye. Given the intensity of the feelings of both, the sporadic turmoil that *both* inflict on local communities from time to time is understandable. It has to do with the fact that neither side sees a way to integrate national longer term values with day to day local values. Each side may feel that the suffering that follows the pursuit of their strategies is justifiable in the short term given long term objectives. In our view however, the levels of suffering both inflict are intolerable. There is a third "conflicting perspective" to which neither pays sufficient attention and that is the one which attempts to maintain some sort of order at the personal level of existence in spite of the surrounding chaos.

The trends amongst the rank and file in the Black and White communities suggest that South Africans are moving away from the expression of religion in active conventional political terms. This does not mean that South Africans have no opinions or affective allegiances to groups operating in the sociopolitical sphere. It means simply that the institutional religions find it extremely difficult and sometimes impossible to satisfy both individual and social needs simultaneously. The divide that exists between the spokesmen for Christian churches and their local congregations, for example, is to be seen in this way. So also is the tension that occurs at leadership level (See Warden, 1983). From the perspective of the national church, what matters most is the national level of concern. This has to do with the role of religion in providing a touchstone for social values. It is not surprising therefore that many church spokesmen in their national councils concentrate their efforts on the sociopolitical expression of religious values. In the local congregation however, it is individual needs that matter most. This in turn has to do with the role of religion in mediating individual life-traumas. It is not surprising therefore that the congregational preference is often for the personal rather than the social function of religion. Leadership tensions arise out of the failure of the leadership group to achieve a consensus as to how to integrate these two roles.

PIETISTIC RELIGION IN THE PROCESS OF SOCIAL CHANGE

The apparent trend towards a pietistic form of religious expression at a time when the public arena is occupied by those who articulate their religiosity in sociopolitical terms raises important questions. Principally, how are we to estimate the role of pietism in processes of social change? We have seen that the divide in religious perspectives in South Africa applies not only to those debating national needs, but also to those for whom the main function of religion is personal as against those for whom it is social and conventionally political. How then can we expect those with a pietistic religious outlook to respond to change? Are those who believe that the apparently pietistic outlook contains a revolutionary potential right; and if so, in what way?

The research of Cumpsty and his team provides some basic pointers with respect to this important question. The religious orientation of the majority in Athlone was pietistic. Even the so-called neutral profile was pietistic in its inclusion of a muted expression of religious values at the "mid-levels" of social aggregation. Yet, clear pointers were found as to the potential of many to become socially active. As Cumpsty *et al* argue (Addendum II), in attempting to resolve this question two factors are vital. The first has to do with the present but inactive emotive affiliations to groups with a sociopolitical relevance that the research uncovered. The second has to do more generally with what now appears to be the basic structure of sociopolitical debate in South Africa.

It is now agreed that the sociopolitical debate on the future of South Africa has become dangerously polarized. A sense of urgency and an emotional intensity charges every debate in a way which contributes significantly to this polarization. For intergroup relations the importance of this process is twofold. First, it eliminates the middle ground of opinion. Second, it forces different groups to unite under the same flag. When this happens the process begins to develop a momentum of its own. What begin as minor issues regularly escalate into major confrontations with the potential for violence. Cumpsty *et al* refer to issues which escalate in this way as "catalytic events" (Addendum II). Catalytic events are not simply heated vocal exchanges, they are potentially violent social processes. Their importance as opposed to that of the merely verbal exchange lies in the *extent* to which they exclude the middle ground. When confronted by a catalytic event, not only is it not possible to mediate the ideological divisions that open up, it is not even possible to remain on the side-lines as a non-participating neutral. "If you are not for. . .", as it were, "then you are against".

Pietism, in the way that it satisfies the religious needs of individuals, is a viable form of religious expression. It is not asocial, as has been pointed out. In fact, it motivates people in a way which enables them to deal highly effectively with their environment. However, whatever might be the reasons, and the reasons surely must be various in South Africa, it is inclined away from the political expression of religious values. Let us reiterate, the problem for this orientation in South Africa is not just that plorization excludes the moderate position, it is more deeply that in the heat of sociopolitical debate non-involvement is no option. This brings us to the significance of the inactive emotive affiliations of those who appear passive. To quote from Addendum II:

> If they (the Neutrals) are the equivalent of the "silent majority", then their latent emotional. . . allegiances are vital, for in the long run it is these allegiances which will play a large part in determining which way they might move when a catalytic event forces a choice.

In an apparently passive group, but one with a significant discontent with the existing national power structure, inactive emotive allegiances become vital when social confrontation has reached the catalytic stage. These allegiances are what help to explain the sudden and unexpected shifts from passivity to activity that we so often see in revolutionary situations.

In Athlone, the allegiances measured were mostly to groups on the more "radical" side of the sociopolitical spectrum. Moreover, surveys consistently show this to be the case with most South Africans other than the Whites. However, when we consider the sizes of the Black Indigenous and Traditional groups it is clear that in South Africa with its great variety of different groups there is likely to be a great variety of such allegiances. Many of these may not be political. Measuring them is clearly vital, not only if we are to understand what concerns and values South Africans have, but especially if we are to do justice to them. The pietistic religious orientation, though it tends to promote harmony between groups at interpersonal and local community levels, is not sufficiently holistic to encompass the forces that are being mobilized at the national level of concern.

POPULAR MOVEMENTS, RELIGION, AND IDENTITY

Catalytic events set in motion the sort of social processes which frequently end with a re-arrangement of social structures and relations. There is a striking feature of the outcome of such processes and that is the regularity with which they disappoint those who participate. If the catalytic event is what sets the process in motion, and if it is the research of Cumpsty and his team which has indicated the role that religion as against latent allegiances might play in this movement; then it is the research of Oosthuizen and his team which explains why it is that disappointment must inevitably follow.

In metropolitan Durban a sense of "ethnic" identity emerged as the most important source of individual and group values. Both religious and racial values were seen to be parts of this sense of identity. In the light of the multipurpose survey, it would probably be more accurate to refer to this sense of identity not as "ethnic", but as "traditional". Traditional values are a shifting complex which is far less determinable than the term "ethnic identity" implies. Response patterns suggested that "religious" and "racial" components were in unrecognized tension in the whole in Durban. The importance of these tensions is that they alert us to the truly delicate and complex nature of "traditional" group entity. This complexity, in conjunction with what seems to be the almost inevitable character of most processes of social change, is at the root of disappointment.

Large popular movements frequently begin with small and apparently insignificant events. The basis for the momentum they develop is the mobilization of deep discontent with existing social structures. As analysts have therefore pointed out, those mobilized are frequently far clearer about what they are reacting against than they are about what they are acting for. In any complex society with a variety of sub-group interests as is the case in South Africa, this must be so. It is only by leaving the alternatives to the existing structures relatively undefined that the differences between those participating in the process can be suspended. The result is that whether change comes about gradually or rapidly, peacefully or violently, the feelings mobilized to initiate change are almost always "narrower" than the total set of emotive and valuative affiliations of those mobilized. Large scale social changes simply cannot embody all those things held dear by the myriad different social sub-groupings that need to be mobilized to achieve it.

To the effective social strategist, all of this is a matter of common sense. What gives the whole process its poignancy however, is that those involved are seldom aware of the depth of impact that change will have. This is what the research of Oosthuizen and his team demonstrates. In metropolitan Durban, religious and racial values were found to be in tension in "ethnic" identity for a large number of those interviewed. This suggested that change would have the following sort of dynamic (using multi-racial worship as an example):

● Initially, those acting for multi-racial worship would express enthusiasm for the fact that the old separation had gone. However, the new relations that the new structures would make possible would soon tap the tensions between religious and racial identity of which people were previously unaware. Many would then discover for the first time that their choice in favour of religious values had consequences for "traditional" identity of which they were not in favour.

● A process would begin in which people sorted through the way in which their existing identity was being infringed by circumstances and attempted to resolve the conflict. In each individual's attempt to spell out what the preservation of their sense of identity involved in the new circumstances, some choice would have to be made to sacrifice either the religious or the racial components of identity (See also Cumpsty, 1983).

● It is the diversity of ways in which a new mix might be created that would turn what began as a problem of individual identity into a problem of group identity. Soon spokesmen would emerge within both the religious and the racial groups to defend their particular versions of identity. What began as a latent tension, buried within the heart of each individual, would then become a problem for relations within and between groups.

● In the end, the few unitary religious and racial groups would become many. New multi-racial but singular religious alliances would form. Others might prefer multi-religious but singular racial alliances, etc. Many might, of their own volition, mark off a seperate territory in terms of, for example, worship or schooling. If multi-group contact were to be preserved, then "higher" values would have to develop to mediate the multiple tensions that might arise as each alliance marked out its "social space".

The metropolitan survey clearly illustrates the general dynamic which must follow any large scale and significant alteration to social structures. Any such change in a complex society like South Africa must involve a failure on the part of the new structures to satisfy the beliefs and values of all those going into them. And as the Durban survey shows, this will be the case even if the changes come about as the result of a popular movement or decision. The fact that values are in unrecognized tension in identity is fundamental to the fact that the grand popular movements in which people indulge later take them unpleasantly by surprise. They are taken by surprise because they are usually not aware of the way that the new social structures for which they have striven will ignite likes and dislikes which they never even knew existed.

SOUTH AFRICA: A SOCIETY WITH NO RELIGIOUS MAJORITY

Fundamentally, South Africa is a society without a numeric majority, it is a society of minorities. To judge by the survey in Durban, a strong sense of identity continues to play a significant role in the way that each minority group understands itself. However, as the Durban survey also showed, there is no simple way to draw lines between minorities. Race and language have been the main tools used to date but the legislative structure which has resulted is harsh and clumsy. In Durban we saw that religion was a better measure than race. Yet, it too is clearly not what matters most to each group as it forms and reforms its sense of identity and values.

In many ways, the environment of South Africa is hostile to the identity of its minorities. There is an irony here, for the policy of apartheid, far from being protective, has often been destructive. In Durban, for example, implementation of the Group Areas Act destroyed much of the infra-structure on which Hinduism depended (See Oosthuizen, 1975; and Oosthuizen and Hofmeyr, 1979 among others). It put the joint or extended family system under severe strain and took Hindus away from their temples. A second group, the Zanzibaris, have left us an absurd record of anomalies as their racial classification has varied from one generation to the next. Thought by most to be the descendants of a Black Mozambiquan tribe, this group are presently living in the Indian township of Chatsworth as "other Asians" (Oosthuizen, 1982).

The history of religion demonstrates the ability of minorities to survive, but this is usually at some cost to their institutional participation in sociopolitical processes. Political non-involvement is a classic measure in defense of minority identity. Over the years, for example, the institutional representatives of Judaism have limited their participation in the national level of debate to muted criticism of apartheid. It has been left to the individual Jew by his political involvement to exemplify the strong Jewish tradition of civil justice (See Muntingh, 1984, for an account of the history of the relation between Judaism and Islam on the one hand, and the government on the other in South Africa).

Presently the Black Indigenous churches must be considered the most important group of non-political minority religions in South Africa. It would be a mistake to suppose however that the adherents of these religions have no political opinions or sympathies. In fact, that they do appear to follow from the results obtained in the multipurpose survey and dealt with in chapter two above. Moreover, the example of Judaism demonstrates that these opinions might well come from the sense of values for which the religion stands. If therefore most South Africans disagree with the way they are governed, then there must be relatively few who see, in the social structure of South Africa, anything which comes close to a system embodying their religious values.

For one who has his gaze focussed on the sociopolitical needs of a society, the non-political forms of religion that we see in so many of South Africa's religious minorities may be seen as a negative phenomenon. This view, as we have argued strongly, does not do justice to the broad range of psychological and social functions which religion is presently fulfilling. Yet, we must agree that there is something fundamentally wrong with a society in which it is impossible, as Cumpsty *et al* have shown, to integrate the personal and the sociopolitical or civil functions of religion harmoniously (Addendum II). Moreover, there is a reservoir of discontent to be tapped and powerful forces have already been mobilized to pursue various sorts of change. Here is the problem, for it is important to bear in mind that popular movements never represent the broad range of minority interests of those participating. In South Africa we already have a situation in which the interests of one minority have dominated all others. There lies ahead the danger however, that no matter who comes to power, the domination of South Africa by a powerful minority will continue with similarly severe consequences for the myriad minority systems of belief and value that matter to South Africans.

HARMONISING VALUES IN A MULTI-RELIGIOUS SOCIETY

While the majority of South Africans are nominally Christian, the fact is that South Africa is a multi-religious society. Our history is already a testament to the damage that religion can do when it is used to entrench an understanding of the identity and values of a particular group at the expense of others. Part of our problem must be to undo the damage still being done and to prevent it from happening again. De Gruchy has expressed it is follows: ". . .the problem remains for us all to ensure that theology does not become captive to culture. . ." (De Gruchy, 1984, p. 52). Since this is a multi-religious society we might wish to re-express these sentiments: The problem remains for us to ensure that no set of symbols with the motivating power of religion becomes captive to the cultural interests of any one dominating group.

The research undertaken for this project has shown how delicate and complex the belief and value structure of each of the many groups in South Africa truly is. Moreover, we have seen that any process of change must, to a certain extent, infringe the things held near and dear by many of the people in those groups. Even should change be "well-managed" therefore, we must inevitably expect radical splinter groups to emerge to defend their particular ideas about social justice. Yet, precisely because of the complexity of our group structure, and precisely because the process of group identity and value formation is so dynamic, there is no way of legislating a structure based on simple criteria that will not ultimately lead to severe trauma for individual South Africans. Harmonising group interests in a multi-religious society cannot be achieved within group boundaries which are, to an important degree, artificial.

If the multiple value systems of South Africa's people are to be harmonized without infringing individual systems of value, then some means must be found to develop values which transcend particular group interests. This has already been suggested above in chapter one, but it should now be clear precisely why this will be such a difficult task. Presently there are no common symbols functioning as the basis of belief and value information at the national level for South Africa's groups (See Cumpsty 1983 for a discussion of the effect that this lack has had on Israel). This is above all due to the way that the national level of symbol formation has been dominated by the interests of only one group. Our hope nevertheless is that some such super-ordinate value system might emerge if sufficient attention is payed to the best values embodied in South Africa's major traditions. With the contribution that the research done for this report has made to understanding the general nature of intergroup processes, it is no longer necessary that the discussion about values be sociologically and psychologically uninformed. To such a discussion we now turn.

CHAPTER 4

BURNING ISSUES IN THE CONTEMPORARY DEBATE

INTRODUCTION

In the previous chapter we focussed on general trends as they appeared from the various research projects. What became clear was not only the great variety of viewpoints which is so characteristic of religious pluralism in South Africa, but also the conflict potential inherent in the situation. There appears to be an urgent need for a common set of values which will be able to transcend divisive group interests. The important question then becomes whether the existing religious traditions in South Africa have such a basic set of values to offer and if so, what these values exactly are. What role do they play in shaping the perception of individuals and groups and in motivating their conduct? In order to find some answers to these questions, we turn our attention in this chapter to three burning issues in the current debate, which all have to do with social justice, namely the theological foundation of human rights, the relationship between economic structures and religious convictions and the problem of violence.

For this purpose, extensive use is made of three independent projects. The fact that all three were conducted from a Judeo-Christian perspective, is in accordance with South African reality (cf. Chaper 2). Each of these projects is based on a different methodological approach and reflects its own understanding of the problem. No attempt is made in this chapter to integrate the various methodologies or to evaluate the underlying theological presuppositions. It can be expected that the various religious groups in the country will react quite differently to the approach and findings of these studies. Nonetheless, they are presented here to provide an insight into the way theological arguments are used and to illustrate the impact religious convictions have on intergroup relations.

It must be clearly stated that the few aspects highlighted here are not meant to be representative of the projects as a whole and do not claim to reflect the viewpoints of the different researchers in all details. For a fuller assessment of the different projects, the reader is referred to the individual reports themselves.

HUMAN RIGHTS IN THEOLOGICAL PERSPECTIVE

ATTITUDES TOWARDS HUMAN RIGHTS

Human rights usually refer to certain unalienable rights which constitute the minimum necessary for a life with human dignity. As far as intergroup relations are concerned, the crucial issue is how these rights are translated into concrete terms when ordering society and how the values underlying these rights influence human behaviour. From the multipurpose survey, it appears that human rights are far more than a theoretical issue. South Africans hold strong views on human rights, with clearly marked differences. In response to the question: What does the term human rights mean according to you?, for Whites the single most important aspect is individual liberty, while Coloureds rate political freedom more important. As far as the participation of religious movements in structural liberation is concerned, the difference in opinion is even more apparent. (Cf. Addendum I and Chapter II for a fuller discussion of the data.)

THE CONTRIBUTION FROM A THEOLOGICAL PERSPECTIVE

In his extensive investigation into the theological foundation of human rights, Du Toit (1984) found that the church — strange as it may sound — traditionally displayed a negative attitude towards the concept of human rights. This attitude changed in the course of time and during the last four decades human rights became one of the prominent themes in church and theological circles world-wide.

If this discussion is compared with its counterpart in a secular context, the similarities immediately become apparent. This raises the question whether theology has in fact a distinctive contribution to make. Du Toit argues that the idea of justice receives a special qualification from the perspective of Christian theology. This relates to two distinctive features of the Christian idea of justice, *viz.* seeing justice as a *gift* from God and understanding its function as *agape*, that is, as love for the unworthy. Justice and human dignity require that man accepts this qualification of the human condition — with regard to himself and to his neighbour. *In the case of the latter, it also functions in the form of agape — love which does not seek worthiness or dignity for itself, but which gives this as instrument of God's love. For the believer this does not mean in the first*

place respect for the rights of his neighbour, but love for his possibilities . . .
(Du Toit, 1984, p. 29).

Because human dignity is not understood as an inherent right, but as a gift and because this potential can only be realized in the context of love, the implication is that the practice of justice is ultimately aimed at the full realization of man's humanity. Therefore all reductionist models of justice are inadequate. Full humanity can only be achieved when all anthropological aspects are taken into account. A further implication is that justice is community-oriented and avoids social atomism and individualism. Because love requires personal involvement in all forms and all situations where human dignity is threatened, it inevitably becomes community-oriented. At the same time it becomes clear that rights always carries with it corresponding responsibilities.

The impression is often created that human dignity is something awarded to man as the result of an effective program for human rights. No doubt many of the external conditions or unjust structures which threaten an existence with human dignity can be rectified in this way. But Christian ethics stresses an equally important aspect, viz. *subjective responsibility* to live in such a way as to express the qualities necessary for a life with dignity. In other words, man has the task to bring to fruition the structural possibilities God has given to him. This includes his relationship to God and to his fellow-man. A life of thanksgiving before God in itself has an enriching and fulfilling effect. Towards his fellow-man, it becomes a life of service in love, which entails much more than merely doing his duty. The significance of the *agape*-service lies in its creative potential to improvise and to transform relations and structures into opportunities for life with human dignity. In this respect the Christian perspective adds an important qualification to the concept of human rights.

Another aspect of significance is the inherent nature of love to "walk the second mile", that is, doing more than what is "legally" required in a specific situation. This includes the capacity and willingness to suffer and to sacrifice — even to forgo one's own rights if necessary. This aspect cannot be formalized as part of a general declaration of human rights, neither can it be expected of anyone but of oneself. Nonetheless, it does underline the specific contribution coming from a theological perspective (cf. Du Toit 1984, p. 31-33).

HUMAN RIGHTS AND THE CHURCHES IN SOUTH AFRICA

Du Toit analyzed the position of the following institutions: the NGK, Roman Catholic Church, SACC, Methodist Church, Church of the Province of S.A., NGSK, Presbyterian Church of S.A., Baptist Union and the NGKA. From this extensive empirical investigation it appears that, in spite of important differences, there exists a surprising measure of consensus on basic issues which makes the prospects of a dialogue not without hope. Du Toit (1984, p 212 ff) summarizes the points of agreement as follows:

● All human beings have a claim to basic or fundamental rights.

● These rights have been conferred by God on man as the bearer of his image and therefore are inviolable.

● Not only the individual, but the community as a community of people, has certain rights.

● A balance must be struck between the claims and rights of the individual and the collective rights of the community.

● All rights are accompanied by corresponding responsibilities and duties.

● A distinction should be made between fundamental rights and secondary rights and privileges.

● Under no circumstances may rights be withheld or suspended. Even secondary rights and privileges may not be withheld when a person or persons have a rightful claim to them.

● Biblical norms relevant to human rights are love, truth, peace, justice, freedom and human dignity. These norms function within the context of the central biblical message of God's creation, salvation and reconciliation in Christ. For a proper understanding of human rights the full scope of a biblical anthropology must be taken into account.

● The value of the concept of human rights lies in its universal appeal and the fact that it is an accepted secular term. Churches should therefore use this concept to express a Christian understanding of its meaning in their witness to the state and to the different groups in South Africa.

● The successful use of the concept of human rights by the churches will, to a large extent, depend on whether they can reach consensus on the content of these rights. In broad terms, the Roman Catholic understanding seems to express what most churches subscribe to: man has a right to life, to corporate integrity and to the basic necessities to sustain life. Further rights are: the right to respect; to freedom in the search for truth; to public and personal freedom of religion; the right to marry and to form and raise a family; the right to work and decent working conditions; the right to just remuneration; the right to property, including the means to be productive; the right to form a community; the right to migrate; the right to participate in public life and the right to be protected by law.

At the same time, the differences between churches should not be overlooked. These pertain to matters like the choice between a more "theological" and a more "political-pragmatic" approach to human rights, the unity and diversity of mankind, and the contrast between individual and collective rights. However, it is only when the socio-ethical implications of these principles are spelt out for South African society that the divisions become visible on another level. This will be the focus of the next section.

THE PRACTICAL IMPLEMENTATION OF HUMAN RIGHTS

When the question is asked how this measure of agreement on basic principles is translated into concrete terms, it appears from Du Toit's research (1984, p. 214-229) that two lines of development can be identified, which, in their turn, are closely linked to two different perspectives of South African society.

These perceptions are confirmed by empirical data from the multipurpose survey. Various questions dealt with aspects of human rights. The greatest differences were to be found between Whites and Blacks, while Coloureds and Indians occupied more or less the middle ground. Differences centred on the redistribution of wealth, separate residential areas, racial discrimination, homelands for Blacks, separate schools, mixed marriages, social contact and political rights. Agreement (or a larger degree of agreement) was found on matters like equal pay for equal work, non-racial sport, promotion on merit, co-operation with other races and the meaning of church and religion.

It would appear therefore that a considerable measure of agreement is to be found even on the level of practical application. Du Toit (1984, p. 256) concludes from the data that the future of human rights in South Africa is not as bleak as some would suggest. The real problem concerns political rights and the system within which these rights are to be exercised. This again ties in with the findings of the multipurpose survey where Blacks, Indians and Coloureds are overwhelmingly in favour of equal rights for all groups in contrast to the only 50 % of Whites who would support equal rights but even then only under certain conditions (e.g. the safeguarding of the position of minority groups). For this reason Du Toit maintains (1984, p. 250) that at the moment political problems stand in the way of a fuller development of human rights in South Africa. The question is whether these rights can be realized within a system based on the concept of separate development or not. The issue has become so polarized and emotional that it is a real question whether a constructive dialogue is still possible at this stage.

PRIORITIES IN THE SOUTH AFRICAN CONTEXT

Despite what has been said in the previous paragraph, there is also another side to the matter. Despite deep divisions, there is a considerable amount of common ground and even shared convictions. Because any future dialogue will, of necessity, focus on these issues, it is important to summarize Du Toit's findings (1984, p. 230 ff) at this point:

● In all churches a strong appeal to a common biblical tradition is made, although differing conclusions are drawn from this tradition.

● All the major churches agree that racism is sin. The NGK has condemned racism because it sees and treats certain peoples as superior and others as inferior. The NGSK has condemned racism as sin and as a form of idolatry. It understands racism as an ideology which includes the belief in the inherent, cultural and biological inferiority of certain races and race groups. It is also a political system which embeds unequal treatment of these groups in laws, structures and institutions. Racism is not merely attitudinal, it has a structural dimension to it. It is a system of political, economic and social dominance. On these matters there is agreement, but opinions differ sharply as to what qualifies as racism in South African society.

● It is commonly accepted that civic rights for all inhabitants of the country are essential and must be respected. There is sharp disagreement about the constitutional model within which these rights are to be exercised.

● All the major churches are convinced that the Law on the Prohibition of Mixed Marriages cannot be defended on biblical grounds. Only the NGK and NHK is of the opinion that the state has the right, in certain circumstances, to limit the choice of a marriage partner. However, the NGK in Suid-Afrika (Western Cape Synod) has stated clearly that the law is in conflict with the biblical understanding of marriage. Most churches feel that this law and also article 16 of the Immorality Act constitute a flagrant contravention of an inviolable and divine right given to man. The Anglican and Presbyterian churches have passed resolutions to solemnise mixed marriages even if it should imply civil disobedience. The Roman Catholic, Methodist, Gereformeerde, Congregational Churches, Felksa, the NGSK and the Baptist Union all have repeatedly called for the repeal of these laws.

● As far as the Group Areas Act is concerned, the NGK has pointed to the violation of human dignity caused by this measure. All churches which are of the opinion that present government policy constitutes an infringement of human rights, reject this act, together with influx control, pass laws and the system of migratory labour. Churches like the Methodist, Anglican, Roman Catholic and the NGSK feel very strongly about the resettlement of Blacks — a measure which has been described as the most cruel piece of legislation to appear on the South African statute book.

● For all the churches the field of economics and labour constitutes an important area where human rights must be upheld. This includes providing adequate job opportunities, decent working conditions and just wage structures. Many churches have pleaded over the years for the recognition of Black trade unions and have supported these unions since their establishment. Equal employment opportunities without racial discrimination and equal pay are important goals. The wages of domestic staff and farm labourers are particularly sensitive issues.

• Migrant labour is considered by all churches as the source of great evil. Each family has the right to live together. Although the system cannot be abandoned overnight without causing more hardship, it has a very detrimental effect on family life. Churches which reject the system of apartheid, see the solution of this problem in the right to free movement for all workers and their families.

• The right to own property and adequate housing is also viewed differently by the churches who oppose "separate development". Permanent occupancy must be given to squatters, while the demolition of squatter dwellings without providing alternative housing is sharply criticized. All churches feel that the causes of squatting must be eliminated.

• Equal education opportunities are considered a priority by all the churches. Churches who reject "separate development", call for integrated, compulsory education for all under one department. The Baptist Union and the NGKA for example, feel that a common education policy and administration will do much to eliminate suspicion and friction.

• Especially the Methodist and Presbyterian churches hold strong opinions on security legislation which impinges on the rights of the individual. Death in detention without trial has made this an intensely emotional and controversial issue. The Roman Catholic church and the NGSK have called upon the government to abandon detention without trial and to respect the "rule of law" principle. The Baptist Union has proposed a system of review in cases where a person is detained for longer than 90 days. The NGK has asked for a balance between the security of the state and the rights of the individual, while the NGSK stated clearly that an ideology which places the security of the state before the upholding of human rights, is to be rejected completely.

• As far as the right to conscientious objection to military service is concerned, the NGK recognizes only religious grounds as a basis for alternative service, while the Anglican, Roman Catholic and Presbyterian churches hold that every Christian has the right to refuse military service on moral, ethical and religious grounds. Acceptable forms of non-military alternative service must be provided in these cases. The Church of the Province especially is convinced that the role of the Defence Force increasingly is becoming one of defending an immoral and sinful situation.

• Other rights discussed by the churches, but less prominent, are the rights of women and the right to life. The latter includes issues like abortion and euthanasia, where biblical anthhropology again becomes important.

• Theological discussions and statements on human rights are accompanied by specific projects to ensure that these rights are applied in concrete terms in the socio-political reality in South Africa. The style in which this is done differs considerably. For example, the SACC has a special study commission and a task force for human rights. On the other hand, the NGK follows the system of liason committees which consult directly with the authorities to bring problems and cases of injustice to their attention.

A THEOLOGICAL CATALOGUE OF BASIC RIGHTS?

From the preceding it is clear to what extent religious values form an inherent part of the discussion on human rights in South Africa. Indications are that this input from a religious perspective is bound to become even more important in future. No doubt a new era in the development of these rights was ushered in by the Universal Declaration of Human Rights of 1948. But since then it has become clear that this Declaration also has some serious shortcomings. One problem is the applicability of these (broadly speaking, Western-oriented) values in a Third World situation where group conflict, social stratification and the position of minorities are important issues. The question is whether a positive contribution cannot be made from a religious perspective by listing the major points of consensus among the various churches. According to Du Toit (1984, p. 259-261) such a catalogue would consist of the following basic rights:

● *The right to life*. In the first instance, this implies the basic means to sustain life, viz. food, clothing, housing and medical care (however contextually determined this might be). It also includes the right to the means to obtain these, viz. the right to work and to its rewards (property). Further — the right to protection of the physical and mental integrity of life, that is, protection by the state and by law against arbitrary execution, abortion, genocide, terrorism, torture, war and the threat of nuclear weapons. At the same time it implies the demand for charity and a just distribution of wealth.

● *The right to fully express one's humanity*. This concerns man as a unique individual created in the image of God. This implies first of all the right to freedom of religion and worship in expressing the priority of the relationship to God. It also constitutes the basis of personal freedom (freedom of conscience and of moral decision/choice/responsibility), the right to be treated with human dignity, irrespective of race, colour, creed, sex or language, the right to personal privacy, the right to develop personal aptitudes and abilities.

● *The right to a life in community with fellow humans*. In its most basic form this is the right to marriage, to a free choice of a marriage partner and to the privacy of this relationship. From this follows the right to form a family and a community and the right to free association (on the political, economical, social and cultural level), the right to identity and the protection of minorities. Finally, this also includes the right to participate in all the political, economic, social and cultural activities of the community in which man lives.

These rights, according to most of the churches, form the core of the Christian understanding of human rights. The "core" is indicative of the fact that most churches feel that a distinction of some sort should be made between "basic" or "fundamental" rights and "secondary" rights which are deduced from these basic rights. But the problem is where exactly the line between the two categories must be drawn. Churches from the affluent West tend to include much more under the first category than the churches from the Third World.

Examples of "secondary" rights would be the following: the right to a just economic system, decent working conditions, autonomous trade unions, freedom of choice regarding education, impartial civil and juridical administration, equal treatment before the law, the right to a fair and undelayed trial, the right to legal representation, the right to freedom in the pursuit of truth and the publication thereof (freedom of thought, speech and a free press), the right to migration and settlement, the right to advanced education, science, art, etc. In short: the broad principles of justice, fairness, equality, freedom and participation in all spheres of life, government, wealth, property and prosperity.

Sometimes even further aspects are added, such as the right to political asylum, privacy of correspondence, hereditary law, the right to petition, vacation, welfare services, unemployment insurance, pensions, the right to cultural privileges, participation in management, etc. It is clear that the further one moves from basic rights, the greater the diversity of opinion will become on what is to be included and what not.

THE CHURCH AND THE FUTURE OF HUMAN RIGHTS

In what has been said thus far, the emphasis was predominantly on the ideal of human rights, that is, on what these rights could and should be. But the question to what extent this ideal has been realized in practice, must also be faced. The high expectations with which the Universal Declaration was launched in 1948, have made way for a sense of disillusionment because of the countless problems encountered in the actual implementation of these rights. In fact, there seems to be a world-wide increase in the violation of human rights. The problems encountered here have to do on the one hand with differences related to the foundation of human rights and on the other hand with factors which obstruct their implementation.

Under these circumstances, the possible contribution from a religious perspective, in order to make some progress, has become a matter of urgency. Du Toit (1984, p. 261 ff) identifies three priorities for the South African situation.

Human rights in a new political dispensation

Despite the consensus among churches that racism is sin there is also a growing awareness that the mere replacement of the present system with an European or North-American model will not necessarily guarantee a more effective implementation of human rights.

The most urgent need at the moment is to find a political dispensation which accommodates both the demands of human rights and the demands of the African continent — without neglecting either of these two prerequisites in the process (Du Toit, 1984, p. 264).

A *declaration of human rights*

Although the formulation of such a declaration will be extremely difficult under present circumstances, it is the task of religious communities to foster an awareness of, and a commitment to, human rights in order to create an atmosphere in which such a declaration can become possible.

Involvement of religious communities

Although religious communities must have no illusions about their own limitations as far as competence, moral influence and specialized knowledge with regard to the implementation of human rights is concerned, they nevertheless have an important obligation to make whatever contribution is possible from their own perspectives. Du Toit (1984, p. 265-284) shows that this potential contribution covers a wide spectrum of activities, including *inter alia* the following: the more effective and consistent use of proclamation opportunities to establish proper values; the openness for a self-critical appraisal of the role religious communities themselves play in this respect; the development of a biblical anthropology; the training of members; the commitment to constructive change and consistency in word and deed. A very real contribution lies in the ability of the church to mediate between ideal and reality. Because of its eschatological orientation, the church has a vision of the future which is presently still unrealized and therefore is in a position to mediate between the future ideal and present reality and to utilize the dynamic force inherent in such a future-directed orientation.

In view of this very heavy responsibility of religious communities, we shall now, in more detail, look at two areas where religious values are of specific importance, viz. economic justice and the use of violence.

POWER, BELIEFS AND EQUITY

INTRODUCTION

It is generally accepted that economic structures have an important influence on group relations. But the question is seldom raised to what extent these structures are shaped by a certain set of beliefs or convictions or whether they operate as independent or "automatic" forces which, in their turn influence beliefs or convictions. The study of Nürnberger investigates economic potency structures in South Africa and their interaction with patterns of conviction in the light of a Christian ethic (cf. Nürnberger, 1984, p. 6 ff).

POWER STRUCTURES AND PATTERNS OF CONVICTION

Power structures can be described in terms of various factors, e.g. the spread of economic potency over geographical space, the distribution of economic power between different sections of the population, the differential relation between economic potency of different groups and their economic needs, or in terms of the causes of unequal distribution of potency in the population.

Patterns of conviction for their part can take different forms, e.g. religion or metaphysical convictions, convictions related to group identity, convictions related to the distribution of economic potential or collective interests.

The interaction between these patterns of conviction can be categorised as follows:

● Conflicts between different convictions. From a theological point of view this is the area of missionary dialogue or evangelization.

● Conflicts between the collective interests of various groups in society. This is the area of social justice. Obviously it has a direct bearing on the demands for structural change.

● The conflict between convictions and collective interests, or more precisely, between normative systems and ideological self-justifications. In theological terms this is the area of justification and sanctification.

THE SPATIAL ASPECTS OF ECONOMIC POWER STRUCTURES IN SOUTH AFRICA

The situation in South Africa provides a very good example of how economic forces and convictions interact with one another. The universal phenomenon of the concentration of economic activity and potential in certain geographical centres and the concomitant relative underdevelopment of their respective peripheries is clearly visible in this country. Here a particularly marked centre-periphery pattern evolved over the last century. The so-called PWV area is in a commanding position while the Cape Peninsula and Durban-Pinetown area form smaller sub-centres. At the same time it becomes clear that the areas reserved for Blacks occupy a peripheral position, with a resultant total dependence of their populations on the economic centres.

Although the concentration of economic activity is not unique to South Africa, certain irregularities are very prominent. Whether the country is seen as a constellation of states or as a unitary state, it does not have any significant effect on the overall picture (see following diagram taken from Nürnberger 1984, p. 65):

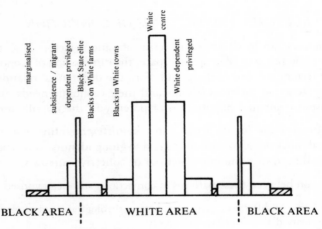

POPULATION-POTENCY RELATIONS

The most striking irregularity is the series of barriers restricting vertical mobility. At least four such barriers can be distinguished:

● The first institutionalised and legalised socio-economic barrier exists between the White population group as a whole and all the other race groups.

● The next line is formed by the Asians and Coloureds (with a slight barrier between these two also).

● The third line is indicative of a definite jump towards the Black population which is firmly established in White controlled urban areas, particularly those who possess Section 10 rights. A minority of them managed to attain relatively high standards of living, but they are surrounded by an outer fringe of the marginalised urban group: i.e. people with casual employment and insecure housing who are constantly in danger of being found and "endorsed out".

74

- Permanent Black labourers on White farms form the fourth line.

- They are followed by tribal subsistence peasants in Black areas who are largely dependent on migrant labour in White areas. The position of migrant workers in White areas is precarious but they have at least a rudimentary base in their "homeland" to fall back on in times of emergency.

- Finally, we have the rural marginalised population e.g. of the resettlement camps. They are totally dependent on migrant labour — or charity.

Against this background, we can now look at the relationship between need and potency in more detail. Results from the multipurpose survey of the HSRC indicate that among Blacks, Coloureds and Indians there is a strong conviction that wealth is unequally distributed in South Africa and that peace can only be ensured if this situation is rectified (MPS/OV/57 item 12(a) and (1)).

NEED-POTENCY RELATIONS

If the relationship between need and income is accepted as an indicator of potency, it becomes possible to highlight some of the important aspects of the South African situation. Of course, "need" implies some measurable lack and the setting of specific standards. We do not intend to go into the debate of a "poverty datum line" or the "effective minimum wage level" (Nürnberger, 1984, p. 70), but are interested in the dynamic interaction between need and income. For this purpose, a distinction between three types of need can be made: basic essentials, social expectations and personal wishes. The intersecting of the three need curves with the income curve divides the field into four categories: absolute poverty, relative deprivations, relative privilege and absolute affluence (Nürnberger, 1984, p. 81). A "poverty gap" develops when income drops below the line of basic essentials, while an "affluence gap" is created when income exceeds personal wishes.

When applied to South African conditions, the need curve — contrary to expectations — has a concave rather than a convex shape. This is mainly due to progressive taxation. Indications are, furthermore, that the need curves display the same sort of "jumps" due to racial and spatial barriers which were found in the case of the income curve. Nonetheless it is clear that absolute poverty occurs especially among the Black and Coloured populations, while a very small overwhelming White minority enjoys absolute affluence. Apart from poverty datum line studies, very little research seems to have been conducted in this whole area and a lot needs to be done before a clear picture emerges concerning the relation between need and income in the different population groups.

CAUSES OF ECONOMIC POTENCY DISCREPANCIES

In order to attain a full understanding of the situation outlined above, it is important to gain insight into its causes and thus into its historical dynamics. Three major factors are at work here: asymetrical interaction on the market place, the role of differential technological advance and volition.

Before discussing these factors in more detail, it should be emphasized that any situation of economic imbalance may be interpreted from different perspectives. The debate in the social sciences concerning economic discrepancies is conducted within the framework of two conflicting paradigms. The liberal school of thought maintains that the cause of poverty in the periphery is backwardness and its cure is modernisation. Modernisation aims at a rise in initiative, productivity, efficiency and organisational sophistication. In contrast, the radical school maintains that poverty is the result of oppression and exploitation and that the cure is liberation. Though the two schools differ sharply in their analysis, there is a common element. Both agree that there are "vicious circles of poverty" and "spirals of affluence" (Nürnberger, 1984, p. 83) and that the problem is due to the way in which access by one group to economic resources is limited by the other. In the South African situation, this is illustrated by the following three interrelated tendencies:

Asymmetrical interaction on the market place

Because of the imbalance in income, purchasing power is concentrated inequitably. The economy shifts to fill the affluence gap.

The effect of technological advance

Technological knowledge and skills form the basis of the modern industrialized world. When access to technological skills is not shared equitably, this produces severe economic disjunctions. Technology outperforms labour in terms of productivity to the benefit of owners and operators. The result is the emergence of a technological elite which possesses secure jobs, receives high incomes and attracts production to its luxury demand. Those with limited access increasingly fall into redundancy as technology advance pushes it out of the market for factors of production. South African racial and spatial policies enhanced this development.

Volitional factors

Economic conditions are not merely the result of certain laws which operate in a mechanical way. Human decisions certainly also have a part to play and can influence the course of events in a decisive way. As far as these imbalances are

76

concerned, man can either enhance or counteract the structural mechanisms which lead to gravitation of potency towards one group. This largely depends on the normative system which forms part of a specific culture. In South Africa, a clash between Western and African cultures has a direct bearing on concepts like private initiative and the profit motive. This motivational imbalance seems to have been a strong contributing factor in the emergence of potency discrepancies.

Thus the mentality of Whites in South Africa, formed by capitalist liberalisms and nationalism has had no scruples in entrenching its own competitive position at the expense of Blacks through institutionalised discrimination.

Structural mechanisms and volitional factors therefore combine to widen the gap in potency between the strong and the weak unless some powerful countervailing forces come into play.

TYPES OF CONVICTION

Once it is accepted that convictions and beliefs do interact significantly with economic structures, it becomes important to realize that the convictions themselves can be of a widely differing nature. Nürnberger (1984, p. 1165) distinguishes at least three and gives concrete illustrations drawn from his research (1984, p. 153-171), namely convictions based on religious or metaphysical presuppositions, convictions related to cultural group identification, and convictions related to the distribution of economic resources.

To this should be added a further type, that of vital interests: These are not identical with basic instincts, needs, desires, but rather needs and desires in an interpreted form, already evaluated and arranged according to priorities.

Convictions and interests often are in conflict with one another. Consequently, a constant interaction between these two poles takes place, which moves along three avenues: perception (guided by values), justification (guided by norms) and motivation (guided by goals).

The most serious clash between convictions and vital interests takes place on the level of justification. When a man has to choose between what he perceives as his vital interests and what his normative system prescribes he finds himself in a difficult dilemma. Consequently, an elaborate system of self-justification or rationalisation has developed. Basically, this is a defense mechanism of the mind. But the more it succeeds to convince both its perpetrators and its social environment the more assertive it becomes. Having re-interpreted the system of meaning and norms or having proved itself to be acceptable before the forum of the latter, it will now usurp the moral authority vested in the system of meaning and its system of norms. It will not only absolutise its own interpretation of the system of meaning but also confirm or question man's right of existence according to its own interpretation of the normative system. At this stage, it becomes an ideology.

This leads to a further strange but common phenomenon: Ideologies develop a life of their own. Obviously there is a constant interplay between vital interests and ideological self-justification. The latter is meant to underpin the former. But because of its self-imposed rigidity, an ideology may generate its own logic and dynamic and move away from the vital interests it is meant to cover. It can also stagnate and remain in an obsolete position when vital interests move away from their previous position because of structural change. In this way, a group can be deceived about what its vital interests are. Although the ideology then becomes dysfunctional in terms of its prime purpose it is still invested with the authority of the system of meaning and the normative system and exercises a considerable amount of power over the minds of decision-makers and followers alike. Which means that an ideology can lead a group into a direction quite contrary to its own vital interests.

Obviously then, there is a lot of tension between convictions and vital interests. But there is a lot of interplay which leads to mutual adjustments as well. An accepted system of meaning and its normative system play a vital role in defining what can become a vital interest in the first place. Obviously they also provide the normative terms of reference for ideological self-justification. Conversely vital interests and their ideological justifications constantly influence the concrete interpretations of the system of meaning and the normative system. Often they go to the extent of changing their entire contents.

STRUCTURE-INDUCED MENTAL DISPOSITIONS

Within the South African context, the interaction between convictions and vital interests has resulted in a series of mental dispositions both in the dominant group and in the dominated group. These dispositions were shaped in the course of South Africa's colonial history. Of particular importance was the threat to the first wave of colonialists (the emerging Afrikaner) by the second wave of colonisers (British imperialists) and by the Black colonised majority. Consequently, the following types of mental dispositions developed (see Nürnberger 1984, p. 142-143 for a discussion of each of the types): Baasskap (lordship), guardianship, separate development, state security and technocracy.

On the other hand, the dominated group also developed a variety of mental attitudes to enable them to cope with the situation in which they found themselves. This development also has a long history, going back to the first liberation and resistance movements. To give an indication of present-day attitudes, a recent survey (1984) by Sociomonitor (Market Research Africa) can be quoted (Nürnberger, 1984, p. 149), which found the following typical groups in Black urban areas:

● The motivated: interested in improving racial harmony; prepared to work hard for better houses, higher standards of living and better jobs; concerned about fitness and health. Stated to cover 31 % of literate urban Blacks.

● The frustrated: resentful of being exploited as consumers and workers; distancing themselves from materialistic goals; not interested in racial harmony and "pragmatism" which in their view brought them nowhere. Most are youths with low educational standards, coming from poor and crowded homes.

● The traditional: concerned about the security, future and wellbeing of authority, elders, and tribal law; reassured by familiar patterns; increasingly involved in religion. Said to cover 22 % in 1982.

● The swingers: youths with frustrated education; very conscious of their image which they display by defiance of authority — particularly over against their own set — the most militant group.

What we see here is the development of a strategy to survive in a period of transition where values change rapidly and often are in conflict with traditional concepts. In such a situation, people are forced to devise subsets of values instead of a holistic approach to reality, in order to cope with the conflicting demands made upon them. In this process, as we have seen in chapter 3, religion can play an important role by providing a broad matrix of values and beliefs within which to hold the subset. By doing this it facilitates the process of cultural transition.

INTERACTION BETWEEN CONVICTIONS AND INTERESTS

It should not be surprising that in the South African context, interaction between convictions and interests for the most part takes the form of the justification of interests. This holds for both the dominating and dominated groups. Research in this area provides us with pertinent examples of the following:

● Justification in terms of religious convictions (Nürnberger, 1984, p. 174-8). The most visible example is when a group understands itself in terms of the biblical concept of the "chosen people" and thereby claiming a privileged status. Another example would be when the biblical message is spiritualised and the social and political sphere withdrawn from the direct influence of religious convictions.

● Justification in terms of cultural identity (Nürnberger, 1984, p. 178-85). The ideal of cultural identity has often been used to protect group interests. An example is the way in which apartheid was defended as a measure to preserve the cultural identity of all ethnic minorities.

● Justification in terms of distribution of economic potential (Nürnberger, 1984, p. 185-191). A good example is the way in which the poor are viewed from a liberal, free enterprise and from a socialist perspective. In the case of the former, the achievement norm leads to the statement that the poor is poor on account of their failure. In the case of the latter, the norm of equality leads to the view that the poor are poor because they are the victims of oppression and exploitation.

The important point is that through the interaction between convictions and interests, the perception of individuals and groups are also influenced. These perceptions are not the result of empirical research or rational argument, but based on gut-level feelings or mental dispositions. ''Yet they lead to sets of rationalisations which do not only determine the behaviour of the man in the street, but also the paradigms of academic enquiries and, in consequence, their findings and recommendations to a very large extent'' (Nürnberger, 1984, p. 192).

The situation is further aggravated by the fact that isolation between groups and individuals encourages the growth of biased perceptions. Nürnberger, (1984, p. 192-193) refers to the findings of Van Wyk (1984) in his research on different elites in South Africa:

● 88,3 % of Whites were convinced that South Africa could win the military struggle against Swapo, 75,6 % of Blacks were convinced that she could not.

● 94 % of Whites disagreed with the statement that the Government exaggerates the communist threat against South Africa, 70,3 % of Blacks agreed.

● 92,7 % of Whites (politicians) disagreed with the statement that Blacks have good reasons to take up arms against the Government, 72,9 % of Blacks agreed.

● 78 % of Whites disagreed with the statement that Whites cannot depend on the loyalty of Black South Africans in a war situation, 72,9 % of Blacks agreed.

''These examples not only show how widely perceptions differ between different interest groups in our society, but also just how dangerous misconceptions, particularly of decision-making elites, could become in real crisis situations. Biased perceptions can lead to vastly inappropriate responses in such cases. The student uprising in Soweto in 1976 is a classical example.

''It also seems to be self-evident that discrepancies in perceptions would not have been able to grow to such proportions if the elites would not have been isolated from each other. A lively dialogue always challenges extreme positions, draws attention to overlooked aspects and makes one aware of alternative perspectives to a situation.

"According to the multipurpose survey of the HSRC, over 60 % of the Whites in the sample (n = 682) believed that the Government is moving in the direction of increased integration, 19.8 % thought that it was moving in the direction of increased apartheid or that there was no real change. Blacks felt exactly the opposite: almost 60 % (n = 914) believed it was moving in the direction of increased apartheid (40,2 %) or that there was no change (19,0 %) while 23,45 % believed it was moving towards greater integration.

"Since Blacks were left out of the new deal, this is hardly surprising. Indians were nearer to the White point of view though with a reduced percentage (41,5 % for integration). Coloureds in-between (29,8 % for integration, 15,9 % for apartheid, 28,1 % for no change)." (Nürnberger, 1984, p. 193).

THE CONTRIBUTION OF A THEOLOGICAL ETHIC

In the face of such deep segmentation in society and such conflicting perceptions of groups and individuals, the question is what contribution a theological ethic can make in these circumstances. In his study, Nürnberger (1984, p. 222) suggests that any such contribution should proceed in three stages:

The missionary dynamic of the biblical message

Because of the radical nature of theological ethics, in the sense that it makes no allowance for social status, rank or authority, but confronts every person on an equal basis and with a universal appeal, it is one of the most penetrating forces at work in society. As such, it can have a very dynamic and regenerating effect, as the history of religious movements amply illustrates. In Christian theology, the doctrine of incarnation means, *inter alia,* God's willingness to enter human history. The message of God's creative and redemptive love is therefore understood as a dynamic historical power, which reaches for ever new phases of history, new cultural contexts, new human situations and conditions. "It enters them, makes itself relevant in them, incarnates itself in them" (Nürnberger 1984, p. 222-223).

It is exactly because the message is seen not as an abstract set of ideas, but as a changing force in society, that a diversity in the application of the message is the inevitable result. This diversity may eventually lead to conflicting perspectives. Because the message becomes so involved with the situation, it might begin to reflect the hopes and fears of those concerned, even support the vital interests and their ideological justifications. Thus the danger is real that the message may simply be incorporated into an existing ideology and greatly reinforce it. Alternatively, it may displace the ideology, but take over its functions of justifying the vital interests of the group in question (Nürnberger, 1984, p. 223).

The ecumenical dynamic of the biblical message

The penetrating and potentially divisive dynamic of the biblical message is acompanied by an "ecumenical" or "cohesive" dynamic. The unconditional acceptance of man by God, implies the unconditional acceptance of man by man in a new community of faith. "But the result is an impossible community. Each member is not just a private person. He is also a representative of some group and thus an element in the social structure. He is Black or White, rich or poor, employer or employee, security policeman or detainee. And so the tensions and agonies of society are reproduced in the Christian community. They are even hightened in this community because the contact is more immediate" (Nürnberger, 1984, p. 225).

When brothers recognize one another as structural enemies, the tendency may be to gloss over differences in order to preserve the appearance of peace. It is of the utmost importance to realize that a common faith can provide the context in which confrontations of the most serious kind can be handled. In the first place, the biblical message horizontalises vertical relationships by treating both elite and underdog as sinners before God. "Thus on the level of consciousness (not yet on the level of social structure) they become equal. They are able to communicate from man to man on the same level without being either condescending or submissive" (Nürnberger, 1984, p. 226). Secondly, a common faith provides the basis for a mutual exposure to conflicting perspectives, revealing the biased and stereotyped nature of the images people often have of each other. It is only when this kind of exchange is refused by isolation or other means that these stereotypes are perpetuated. "The overall effect of an honest ecumenical confrontation is that religious and ideological syncretisms begin to be filtered out" (Nürnberger, 1984, p. 227). The result is not a "pure" form of the message, but rather a revitalisation of its creative and restoring force.

The move from church to society

Confrontation does not only challenge the perceptions and interpretations of the biblical message, but also the perceptions and interpretations of the social reality of each partner. Shared religious convictions therefore can also provide the basis for a common analysis of the situation and the context for a joint strategy. In this way, religious communities, such as churches and similar institutions, can function as some of the most powerful instances to de-absolutise extreme positions and to mediate between conflicting perspectives in a plural society. This presupposes, however, that the insights and motivation of the community of faith is carried into society. It is often argued that what is possible in the church is impossible in the world.

But the church is not a redeemed community removed from the depravity of this world. It is still part of an unredeemed world and subject to the same conflicts and biased perceptions. The difference is that the church can provide the context where these perceptions can be changed. And as each member moves in its social context, these insights are being carried into society. ". . .the church . . . can do the country no greater disservice in the structural sphere than allowing the present large-scale distortions of perceptions, justifications and motivations to continue unchallenged by isolating different ecclesial and racial groups from each other. If I were to make recommendations on the basis of this study, I would certainly make this my first priority" (Nürnberger, 1984, p. 232).

The question is whether the ministry of the church does in fact play a significant role in the changing of attitudes and perceptions. Although much empirical research is still needed in this area, the study of Müller on the preaching in certain churches provides us with some important insights (Müller, 1984).

BIBLICAL PARADIGMS FOR THE USE OF STRUCTURAL POWER

In applying the insights of his study to the South African society, Nürnberger outlines how a transition can be made in terms of three biblical paradigms. The principle of survival where vital interests play a dominating role, must be superseded by the principle of justice, where the right of every individual or group is guaranteed to share in the economic potential of society. But justice in its turn should be encompassed by the principle of concern, that is, by the willingness to share one's right with a person who has forfeited his right. In this way, the goal of survival is fulfilled in justice and the goal of justice is fulfilled in concern (Nürnberger, 1984, p. 234).

It is important to stress that Christians do not have the monopoly on these values. In the section on human rights, it has become clear that it was often non-Christian or non-religious movements who upheld these values. Nonetheless, no institution is more favourably placed in society than the church to give substance to these values. The church has both the opportunity and challenge to innovate within its own structures and if viable solutions are found, to present these to wider society.

A STRATEGY TO OVERCOME STRUCTURAL IMBALANCES

In concluding his study, Nürnberger gives some concrete guidelines of how his findings can be implemented in the South African situation. These focus on three main areas: measures to redirect the economic dynamic of the centre, measures to develop the economic potential of the periphery and measures to neutralize the effects of the asymmetric interaction between the two, as illustrated by the following diagram:

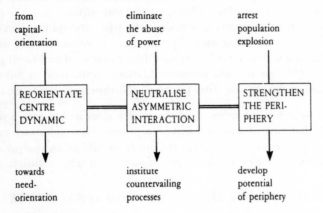

from capital-orientation   eliminate the abuse of power   arrest population explosion

REORIENTATE CENTRE DYNAMIC — NEUTRALISE ASYMMETRIC INTERACTION — STRENGTHEN THE PERIPHERY

towards need-orientation   institute countervailing processes   develop potential of periphery

Nürnberger (1984, p. 245) sums up his recommendations as follows:

"Concerning the asymmetrical interaction between centre and periphery, we suggested that all discriminatory measures and institutionalised abuses of power should be removed and some countervailing processes institutionalised to balance out structural mechanisms. We suggested secondly that the power of the centre needs to be redirected away from its orientation towards capital to an orientation towards needs. Thirdly, we suggested that the impotence of the periphery should be overcome through a serious effort to develop its potential and a reduction in the birth rate, assuming that these two aspects depend on each other. Finally we argued that economic equity presupposes democratization in the political sphere."

FROM IDEAL TO REALITY

What Nürnberger describes as the role of the church in overcoming structural imbalances, points to a potential contribution of considerable importance. But this contribution will depend on the ability of the church to influence the convictions of its members with regard to social and economic justice. How effective is the church in fulfilling this role? To answer this question, empirical evidence is needed to measure in some way the effectiveness of the church's proclamation. The research project led by Müller (1984) had exactly this kind of evidence in mind. The team pioneered a novel approach in the evaluation of the public proclamation of the main churches in South Africa. In co-operation with the HSRC, the basic techniques of content analysis were adapted to suit the specific needs of evaluating that type of literature. After breaking down the various topics relating to intergroup relations into 145 different categories, their frequency of occurrence was recorded as well as their combination with specific predicates. In this way a quantitative and qualitative analysis became possible.

A sample of *written* sermons which appeared in official church magazines and in published collections of sermons over the past decade was analysed. The researchers decided on written sermons because of their general *availability*. Also, being in published form and made available to the general public, one could presuppose that they had been weighed by the author for *correctness, directness and brevity* — thus easier to break down for coding purposes than the general, rather vague rhetoric expressions in oral sermons. Because they were written not primarily for theologians, but for the general rank and file of church members, they can be regarded as representing the *most wide reaching form of preaching in the country:* at the same time they represent a good cross-section both with regard to the different authors of the sermons as well as the different types of congregations receiving sermons.

The same method was used to analyse leaders in official church magazines in order to see whether there were any differences in the frequency and style of expressions about intergroup relations.

The project covered sermons from twelve of the largest churches in South Africa and the leaders of eight official church magazines.

The overall impression gained by the research is that the public preaching does not give clear guidance on the sensitive issues of intergroup relations and in fact seems to avoid these problems because of their controversial nature. Although there is a clear qualitative difference between the churches in the *mood* in which statements are made, the most common tendency is to speak in a very general way, to stick to hackneyed cliches which say very little and which leave ingrained convictions and values intact. With a few noticeable exceptions where ideological sanctions were transgressed and concrete applications were made, the general tendency is to play safe and make only "tactical" pronouncements. There is a great danger that the church will become irrelevant in its proclamation if it provides no new perspectives and no clear guidance to members how to cope with intergroup relations in a time of rapid cultural and social transition.

THE PROBLEM OF VIOLENCE

INTRODUCTION

After discussing human rights and economic justice, we shall now focus on the problem of violence. When we look at this phenomenon from a historical perspective, we once again encounter an ambiguity in the role religion plays, this time in relation to violence. On the one hand, if one remembers the violence and tortures done in the name of religion, there seems to be a definite compatibility. On the other hand, if the testimony of the martyrs and the long pacifist tradition is taken into account, religion and violence represent opposite poles. There are at least two compelling reasons why we must give attention to this problem in this report. Firstly, in many respects South African society is already perceived as being unacceptably violent, and further; unless a greater degree of social justice is not speedily achieved, the present level of violence is likely to escalate incalculably. Secondly, because of certain developments both on a local and international level, the question of violence and non-violence has become a religious issue par exellence. Not only Christianity, but also other religious traditions like Judaism and Islam are confronted with the same problem. As far as intergroup relations are concerned, it is without doubt one of the most critical issues facing religious communities, involving as it does questions of justice, freedom and individual responsibility.

It is important to realise that the phenomenon of violence can never be considered in isolation from the situation from which it emerges. Many different factors and forces often unrelated to one another may be involved in creating an atmosphere where violence finally rises to the surface. Religious convictions may or may not play a role in these developments. It is not our intention to discuss all these different aspects. Even more explicitly, it is not the aim of this section to offer a theological critique of the different positions and the usual lines of argumentation followed in a debate of this kind. Our only purpose is to highlight the effect this issue already has had on intergroup relations so as to understand as clearly as possible its potential to influence future relations.

SOME BASIC CONCEPTS

In order to do this, it is important to clarify first of all some of the concepts involved in this discussion. (Grateful and extensive use is made here and further in this section of the recent studies by Villa-Vicencio (1980), De Villiers (1983) and Russel (1984)).

There is a fundamental problem in defining violence, as the very choice of words may already indicate a certain positive or negative evaluation of the phenomenon. The description of a specific action as "physical", "effective" or "criminal" will certainly differ depending on whether the speaker is administering or undergoing the action. A further complication is that the same words may be used to make an exaggerated claim or to point to genuine atrocity. Each abuse of the term desensitizes people to the occurence of real violence and in the long run makes the latter a tolerated if not accepted part of society. Despite these problems of definition, it can be said in general that violence presupposes a situation of power or the lack of power, an interplay between force and the resistance to force. For the purpose of this study, we distinguish between the following concepts:

Power is the capacity to alter or influence a situation either in its personal or material dimensions. It is a capacity inherent in being human. As such, it is ethically neutral and may be used for good or evil purposes.

Force is physical power. It is usually understood in conjunction with the term coercion. To coerce is to constrain or restrain by force, or by authority resting on force. Since force, like power, is a phenomenon inherent in, and necessary for, human existence, it must be said that it too is ethically neutral and can be used for good or evil purpose.

Violence is both intentional harm done to another and the serious abuse of power. Both dimensions of this definition need to be upheld. This again underlines the fact that violence remains an inherently ambiguous term. In this study we shall concentrate on the second dimension and can refer both to the unethical use of force and what has come to be described as structural violence.

Non-violence is the avoidance of all forms of violence. It is difficult to delineate non-violence in any pure form, because of the inherent ambiguity of the term, and because it is often understood to be synonomous with inaction. There are circumstances in which a "non-violent" inaction becomes effectively a "violent" action — ethically speaking.

Pacifism is a complex term denoting, in the first place, a commitment to avoid the use of all forms of violence. It is also a relative concept indicating a spectrum of positions, each with its own borderline beyond which the use of force is regarded as unethical. It is seldom, if ever, found in the form of an absolute and universal ethical rejection of the use of force. (Russel, 1984, p. 18-19).

VIOLENCE IN ITS SOCIAL CONTEXT

The occurrence of violence is usually interpreted as an indication of serious defects in a given community. As already pointed out, violence can never be treated as an isolated phenomenon. It is always part of a field of forces and a function of the interplay between these forces. Most important in this respect is the relationship between violence and powerlessness. It is often accepted that powerlessness provokes violence and that those who have no power are inclined to resort to violence. According to this view, this happens when conventional political options are no longer effective or are denied to the persons concerned. In their sense of powerlessness, they either capitulate into submission or resort to violence to affirm their humanity and determination to be. (Villa-Vicencio 1980, p. 4). If the first has led to dehumanization, the second all too often has ended with inhumanity.

However, violence can be indicative of more than powerlessness. Hannah Arendt contends that violence enters the field when power is in danger. According to this view, power and violence are opposites — where the one rules absolutely, the other no longer exists. Violence would then be a sign of a government losing its grip on society, an indication that it no longer can rely on popular support for its policies.

TYPES OF VIOLENCE

Violence not only forms part of a complex interaction of forces in society — in itself it is a multi-faceted phenomenon. Various types of violence can be distinguished. Helder Camara, writing against the background of the Latin America of recent decades, suggests that there are three kinds of violence:

- The violence of injustice (violence as unjust oppression) (violence no. 1).

- The violence of the oppressed (violence as rebellion against this injustice) (violence no. 2).

- The violence of repression (violence as repression of such rebellion) (violence no. 3).

Violence thus attracts violence and gives rise to what Camara calls a "spiral of violence". Villa-Vicencio (1980, p. 5-6) sums up Camara's argument as follows: "It begins . . . as the egoism of some privileged groups drives other human beings into sub-human conditions, where they suffer restrictions, humiliations and injustices without prospects for a better deal and without hope. Within this condition violence is manifest in various forms: both in the institutionalized restrictions and humiliations imposed upon people and in the violence which so often emerges among some members of the oppressed groups who have few others ways at their disposal, through which to express their energy and frustration. Established violence, violence no. 1 attracts violence no. 2, as either the oppressed as a group or certain individuals within it come out in revolt and fight for a more just and humane world. These sporadic revolts and at times sustained revolutions are inspired by various ideologies, cadres, "subversive elements" and "agitators" at different times of history in different parts of the world. They all however, have one ingredient in common: whatever the motivation of the instigators the people are receptive to such instigations and respond for a similar reason — the desire to overcome their oppressive state and to institute a more just society.

This violence no. 2 is followed by violence no. 3, the violence of repression in which violence no. 2 is countered by police or military action, in order, firstly, to resist the change proposed by those perpetrating violence no. 2 and, secondly, to maintain the *status quo*.

Villa-Vicencio (1980, p. 6-7) then proceeds to offer the following comments of his own: "It could be argued that the violence proposed by some groups is anarchistic and merely destructive, or that it is imperialistically designed to captivate and control a people to the advantage of one or other world power. It could also be argued that an ordered and controlled form of violence no. 3 is legitimate if it is used to prevent total chaos and destruction. It is contended that this is better than anarchistic revolution and thus the better of two evils. Others argue that violence in any form is totally wrong and not to be condoned at all. Others argue that there is a just, or at least a justifiable form of violence which could be permitted in certain circumstances. The question then arises as to whether this form of violence is legitimate for both the authorities as well as oppressed or opposition groups. Still others contend that perhaps some form of total destruction is necessary in an unjust society. Was Israel not destroyed in this way by the Babylonians, presumably in accordance with the will of God?

Perhaps the most common rationalization of violence no. 3 is that law and order must be maintained at any cost so that any necessary change may be peacefully and orderly negotiated. The opponents of this position argue, however, that while all military force is in the hands of the authorities there is little chance that the demands of the oppressed will either be heard or complied with. This is the argument of certain ethicists and others who argue for a so-called balance-of-power ethic within which there is sufficient military or at least some form of manipulative leverage at the disposal of both sides to persuade their opponents that it is in their interest to change."

Important for the understanding of the present debate in South Africa is the broadening of the concept of violence to include more than what traditionally is covered by this term. Of special significance is the new emphasis on "structural violence" — the idea that some measures of restrictions in themselves contain an element of violence, or in a more extreme sense, that these measures are themselves nothing but instances of violence. Usually a distinction is made between those laws and restrictions necessary for the orderly functioning of society and which are sanctioned by common consent and those measures which are based on unjust principles. The latter, according to this view, leads to instances of injustice and finally results in injustice becoming institutionalised.

VIOLENCE AND RELIGION

Introduction

What has been said up to this point pertains to violence as a general phenomenon. No specific religious or theological dimensions have been introduced. But before doing so, it should be pointed out that the issue of violence provides a dramatic illustration of the conflicting perspectives inherent in the South African situation. What to one person is a "freedom fighter", is a "terrorist" to the next. The presuppositions of the interpreter, the way in which he imposes a predetermined grid on the available data and the position he himself occupies within society, are all of decisive importance for the shaping of his understanding of a given situation. Intergroup relations are to a large degree determined by perceptions of this kind.

Once the problem of violence is raised within a religious and more specifically, a theological context, a number of critical questions emerge. To quote Villa-Vicencio (1980, p. 9-10): *Violence is part of man's experience as we know it; it is entangled in history; it raises the most profound anthropological and theological questions and it is the most inclusive and urgent question facing contemporary man. It is inclusive because all kinds of other ethical problems, racism, economics, politics, lifestyles and so many more, threaten to end in violence. It is urgent for the obvious reason that modern man's violence is more destructive than anything history has ever known. Violence is therefore central to all contemporary ethical problems and we can only ignore it at our peril . . .*

All these issues are related to one basic question: Is the use of violence justifiable on religious grounds? The answer to this question is indicative of two basic positions in religious thought. A negative answer represents a long tradition of non-violence and pacifism, most clearly manifested in the South African context by the debate on conscientious objection to military service. A positive answer for its part can appeal to a long list of religious authorities, ranging from Augustine to exponents of liberation theology, culminating in the concept of a "just war", and recently in its modern counterpart, also very prominent in the South African debate, the concept of a "just revolution".

Before discussing these conflicting traditions in more detail, it is important to realise that in the religious context, a further dimension is added to the question of violence, which makes the problem even more acute. As soon as a divine prohibition or a divine imperative is attached to the use of violence, this can act as a very powerful deterrent or as an equally powerful incentive. In a situation where violence is already being considered as a practical option, a divine sanction and even a divine command might provide the final motivation to proceed with this course of action.

"Just wars" and "just revolutions"

When examining the concept of violence in various religious traditions, it appears that a high premium is placed on non-violence in many of the major world religions. As far as Christianity is concerned, the attitude of Jesus towards his captors and the authorities during his life and especially his cruxifiction, has played an important role and there is evidence of a very old pacifist tradition in the Christian church. (This interpretation has been challenged by recent studies which present Jesus as a revolutionary figure). As far as warfare and military service in the period 173 to 314 is concerned, the attitude was distinctly negative. This view was based not only on the early Christians condemnation of idolatrous malpractices in the Roman army, but also on their conviction that Christians should strictly obey Biblical prohibitions against bloodshed (De Villiers, 1983, p. 21).

After the conversion of Constantine in 312, a rather drastic change (as in so many other aspects) took place in the attitude of the Church towards warfare and military service. Where the Christians had previously only been a minority group in the Roman Empire, constantly submitted to the threat of persecution, they now became the majority group that had to shoulder a substantial burden in the responsibility of the ruling and defending the Roman Empire. In this situation the viewpoint soon gained influence that there could be wars that were justified and in which Christians might do military service. (De Villiers 1983, p. 22).

The chief proponent of the ''just war'' theory was Augustine who insisted that warfare might not automatically be labelled as murder. As long as the following three conditions were met, a war could be called just:

- The war had to be declared by a legitimate authority.
- The cause had to be just.
- The goals had to be just.

This theory was developed further by other theologians and subsequently three further conditions were added to the list:

- The means employed had to be just. This related both to the immunity from direct and intended attack on innocents and non-combatants, and to the proportion between the means and the goals.
- War had to be undertaken as a last resort, after all other means had failed.

- There had to be a reasonable chance of success, that is, of winning the war and of attaining the just goals. (De Villiers 1983, p. 22).

The "just war" theory became the official viewpoint of the Roman Catholic Church and later also of most of the churches that developed out of the Reformation. For centuries the pacifist viewpoint was held only by small minority groups that operated in opposition to the main churches. Behind the theory of the "just war" stood a notion of a corpus Christianum with its need for both internal peace and external peace with heathen neighbours (to whom it owed the gospel). It could be argued that the theory was designed to limit the damage Christians did to one another. Almost simultaneously it had to be accepted that violence had crucial limitations when it came to converting the heretic or the heathen. The revolutionary and Napoleonic wars ushered in both the concept of a national army and a secular state in which the old limitations disappeared. The national state became absolutely sovereign not only over its own people, but also in regard to its neighbours. The stage was thus set for both totalitarian wars and totalitarian revolutions. What Europe's experiences in 1914-1918 adumbrated, was realized world-wide between 1931 and 1945.

It could therefore be asked if the "just war" theory did not in fact pave the way for unrestricted warfare. The original intention was exactly the opposite — war should be avoided if at all possible, but situations may occur where it becomes necessary if total chaos in society is to be avoided and order and peace is to be restored (De Villiers 1983, p. 23). The "just war" theory is based on the prior conviction that it is necessary and proper in the conditions of a fallen world to use coercive force in the form of a police function, to maintain peace and just order. It derives from the conviction that given the reality of the abuse of power, action must be taken to control, stem and prevent this abuse of power (Russel, 1984, p. 246).

The "just war" theory has provided the analogy for a related concept, but with diametrically opposed implications in the South African context, namely the idea of a "just revolution". Already the Scottish reformer, John Knox, advanced the basic arguments for this position. In the last analysis, the believer has to obey God, not man. It is therefore the responsibility of Christians to resist and oppose rulers whose commands are contrary to the will of God. In this case, revolution would be justified. This concept has been developed extensively within the context of liberation theology and the World Council of Churches Program to Combat Racism. Crucial for this theory is of course, just as in the case of the "just war", the decision when a given situation has reached the point where violent resistance is justified and the criteria on which such a decision should be based.

TWO ILLUSTRATIONS FROM THE SOUTH AFRICAN DEBATE ON VIOLENCE

Despite the contrast between the pacifist and just war/revolution traditions, it is surprising to see how often a combination of conflicting perspectives occur. Within the South African situation, some on the basis of a particular interpretation of Romans 13 condemn all violence while at the same time condone the violent suppression of any uprising. Others justify violent resistance to oppressive laws while at the same time urging conscientious objection to military service. Inconsistencies of this kind would seem to indicate that more than religious convictions play a role in determining attitudes and shaping intergroup relations. Indeed, indications are that the potential for conflict is extremely high in these cases. In order to give a concrete illustration of these tendencies, we shall take a brief look at two issues which attracted a lot of public attention, *viz.* the Program to Combat Racism (PCR) as initiated by the World Council of Churches and the debate on conscientious objection to military service, which resulted in certain amendments to the Defense Act being passed in Parliament.

The Programme to Combat Racism

After a long history of involvement in Southern Africa and the problems of the sub-continent, the Central Committee of the World Council of Churches (WCC) in 1969 endorsed a proposal for the establishment of a Programme to Combat Racism (PCR). This programme heralded a new era in ecumenical relations. The commitment was made to eliminate racism throughout the world — not only in word, but in deed. In 1970, the executive meeting of the WCC held in Arnoldshain in the Federal Republic of Germany decided to give financial support to various movements engaged in military conflict against what were described as the unjust White minority governments in Southern Africa.

The decision sparked off a controversy unparalleled in its scope and intensity. Despite repeated assurances by the WCC that their funding was solely for humanitarian purposes consonant with the aims and policies of the WCC, critics of the world body maintained that the PCR in effect meant that churches were condoning and giving concrete support to acts of violence and terrorism whereby the lives of innocent people were put in jeopardy. Within South Africa, the WCC's decision caused a polarization between churches and individuals which severely damaged intergroup relations. The WCC was accused of naiveté in assuming the funds would be used only for humanitarian purposes when no form of control over expenditure was envisaged. Further criticisms were that the task of the church is to find other ways than violence to solve political differences, that violence in the end breeds more violence, that the exclusive identification of the church with one group casts doubt on its impartiality and jeopardizes its role in bringing about reconciliation. The most serious criticism was directed at the theological justification of the concept of a "just revolution".

For their part, the WCC insisted that their support should be seen as a sign of solidarity, clearly to be distinguished from identification with any movement, that the decision of those who were the victims of violent measures which denied basic human rights and who had decided to wage an armed struggle, should be respected and understood, that the WCC had a long record of humanitarian aid to all victims of war, irrespective of the group to which they belong. Again the argument was used that the continual infringement of human rights constitutes grounds for a legitimate right to resistance, including armed resistance if no other alternatives appear to be left.

Without going into more detail concerning the debate itself, it can be said without fear of contradiction that the PCR represents a watershed in the debate on violence. Attitudes on both sides hardened and are likely to remain so for quite some time. What is further of importance, is the fact that the "just revolution" forms the pivotal category of the debate (Villa-Vicencio, 1980, p. 21). The concept itself is problematic — if by "just" is meant that which is acceptable to God, it can hardly be used to describe an event which is marked by the loss of life and often ends in chaos and anarchy. (The same criticism would apply to the expression "just war"). Because of these difficulties, the concept of "justifiable resistance" has been proposed (Villa-Vicencio, 1980, p. 58). As far as intergroup relations are concerned, the critical issue is: At what point does violence become justifiable? Since the perception of reality appears to be a crucial factor in intergroup relations, the answer to this question will depend entirely on the position of the individual or group concerned and of their evaluation of the situation in which they find themselves. We shall return to this aspect in due course.

The debate on conscientious objection to military service

The second illustration of how concepts of violence affect intergroup relations is taken from the current debate on conscientious objection. We have already seen how the initial pacifist tradition of the early church was replaced by the "just war" theory after 312. But conscientious objection to military service only becomes a serious problem in a society when conscription is introduced as a way of recruiting soldiers. In the case of a volunteer or professional army, conscientious objectors need not come into conflict with military officials. Conscription was for the first time introduced in France after the French Revolution. The idea was that every citizen who has the right to take part in government should also be responsible for the military defence of his county.

Interestingly enough, conscription was introduced in South Africa only in 1966 (cf De Villiers 1983, pp. 24-5). During the Second World War, the authorities (unlike the rest of the Allies) refrained from doing so because of the deep political divisions in the white ruling group. The event that really initiated the current debate was a controversial resolution adopted by the South African Council of Churches (SACC) at its annual meeting at Hammanskraal in 1974. In its preamble, the motion stressed ultimate obedience to God, argued that South Africa is a fundamentally unjust and discriminatory society and therefore the real threat to peace and finally questioned whether it is consistent to condemn only revolutionary violence while remaining silent about the institutional violence of the state.

De Villiers (1983, p. 24) continues: "The motion questioned whether it was the duty of those who followed Christ, the Prince of Peace, to engage in violence and war when the state demanded it. It argued that the only possible case for this demand, if any, was in the case of a just war, which could not be in defence of an unjust society. It was resolved, inter alia, to deplore violence as a means of solving problems and to call on its member churches to consider whether Christ's call to take up the cross and follow Him in identifying with the oppressed, involved also becoming a conscientious objector.

This resolution met with fierce opposition from the government, some of the churches and a large section of the public. It prompted the government to pass the Defence Further Amendment Act. This legislation provided, inter alia, for a fine of up to R5 000 and imprisonment up to six years for anyone who "uses any language or does any act or thing with intent to recommend to, encourage, aid, incite, instigate, suggest to or cause any other person or group of persons in general to refuse, to fail to render their national service".

The response of the churches to the SACC resolution was mixed. The White Afrikaans-speaking churches rejected it outright. The NGK, for example, declared at the general synod meeting in October 1974 that it was in conflict with Romans 13. The Baptist Union of South Africa also dissociated itself from the resolution although all the other mainline English churches supported it in varying degrees. The Baptist Union, however, joined the other English churches in stressing the supremacy of the individual Christian conscience and in regarding conscientious objection as a legitimate Christian option which should be provided for by alternative forms of national service.''

The Defence Force had always had to cope with a number of conscientious objectors. These almost invariably were Jehovah Witnesses who refused military service because of the official pacifist viewpoint of their organization. In contrast, the trials of the first public conscientious objectors coming from the mainline churches, received very wide press coverage. The first six were Peter Moll (1979), Richard Steele (1980), Charles Yeats (1981), Mike Vivieros (1982), Neil Mitchell (1982) and Bill Paddock (1982). From the reasons given for their refusal, it appears that some had "universal" pacifist convictions, while others took a "selective" pacifist position. The latter based their argument on the "just war" theory. Although they were not in principle against military service, they refused to participate in the present border war which, to their understanding, was unjust insofar as it was in defence of an unjust society. Furthermore, seen from the type or service these objectors were willing to perform, the following main categories of objectors can be distinguished:

● Conscientious non-combatants: people who have conscientious objections to doing their military service in a combat capacity only.

● Conscientious non-militarists: people who have conscientious objections to doing all military forms of national service.

● Conscientious non-conscriptists: people who have conscientious objections to being conscripted for national service. (De Villiers, 1983, p. 26).

As a result of the critism of the Defence Act and the treatment of the above-mentioned objectors, the Naude Committee was appointed in 1980 to investigate the whole issue of conscientious objection to military service. The proposals of this committee formed the basis of the new Defence Amended Act. Inter alia, the Act provides for three categories of objectors:

● Bona fide religious objectors with whose religious convictions it is not in conflict to render service in a non-combatant capacity in an armed force. They would have to perform service in the SADF in uniform, but in a non-combatant capacity, for the same duration as non-objectors.

● Bona fide religious objectors with whose religious convictions it is not in conflict to perform prescribed maintenance tasks in military forces in a prescribed non-military dress. The length of their service would be one and a half times the length of the current military service, together with camps. This would amount to three years initial service and three years of service in camps afterwards.

● Bona fide religious objectors with whose religious convictions it is in conflict to render any service in any armed force. Initially it was stipulated that they would be required to do an alternative form of national service in other government departments for an uninterrupted period of eight years. During the debate in parliament this was changed to an uninterrupted period of six years of alternative service.

By "bona fide religious objectors" are meant only total pacifists who, for purely religious (not necessarily Christian) reasons, object to direct participation in violence. Selective pacifists, who object to participation in a particular war which they regard as unjust on religious, moral or political grounds, are not recognised as *bona fide* religious objectors. Nor in their case is provision made for alternative national service. (De Villiers, 1983, p. 27-8).

As far as intergroup relations are concerned, it is likely that the Act in its amended form will remain a point of friction, because of the non-recognition of selective conscientious objection. The issue is a highly sensitive one. At the moment we have the remarkable position that provision is made for the total pacifist, but not for selective conscientious objectors. But at the same time, it is also understandable. The total pacifist position implies a rejection of violence in any form, regardless of the motivation for the war or the social conditions in a given society. Selective conscientious objection implies a negative judgement of a specific situation, i.e. that a specific war is unjust or that an unjust society is being defended. It has been argued by supporters of the Bill that selective conscientious objection in the final analysis is directed against the existence and orderly function of the state and therefore cannot be tolerated. In constrast, it has been argued that this is not necessarily the consequence of such a position, as the "just war" concept does recognise the duties of the state and even the necessity of a just war.

From this discussion, the dilemma for intergroup relations becomes clear. If unqualified obedience to the state is demanded, no room is left for the "just war" theory to function. If, on the other hand, it is left to the individual to decide whether a war or society is just or unjust without a clear and accepted set of criteria, the danger of subjectivity is real. It is for this reason there is an urgent need to reach concensus on basic human rights, as discussed in the first section of this chapter. But even when this is done, some questions will remain, e.g.: Will it be possible for the state to resile from totalitarian concepts of sovereignity to one in which the powers of the state are in some respects limited (by human rights) without such limitations being exploited for subversion? Where the government itself claims to have a religious foundation and motivation, how is it possible to provide for alternatives to civic religion (i.e. for dissenters and heretics)?

EMPIRICAL DATA ON ATTITUDES TOWARDS VIOLENCE

What has been said up to now, has to do mainly with the influence of religious convictions on attitudes towards violence. When these views are compared with empirical data drawn from the multipurpose survey and other HSRC investigations, it appears that violence is no longer merely a theoretical option in the South African context. On the one hand, there is a certain measure of optimism that relations will improve in future. A majority of Coloureds (68 %) and Indians (64,9 %) expect that relations between the different population groups will improve within the next five years, over against 48,3 % of the Whites and 47,6 % of the Blacks. This would seem to tally with the 79,1 % of Coloureds and 79,9 % of Indians who think that changes can take place quickly enough without violence. On the other hand, there are signs that violence is being accepted as inevitable by a growing number of people. While almost all Whites (92,1 %) disagreed with the statement that protests in which some people are killed are necessary for accelerated political change, the figures for Coloureds and Indians were 72,9 % and 74,5 % respectively. A significant minority of Coloureds (11,9 %) and Indians (12,9 %) in fact agreed with the statement. But most revealing was the reaction to the question whether the use of violence is permissable in order to achieve political objectives in South Africa. Clear majorities in the case of Whites (70,1 %), Coloureds (62,5 %) and Indians (59,8 %) were against the use of violence, while in the case of Blacks it was a clear minority (36,6 %). In fact, 14,4 % of the Blacks thought it was permissable under all circumstances and 30,9 % under certain circumstances (18,1 % unsure). This means that almost half of the Blacks are not averse to the use of violence, which is an indication that the possibility of violence is increasing for this group.

THE WIDENING SPIRAL OF VIOLENCE

In a previous section, we focussed on only two areas where the issue of violence became especially visible in the South African context. As we have seen in the previous section, indications are that the scope of violence is indeed expanding and spreading to other areas. The inclusion of at least two more population groups in the new constitutional dispensation, means that the issue of military service will not be confined to the White group in future. Whether conscription will be extended to other groups is uncertain at this stage, but it can be anticipated that the introduction of such a measure will increase rather than decrease problems related to conscientious objection.

The increase of resistance to government measures and therefore the possibility of a higher rate of violence type 2, is likely to result in an increase of violence type 3, that is, repressive violence. The disturbing aspect of such a development is that repressive measures can be expected from quarters other than the official authorities. Indications are that radical groups to the right of government might also resort to violence. Certain isolated incidents have shown that this is not merely a hypothetical possibility and that an escalation of violence type 3 can be expected as changes in the present system continue to take effect. Against such a possibility must be reckoned the increased violence that can be expected if such changes do not take place.

The scope of violence may expand in yet another direction. The interaction between violence no. 1 and no. 2 is not confined to the military field. When the just/unjust society becomes a criterion for deciding the response of individuals on groups, the problem is bound to spread to all law-enforcing agencies. The police especially becomes a focal point — being at the same time the actual instrument enforcing government measures and the first target for resistance against these measures. The total pacifist tradition has developed a strong case against the participation of Christians in any police action because of the coercive force involved (Russel, 1984, p. 167). But it is also admitted that law enforcement is inevitable if the state has the obligation to serve God by encouraging the good and restraining evil. The consequence of such a position is that it is left to non-Christians to undertake the police function in society. This view has found little support and has in fact been severely criticised, but it did serve to focus attention on the issue of violence with regard to other law-enforcement agencies.

THE CRUCIAL QUESTION: WHAT KIND OF A SOCIETY IS SOUTH AFRICA?

In the preceding sections we have looked in a very selective way at some aspects of violence in the South African context. There are many other non-religious factors which would affect the "threshold of violence" in a given situation. We were only concerned with the relationship between violence and religious convictions. It is clear that a new awareness of the role of violence (potential or real) has emerged and that this theme is bound to become more prominent in intergroup relations. In summary, the following points can be made:

● The most striking feature of the debate is that for all parties concerned, the case for or against violence is finally decided by the answer to the question: In what kind of a society are we living in South Africa?

The diverging answers to this question illustrate the dilemma in which we find ourselves.

Some would say that the country is in the painful process of transition towards a more open and just society. Everything should be done to strengthen and accelerate this process. To this end, the preservation of law and order is essential and the state has both the right and duty to take all necessary measures to ensure an orderly transition.

Others would argue that the new dispensation is a further entrenchment of injustice, that all efforts to bring about change by non-violent means have failed, South Africa is already in a state of civil war and that the use of violence is therefore justified to overthrow the present regime.

Still others would argue that present changes are the first signs of capitulation by the dominant White group — a process which should be resisted by all possible means, including force, as it has become a struggle for survival and the preservation of civilized standards.

Attitudes towards the defence force and the police are a function of these conflicting perspectives , which on the one hand would make military service a Christian duty and on the other hand make the refusal to do so, a Christian imperative.

It is clear then, that religion plays an ambiguous role, in the sense that it can act both as an incentive for and as a deterrent against the use of violence. The deciding factor is our perception of the reality in which we find ourselves.

● A very disturbing feature of the situation is the rigid way in which the South African society is already categorized by different sections of the population. When reading resolutions passed by various church bodies, one is struck by the cliches in which the situation is described. A complex and widely differentiated society is thus reduced to rigid, uncompromising, opposed abstractions, which leave no room for movement of any kind.

● This tendency is strengthened by the challenge of contextual theology to the church to abandon its neutrality or aloofness and to "take sides", to identify with a certain group, namely the poor and oppressed (Villa Vicencio, 1982, p. 63; Russel 1984, p. 32). Solidarity is indeed an important biblical theme, but when it takes on exclusive forms, the church abandons its call to minister to all sinners and becomes one more factor in a series of instances opting for an exclusive position. A church indifferent to its own divisions and inequities should begin by abondoning its pretensions as a reconciler, as its credibility depends on whether it displays unity in its own ranks.

● In this situation, two urgent tasks face all involved in the religious field:

* To harness all forces to move as rapidly and decisively as possible towards a society which would in the understanding of the majority of people as being more just than the present.

* The greatest challenge is perhaps to de-absolutize positions, to show how the same set of data become completely opposing realities if viewed from different perspectives. In doing so, religion may prepare the way for an alternative society.

CHAPTER 5

FINDINGS AND RECOMMENDATIONS

FINDINGS

RELIGIOUS AFFILIATION IN SOUTH AFRICA

1. Most of the world's great religions are represented in South Africa, but the majority of South Africans (at least 75 %) claim to be Christian.

2. Christianity is extremely diverse. The conventional Western churches represent fewer than half of South Africa's population. Deep divisions, both political and doctrinal, run through South African Christianity. Functionally therefore, South Africa is best described as a multi-religious society though Christianity provides a common framework of religious symbols for many.

3. The most significant trend in religious affiliation at the present time appears to be the growth in the Black Indigenous churches. This growth has confounded predictions that these churches would decrease in importance as literacy increased. Black Indigenous churches now represent 39 % of the Black Christian population of South Africa.

THE DEFINITION OF RELIGION: ITS IDEAL FUNCTIONS

1. When we speak of religion we have in mind certain ideal functions which it is supposed to fulfil:

● Religion is supposed to be integrative, both for the individual and society. To individuals it is supposed to provide a sense of meaning and an orientation to life. In groups it is supposed to bind people together within a shared sense of reality and in accordance with shared values.

● When it succeeds in its integrative function, religion is highly motivational, both for the individual and for groups. It supplies over-arching beliefs and values which act as the touchstone for individual and social activity. In this sense it is supposed to be the primary motivating factor in human life.

2. There are two ways in which religion can malfunction relative to these ideals. First, it can fail in its integrative task and thereby fail to motivate. When this happens we speak of it as "dead" (rather then "alive"). But second, when motivationally successful, it may have harmful rather than helpful consequences. Motivated religious people are not always good for society. When its consequences are harmful it makes sense to refer to religion as "sick" (rather than "healthy").

RELIGION IN SOUTH AFRICA: THE PATTERN OF EXPECTATIONS

1. Research shows that the ideal function defined above are important for the majority of South Africans. Most South Africans indicate a basic personal religiosity and most of them expect religious movements to play a conciliatory social role. However, the expectations that people have of religion relate intimately to their life-experiences. Thus, the way in which South Africans expect religious movements to fulfil its ideal functions varies widely between groups. This variation is exacerbated by the highly differentiated nature of South African society.

2. In the social sphere, there are significant differences between Whites and the rest in what they expect from religious movements:

● The majority of South Africans agree that religious movements ought to promote justice and human values. However, Whites differ dramatically from the rest by their failure to connect the abstract ideas of justice to oppressive features of the social structure of South Africa. Thus, while the majority including Whites agree that religious movements should counter oppression, Whites are against the involvement of religious movements in protests against racial and other oppressive legislation. Many Whites appear to be unaware of the suffering caused by such legislation.

● Although it is hard to imagine that the majority of South Africans should not believe that religious movements ought to fulfil a conciliatory role, they differ fundamently in their understanding of how that should be done. Whites appear to believe that the conciliatory role of religion is best fulfilled by keeping the race groups apart. The other groups expect religious movements to bring the population groups together.

● Expectations of religious movements extend to the socio-economic sphere. Large proportions of those who are not White agree that religious movements ought to contribute to supplying the basic material needs of their members. By contrast, the proportion among Whites who believe this is lower.

3. The above pattern illustrates the way in which the religious expectations of South Africans vary with their social circumstances. Yet, there are some important anomalies. Blacks, Coloureds and Indians expect religious movements to oppose race legislation. In the case of Blacks and Indians, this extends to the

use of violence where human values are infringed. Yet, the majority in all the groups believe that religious movements should not be involved in politics.

4. Expectations do not appear to be matched by confidence in the efficacy of organized religion. All but the Afrikaans White group and those in some of the smaller groups e.g. Islam and Buddhism, indicate that religious movements may be failing to fulfil their needs. Many English-speaking Whites express a personal religiosity which is not tied exclusively to any particular religious group or even tradition. Among Blacks, Coloureds, and Asians, significant proportions record that they often or sometimes think life might be meaningless. A large number of South Africans, particularly Blacks, do not believe that religious movements are capable of solving social and economic problems. We must note however that this negative perception of organized religion in general may not extend to the particular religious group to which individuals belong.

PROBLEMS OF INTEGRATING THE BROAD ETHICAL ROLE OF RELIGION IN SOUTH AFRICA

1. Ideally religion ought to be a source of ethical values in the personal, social, and political sphere. Research indicates however that South Africans are experiencing difficulty integrating these various aspects of religious ethics. This difficulty appears to be endemic to the present structure of South African society.

2. At the heart of the problem lies the conflict that many religious people feel between the pursuit of religious values in the political sphere on the one hand, and in the personal and local community spheres on the other. To many, it no longer seems possible to initiate changes towards a more just society without causing local turmoil. To others, the chaos that the pursuit of justice seems to require is not religiously justifiable. We must emphasize that both represent a religious point of view.

● Many South Africans respond to the above difficulty by emphasizing one sphere at the expense of the other. There appear to be three typical responses: (i) Those whose religious activity relates to personal ethics and disavows both charitable social activity and politics; (ii) Those who include an element of social concern in their religious ethics, but without a conventional political aspect; (iii) Those for whom the overt expression of religious ethics covers all aspects, personal, social, and political.

● The third group above includes people who make a serious attempt to integrate their religious ethics at every level, but who would be willing to tolerate suffering themselves, and to see turmoil created in local communities if they believed that it would contribute to the achievement of a more just society.

• In the churches, the dilemma is reflected in the gulf that has opened up in many churches between the leadership and the membership. While members in these churches expect to have their personal needs ministered to, many leaders have tended to focus on the need for sociopolitical action. In some of the larger churches this tension has led to considerable debate and tension among leaders themselves who are unsure of their role.

• Among the under-privileged the dilemma has led to forms of religion which minister to personal needs but are overtly non-political. This is indicated by the growth of the Black Indigenous churches. Yet, surveys indicate that the sociopolitical sympathies of the under-privileged lie with what might be called the more radical sociopolitical groupings in the South African environment. Among many of these people therefore there is a tension between their religious orientation and their sociopolitical affinities.

We must emphasize the broad functional adequacy of the overtly non-political religious orientations. They represent a rational choice to ally a religious orientation with a general social orientation which meets personal and socio-economic needs even though it does not address socio-political problems directly. Given sociopolitical affinities of such groups however, they have the potential to become politically active.

3. The narrow application of religious values to either the personal or the social levels has harmful consequences for interpersonal and intergroup relations. The first does not contribute directly to the need to base social life on just and human structures. The second allows chaos within communities in the pursuit of social and religious values at the expense of other equally viable ways of engaging social problems.

4. To summarize: The research reflects a society in which the expression of religious values in either the personal or the socio-political sphere appears to involve sacrificing its expression in the other. This has had and will continue to have extremely damaging consequences for human relations in general. It has already been a source of severe trauma within many religious communities. We must emphasize that either way, the choice is a genuine religious choice.

THE USE OF RELIGION TO LEGITIMATE SPECIFIC GROUP INTERESTS

1. Religion ought to play a constructive rather than a destructive role in interpersonal and intergroup relations. By this is not meant a situation in which disagreement does not occur. Rather, it is a situation in which "ground rules" establish a common framework within which disagreement can be mediated.

2. Research shows that religion tends to function destructively when it is allied too closely to the identity and socio-economic and political interests of one group at the expense of others. This is especially the case when that group is in or

seeking power. Under such conditions religious symbols play a powerful motivating role in reinforcing the identity, attitudes and values of that group.

• In South Africa with its different groups vying for power and influence the appropriation of religious symbols to serve particular group interests has already had profoundly destructive consequences for intergroup relations. This occurred in the congruence established between the attitudes encouraged by the NGK on the one hand, and Afrikaner Nationalism on the other. There is a danger that the same might happen in the interaction between, for example, the predominantly Black churches, Black Consciousness, and the SACC. Religious symbolism, particularly that of Christianity, is presently being used to legitimate the political and social values of widely different and diametrically opposed sociopolitical groupings.

• In the economic sphere a similar process applies. In order to protect their own economic interests, those in positions of privilege appropriate philosophical arguments to justify their economic behaviour. Presently this is true of the entire White community which is not prepared to take a drop in the standard of living in order to achieve a more equitable distribution of economic potency. The most common rationalizations used to support such behaviour are those of neo-classical economic theory and the idea of enlightened self interest.

• In order to be relevant, religion has to reflect the needs and life-experiences of people. In this way it inevitably comes to be allied with specific group interests. In South Africa with its highly differentiated and heterogeneous society, we should expect therefore that different groups will have different expectations of religion and that religion will be used to justify incommensurate view-points.

• The fact that most South Africans are Christian and therefore ought to draw on essentially the same pool of symbols and teachings has not been enough to overcome the tendency of religion to serve particular group interests. When one dispassionately views the evidence about the actual way that religion functions, then the task of changing this tendency can be seen to be extremely difficult. The extent to which the values and interests of a particular group get buried in its religious point of view means that even under the most rigorous self-examination, a particular interest group seldom understands the full extent of its biases.

TRADITIONAL VALUES AND THE ROLE OF RELIGION

1. South Africans of different groups express a strong sense of their identity and a desire to preserve their traditional values though for the majority there is no need to do so by implementing seperatist legal structures.

2. Research indicates that group identity is an extremely delicate and complex phenomenon in which many factors play a role. Local community, language, religion and race are among the contributing factors. While religion as a source

of ultimate values ought ideally to play the dominant role in individual and group identity, in fact it does not. Research suggests its role to be an important but not determining factor.

3. Because individual and group identity is such a complex amalgam of different factors, many people embody contrary and mutually incompatible values in their individual and group identity. Religious values are not the dominant factor and do not therefore have the power to mediate these incompatibles. The problem with such latent tensions for intergroup relations is that they are frequently hidden to the individuals who embody them. They only become apparent when social change creates new social relations and brings hidden tensions to the surface. Then changes which were intended to improve intergroup relations simply result in new tensions replacing the old.

4. The importance of traditional values to all the groups cannot be used to justify the preservation of South Africa's present sociopolitical structure. It must be noted that the under-privileged groups do not perceive any tension to exist between the elimination of the existing discriminatory structures and the preservation of their traditional group values. From an ethical perspective, one of the most damaging aspects of government policy to date has been the harsh way in which it has broken up the community networks by which traditional values are preserved.

RELIGION IN A POLARIZED SOCIETY

1. It is a common-place that the sociopolitical debate on the future of South Africa has become highly polarized. As a result, people are forced to choose sides in a way which not only eliminates the moderate position, but also makes it impossible to withdraw and be uninvolved.

2. Research suggests that the existing sociopolitical options offered by the major sociopolitical parties and groups in South Africa do not represent the myriad concerns embodied in the complex identity of most South Africans. Yet, the polarized nature of the debate forces people to choose one side or the other. In this way tenuous and deceptive alliances are created between people who have little in common except that they disagree with each other less than they disagree with the rest.

● In a situation of forced choice, people are likely to support those groups with which they express an affinity. For many South Africans these are what are refered to in the media as the more radical sociopolitical groupings. The polarized situation is then one in which support which may previously have been verbal only, becomes active.

- In the area of religious identity, the above forced choice makes the overtly non-political religious orientations untenable. In the process it eliminates religious forms whose broad social orientation is viable and rational in socio-economic terms, but whose orientation is not equipped to deal with sociopolitical forces. There is a very real possibility that the religious and traditional values of many South Africans will not be able to withstand sociopolitical forces.

RELIGIOUS VALUES AND HUMAN RIGHTS

1. The concepts of justice and human rights are abstract and need to be given content in terms of local circumstances and values.

2. Traditionally there have been wide differences between the Afrikaans and English churches on the issue of human rights. Recently however, human rights has featured more prominently as an issue in the Afrikaans churches. There is now a surprising consensus within the most important church-groupings in South Africa as to what constitute basic human rights. Agreement also exists in this regard between theological and so-called secular views. The problems arise when specific content is given to these abstract terms.

3. Research suggests that human rights priorities could be formulated within the following guidelines:

- The right to life;
- The right to fully express one's humanity;
- The right to a decent quality of life.

These guidelines have direct consequences for the following aspects of South African life: The Mixed-Marriages Act, the Group Areas Act, Influx Control, Ownership of Land, Property rights and Housing, Equal Education Opportunities, Security Legislation.

4. In the formulation of human rights the Christian tradition has a contribution to make, particularly in the affirmation of the Biblical tradition of solidarity with and concern for the poor. Beyond Christianity, all the religions have a contribution to make as a resource for the discussion and analysis of social values. In spite of its many and almost inevitable historical abberations, religion remains the only aspect of human endeavour in which a cónscious attempt to transcend particular group interests is made.

- The Afrikaans churches have neglected their task of keeping people sensitive and aware of the need to have a society based on human values. Whites on the whole are extraordinarily insensitive to the suffering which existing social structures inflict on those who are not White.

5. We recognize that the discussion of values frequently takes place in an abstract way and in a way which is *dangerously* uninformed by a proper understanding of social processes. In any attempt to define human rights therefore, attention needs to be paid to the complex nature of social and human reality. However, narrow utilitarian approaches to social problems have proven themselves equally catastrophic when uniformed by a basic understanding of what is human and just. It is the task of religion to ensure that the people in a society remain sensitive to human suffering. The presence of suffering is the most basic indication that the society is being governed badly. No technocratic approach to the management of society has yet proved itself adequate and in the present primitive state of the human sciences there is no reason to believe that any one will in the near future. Precisely for that reason, a proper sense of what is human must remain a basic tool of government, and a proper sensitivity to the existence of suffering must remain a basic guide to the adequacy of policy.

* * *

RECOMMENDATIONS

The following recommendations are presented in the clear understanding that the establishment of proper values will be of little significance for intergroup relations if they are not informed by workable strategies. Furthermore, while full recognition is given to the incongruence between ideal and reality, it is the Work Committee's view that this disparity should not inhibit, but rather stimulate the pursuit of these values.

The Work Committee decided to be more specific with regard to the instances to whom its recommendations are addressed. The following categories were identified:

- The Main Committee
- Religious communities (e.g. the churches)
- The academic community
- The (political) decision makers.

MAIN COMMITTEE

1. Within the South African context, insufficient recognition is given to the crucial role religion can and does play in the shaping of intergroup relations. Steps should be taken to heighten the awareness of all groups to both its positive and negative potential.

2. A better understanding is needed of the ambivalent nature of religion, both in its constructive and destructive dimensions. It can be a strong motivational force for the improvement of group relations, but it can also be used to legitimize

group interests. It can stimulate, but also inhibit change. It can be used to mediate in situations of conflict, but also to incite violence. It can be a strong uniting, but also a very divisive force. The challenge is to understand under what conditions it functions in these different ways.

3. More extensive and sustained research should be undertaken on the role of religion, preferably in a multidisciplinary setting.

4. More research is needed on the relationship between values and culture and the influence this relationship has on the way human rights are interpreted.

RELIGIOUS COMMUNITIES

1. Religious communities are invited to compare the findings of the report with their own experiences both in order to check what is written here about religion and perhaps to assist them in understanding better the role of religion in the broader South African context.

2. Research on a regular basis should be undertaken by religious communities among their own members, especially on matters relating to intergroup relations. The committee found a considerable gap between church leadership and lay members on a variety of issues. The expectations members have of their group often differ radically from what the leadership perceives as the group's main objectives.

3. Religious communities should take note that research also revealed that although people generally have a high expectation of the role religion ought to play in intergroup relations, there is doubt about the ability of existing religious institutions to fulfil that function.

4. There appears to be a remarkable degree of consensus among religious communities on the need to define basic human rights. This measure of agreement should be used as a starting point to enter into dialogue with one another in order to give further substance to these basic rights. Religious communities have the responsibility to create a climate in which this discussion can progress. At the same time, due recognition should be given to the fact that the way in which these rights are concretized in a given situation may differ from community to community. Communities should therefore be allowed to define these rights for themselves, but this does not imply the licence to abrogate basic human rights.

5. There is a need to develop a more adequate pastoral theology and practice in order to provide pastoral care in a rapidly changing society, characterized by uncertainty, insecurity and social crisis. Care should be taken that an effective ministry is provided for needs on both the personal and sociopolitical level.

6. Because many religious communities have a vision for the future which is presently still unrealized, they are in an excellent position to mediate between the future ideal and present reality and to utilize the dynamic force inherent in such a future-directed orientation.

7. One of the findings of the committee was that preaching often does not provide clear-cut and concrete guidance on intergroup relations. Principles and practical guidelines should be clearly and unambiguously expressed in the church's preaching.

8. Both the vertical and horizontal dimensions of theology should receive attention within an ecumenical context. The revolutionary atmosphere in South Africa is not merely due to a so-called one-sided radicalization, but also to a conservatism which justifies the *status quo* on theological grounds irrespective of the social injustices it upholds.

9. There is a need to affirm in practice the biblical tradition of solidarity with the poor. Because of the complex nature of modern society, this will require critical reflection and a sophisticated understanding of present-day economic forces. However, the aim should be to affect equal access to the resources of the country.

10. Churches should be sensitive to the fact that clashes between vital interests and religious convictions can give rise to rationalisations which in their turn can lead to religion being used to support biased perceptions and ideological positions. The churches must be ready to counteract any such tendency.

11. The 1980 census shows that 75 % of the population is (nominally) Christian. This places a heavy responsibility on the churches to build bridges in a deeply segmented society and to provide the context where conflicting perspectives can be confronted with one another without necessarily erupting.

12. By the building of bridges is not meant in the first place the striving for doctrinal unity, but the commitment to a common framework of values, which creates the context where differences can be raised and even confronted with one another without fear. This "relativizing" of these positions may be the most urgent task facing religious communities today.

13. Research indicates that most groups have an earnest desire to know more about other groups, but that isolation and polarization have made this virtually impossible. Religious groups could fulfil an important role by seeking ways and means to facilitate constructive interaction between individuals and groups.

14. Churches should give closer attention to the relationship between church and state in order to give guidance to its members in a highly politicized situation. Research highlighted the tragic consequences when the witness of the church becomes ineffective because of a too close identification of church and state. At the same time it was found that the situation in South Africa is so confused and complex in terms of political structures, that it is almost impossible to talk meaningfully about the relationship church and state. As the traditional formulae for expressing this relationship appears no more to be applicable, a careful study should be done to establish what is meant by these two terms in the present political dispensation.

THE ACADEMIC COMMUNITY

1. The research done for the report has uncovered vast unresearched and under-researched areas. The list of research priorities as identified by the committee and published in the Intergroup brochure, is recommended to the research community as a guideline for further research.

2. High priority should also be given to research in a multidisciplinary setting. To achieve this, theologians should seek closer co-operation with their colleagues in the social sciences.

3. There is a need to establish effective measures of religion not tied too closely to conventional institutional measures, because without such measures, religious processes will not be adequately understood.

THE (POLITICAL) DECISION MAKERS

1. We want to draw attention to the destructive consequences of polarization in South Africa, which is becoming more intense and dangerous, not the least within religious communities. As a result, the option of a middle group in such a situation is less and less available and people are forced either to defend or attack the *status quo*.

2. The authorities should take cognizance of the ambivalent way in which religion functions in South Africa.

3. Due attention should be given to the Black Indigenous churches which are the fastest growing religious group and which will play an increasingly important role in future.

4. The stigma of discrimination attached to Indigenous and other churches among Blacks because of the fact that unregistered churches were denied certain privileges by the government, still remains, despite the fact that since 1966 churches are no longer registered by the Department of Co-operation and Development. More attention should be given to their requests and those of other religious groups for sites for religious buildings, telephone services for their leaders/ministers and applications which comply with the usual requirements for appointment as marriage officers. This recognition can have an important stabilizing effect on society.

5. Care should be taken to uphold religious freedom which implies on the one hand the right of individuals and groups to fulfil their own commitments and on the other hand the equal treatment of religious communities by the state.

6. From a religious perspective, law and order can never be maintained on the basis of injustice. Dehumanizing laws and practices which reduce people to a continuous marginal existence are in conflict with basic religious values and should be removed in the interest of a more just and stable future.

BIBLIOGRAPHY

BOSCH, D.J. 1984. "The roots and fruits of Afrikaner civil religion", In Hofmeyer, J.W. and W.S. Vorster, *New Faces in Africa,* Pretoria: Unisa, pp. 14-15.

COETZEE, J.K. 1984. "Religie as inisieerder, begeleier en inhibeerder van sosiale verandering" (Report: HSRC investigation into Intergroup Relations). Bloemfontein.

CRAFFORD, D. 1984. "Pluralisme as religieuse verskynsel: Die onafhanklike Swart kerke en bewegings en groepsverhoudinge in Suid-Afrika". (Report: HSRC Investigation into Intergroup Relations). Pretoria.

CUMPSTY, J. 1983. "A Year and a War Later: Some Lessons in Religion as Belonging drawn from Contemporary Israel". In *Religion in Southern Africa,* 5, 2.

CUMPSTY, J., J. HOFMEYR and G. KRUSS. 1984. "The role of religion in motivating or inhibiting socio-political action and ensuing counter-influences on the group." (Report: HSRC Investigation into Intergroup Relations). Cape Town.

DE CRUCHY, J.W. 1984. "Response" to Maimela (1984) In *Scriptura* 12, pp. 50-53.

DE VILLIERS, E. 1983. "Putting the recent debate on conscientious objection into perspective", In *Scriptura* 8. pp. 21-33.

DU TOIT, D.A. 1984. "Menseregte: 'n empiriese en teoretiese ondersoek vanuit teologies-etiese perspektief" (Report: HSRC Investigation into Intergroup Relations). Stellenbosch.

HOFMEYR, J. and G.C. OOSTHUIZEN. 1981. "Religion in a South African Indian Community" ISER. University of Durban-Westville.

HSRC. 1983. Results of surveys MPS/OV/56-59 and MPS/OV/71-74. (Document containing results in possession of writers).

KINGHORN, J. 1984. "DRC Theology: A Theology of Exploitation?" In *Journal of Theology for Southern Africa* 49, pp. 4-13.

KRITZINGER, J.J. 1984. "'n Statiese beskrywing vandie godsdienstige verspreiding van die bevolking van Suid-Afrika" (Report: HSRC Investigation into
Intergroup Relations). Pretoria.

MAIMELA, S.S. 1984. "Black Power and Black Theology in Southern Africa"
In *Scriptura* 12, pp. 40-50.

MARKINOR, 1982. "South African Social Values Survey". (Report compiled by
Markinor in conjunction with Gallup International).

MÜLLER, B.A. 1984. "Die openbare verkondiging van die kerk as medium van
verbetering en verandering van tussengroepverhoudinge" (Report: HSRC
Investigation into Intergroup Relations). Stellenbosch.

MUNTINGH, L.M. "Selfhandhawing deur Jode en Moslems as minderheids-
en godsdienstige groep in 'n oorwegend christelike Suid-Afrikaanse
gemeenskap" (Report: HSRC Investigation into Intergroup Relations)
Stellenbosch.

NICOL, W. 1984. "The Churches in Southern Africa and the Poor — An
Urgent Task". Paper read at a conference of the IRS, Potchefstroom,
November 1984.

NÜRNBERGER, K. 1984. "Power, Beliefs and Equity. Economic potency structures in South Africa and their interaction with patterns of conviction in
the light of a Christian ethic" (Report: HSRC Investigation into Intergroup Relations) Pretoria.

OOSTHUIZEN, G.C. 1968. "Causes of Religious Independantism in Africa".
Fort Hare Papers. Alice.

OOSTHUIZEN, G.C. 1975. Pentecostal Penetration into the Indian Community in Metropolitan Durban. HSRC Publication Series No 5, Pretoria.

OOSTHUIZEN, G.C. and J.H. HOFMEYR 1979 "A Religious Survey of
Chatsworth", ISER. University of Durban-Westville.

OOSTHUIZEN, G.C. 1982 "The Muslim Zanzibaris of South Africa". ISER.
University of Durban-Westville.

RUSSEL, D. 1984 "A theological critique of the Christian pacifist perspective
with special reference to the position of John Howard Yoder". PhD-Thesis
submitted in the Department of Religious Studies, University of Cape
Town, Cape Town.

STRYDOM, H. and I. WILKINS. 1978. The Super-Afrikaners. Jonathan Ball:
Johannesburg.

SUNDKLER, B.G.M. 1961. Bantu Prophets in South Africa. Oxford University Press.

VILLA-VICENCIO, C. 1980. Unisa Study Guide on Political Ethics (THE 304), Pretoria.

VILLA-VICENCIO, C. 1983. "Church Unity and Political Diversity." In *Journal of Theology for Southern Africa* 43, pp. 35-45.

WARDEN, J. 1983 "Mitres and Movements: A Paper on Bishops in a Time of Crisis". (Privately printed paper submitted to the editorial committee for consideration).

ADDENDUM I

RELIGION AND SOCIAL CHANGE

J.K. COETZEE

In a deeply segmented society such as that in South Africa, intergroup relations are closely concerned with ongoing negotiation for power (as in all plural societies). The central issues of living together thus entail, largely, the handling, accommodating and continuous adaption to the diverse opportunities of access to power. Accordingly, the possibility of conflict arising from the unequal distribution of power between dominant and subservient groups must be borne in mind all the time. On the one hand dominant groups deriving the most benefit from the maintenance of the structural inequality will consider social change qualitatively and institutionalize it. On the other hand minority groups will focus on altering especially the power relations between themselves and the dominant groups, in their striving for more equality.

This process of negotiation occurs throughout all institutions in society. In the South African society religion and religious collectivities or movements play a pertinent role in intergroup relations. This addendum focuses on religion and social change within the South African social structure. To this end the process of bestowing religious meaning, on one hand, and the ensuing social involvement on the other hand, are analysed. Empirical data was gleaned during a multipurpose survey conducted by the HSRC in 1983, which involved all South African population groups.*

RELIGION, RELIGIOUS INSTITUSIONALISATION AND SOCIAL CHANGE

The concepts which are central to this addendum are highlighted by means of conceptual analyses in this section. The analyses are supported with available empirical data regarding the broad religious scope in South Africa and with

---

* Complete details regarding the multipurpose surveys MPS/OV/56-59 and MPS/OV/71-74 appear in Coetzee, Jan K. *Religie as inisieerder, begeleier en inhibeerder van sosiale verandering* (HSRC National Investigation of Intergroup Relations, 1984).

specific findings obtained from the multipurpose surveys (MPS/OV/56-59 and MPS/OV/71-74) conducted by the HSRC.

RELIGION WITHIN THE SOCIAL STRUCTURE

Religion may be defined as a coherent whole of religious convictions or opinions regarding the transcendent or supernatural on one hand, and specific practices or actions on the other hand. Religion contains an aspect of faith manifested in certain forms of consciousness or orientations through which the followers of a religious orientation act collectively and in a significant relation to the ultimate or supernatural. Simultaneously religion also manifests religious convictions or ideas on transcendent aspects functionally. The substantive aspect of religion is embodied in the way in which people organise and experience their everyday lives. Thus a certain faith or experience underlies the practices which make religion visible in society (J. Wilson, 1978, p. 10-11) thus forming the functional aspect thereof. The integrated whole of symbols as adhered to by the followers of specific religious groups holds further implications for the way in which such groups confront everyday social realities.

The concept religion implies not only that people share a particular religious orientation and set of expectations or opinions regarding the supernatural, but also that a religious group as such emerges when people place their confidence in a series of principles, existential ideas, objects or phenomena collectively. This collective confidence posits a core of conceptions of reality and meanings based on specific actions that occur in the concrete reality of everyday existence.

The concrete realisation of religion occurs in its establishing a structure, by means of relatively stable grouping of concepts of reality and behaviour prescriptions, and which results in behaviour and actions which are reasonably patterned. Such an accepted frame for action and behaviour provides the realisation of a prerequisite for communal human life, viz. a broad guideline for shared ideas and a measure of compatibility regarding actions. This creates a frame for channeling individual expression of specific expectations (in so far as these are in line with the wider spectrum of practices sanctioned within the particular religion).

As an institution religion can be an agent of social change or the inhibitor of social change in a number of ways. As the following and impact of religion increases in a society, the contribution toward the broad encompassing reality found in the society increases accordingly. This encompassing reality guides the collective consciousness of the society and in return is also influenced by the collective constitution of meaning of significant groups, of which religious groups are an

118

example. In cases of other aspects than the religious exerting influences on the broad societal collective consciousness (such as political development, economic aims or educational tendencies) the religious basis can resist or even neutralise change.

It is when a significant number of religious convictions emerge on microlevel and attain a wide enough range through the accumulation of collective convictions to alter or influence the encompassing reality within the society significantly, that religion becomes the initiator of social change. In this way religion can contribute toward social change. Similarly religion can resist or inhibit the process of social change which appears in political, economic and other spheres, if the input of the existing religious basis is effective enough to shape the broad, encompassing reality of the society to an extent that elements of political, economic or other social changes within the society can be monitored or deterred completely. In South Africa religion functions both in terms of an appeal for change as well as in terms of an establishing mechanism of existent social structures.

In this addendum social change is used in the sense of processes occurring within the society which introduce alterations or shifts in the nuance of the total societal reality. The central issue at stake is determining whether a specific religious perspective could change the economic, political and social dimensions of the society effectively, provided it is supported sufficiently and its influence could accumulate. The assumption in this regard is that as an institution, religion is capable of instigating structural changes in society.

RELIGIOUS INSTITUTIONALISATION AND EXPRESSION

The institutionalisation or emergence of religion cannot occur within a sociocultural vacuum. Where people associate for the sake of a shared religious constitution of meaning, institutional structure formation occurs with relation to, and interacting with such other institutions as the educational, political and economic institutions. Religious institutionalisation comprises more than an isolated incident of constituting meaning; the process of bestowing meaning to the religious lifeworld is perpetuated continually. In this process of continual constitution of meaning, the simultaneous process of influencing by intervening institutions must be considered. Religious institutionalisation cannot be viewed apart from the influences that arise from the political, economic and other institutions.

A relationship and mutual influencing are to be found between religion and religious manifestation on the one hand, and the rest of society on the other hand, because, according to Gerard Dekker (1982, p. 11), both religion and religious manifestations do not only influence the rest of society but are in turn influenced by the situation of and the development within society. It follows that religion plays an important part in individual constitution of meaning to the everyday lifeworld. Religion and religious collectivities no longer assuming the same role in the modern society as in the traditional, undifferentiated society, there are sufficient indications to assume that the role of religion has become far more limited especially for some population groups (for example, the Whites). Regardless of the nature of religious meaning in the society, the presence of such an influence is not to be denied.

To determine the role South Africans attribute to religion, an attempt to measure the importance of religion was made, by considering the responses of every member of the investigation group regarding issues such as

• the influence in general of religious movements on South African society;
• the role religion plays in his own life; and
• the role a religious movement has played to change his opinions or beliefs.

An analysis of the four population groups (Empirical data: 2) reveals that the percentage of respondents allotting an important or very important role to religion, is highest in the case of Coloureds (68,6 %), followed by the Indians (62,6 %), Blacks (59,5 %) and Whites (50,4 %).

Analysing the responses of the four groups, on the specific question regarding the influence of religious movements in general within the South African society, brought to light quite different aspects than the collective responses to the theme of the importance of religion for the individual and in society. In contrast with the lowest percentage regarding the importance of religion (Empirical data: 2), viz. 50,4 %, 79,5 % Whites stated that religious movements influenced the RSA in an important or very important way. The percentage for Coloureds was 75,9 % and for Indians, 70,5 %. Black respondents (of whom 61,5 % had considered the influence of religious movements in the RSA to be important or very important) probably ascribed a lower influence level to religious movements because the dominant structure in the RSA has a Western orientation with which the Black religious groups (as well as the Indians who had the second smallest percentage) relate the least (Empirical data: 1).

The above tendencies must be viewed in the light of the different dimensions of religion as has been pointed out. Besides the reflection on the supernatural, religion contains an element of empirical orientation. If religion is to remain meaningful and relevant to the follower, it must be made ''true'' every day. In the case of the Whites (of whom the majority adhere to Christian religion) the ascribed influence of the Christian religion on the South African society may seem self-evident. One may refer to a form of civil religion, because the Christian religion has been largely institutionalised in the society. The opinion on the influence of religion in South Africa thus differs from that on the wider theme (importance of religion). It would appear that while the role of religion has limited impact in the personal life of the individual respondent, its influence on society is deemed considerable.

Where religion and religious collectivities, on one hand, and social criticism or social change, on the other hand, are involved, one must assume that the process of religious institutionalisation remains subject to certain problems or dilemmas which take place in all spheres of human behaviour. Examples would be especially the dilemmas in the process of religious realisation (institutionalisation). Especially the symbolic dilemma connected with tensions between religious experience, and its visible form of expression are important here. Closely connected is the permanently present dilemma of the tension which is generated regularly when the religious message has to be translated into concrete terms for everyday living (O'Dea in Tyriakan, 1963, pp. 71-91).

These dilemmas correlate with the fact that religious constitution of meaning is directly attached to and occurs in interaction with the way in which individuals are permanently giving meaning to their lifeworlds. Those factors which are important for the individual within his daily existence are expressed in some way as he interprets religious aspects in his life and assigns a place to each. This implies that man uses both his own position and the general circumstances of the majority of members of his religious collectivity, as basis for organising his religious set of thought and lifeworld. His daily position and general life circumstances are important for the way that his religion becomes meaningful to him, and influence his constitution of meaning to his religion. This would mean that not only those whose existential circumstances are attached to suffering, subjection and injustice (as defined by them) will imbue religion with the function of eliminating these conditions; also those in a privileged position (regarding material and political power) and who do not experience any threat or specific preoccupation regarding the maintenance of their privileged position, could assign a function of social criticism to religion.

The fact that individual members of a faith find their daily existence contributing toward the attitude of the religious collectivity toward social reality, necessitates further illumination. Research has revealed that religion functions in diverse ways in relation to social change. Gary Marx (Glock, 1973, pp. 62-65) indicates that religion can be made a mechanism for inhibiting social change. On the other hand the most incisive instigation for radical social change has been found within religious collectivities. In this addendum such a spectrum of possibilities are assumed to exist within the South African society. A predisposing factor is that both the more radical propagandists for change, and those pleading for the maintenance of the *status quo* exhibit religious devotion to a large extent. Extreme stances within religious collectivities cannot be brushed aside as mere examples of the application of religion for accomplishing other (e.g. political) ends. The well-known dictum of W.I. Thomas, ''If I define a situation as real, it is real to me in its consequences'', becomes relevant.

CONSTITUTION OF MEANING WITHIN A RELIGIOUS ENCOMPASSING REALITY

In this section attention goes to the fact that the involvement with a particular religious orientation usually presents consequences for the everyday reality surrounding people. On the other hand it can be assumed that the factual situations within which people find themselves will contribute to the way in which they realise their religion in society. This implies that preference will go to certain groups, aspirations and aims, in accordance with the religious reference frame. Such preference cannot be separated from the individual's personal circumstances and position in society.

INCREASING INVOLVEMENT IN THE PRESENT-DAY CONSTITUTION OF MEANING

A larger extent of involvement in the active process of constituting meaning seems evident in contemporary society. Gerard Dekker (1982, p. 19) indicates that the nature and character of religion has undergone change in today's society. This change correlates with general societal changes. A specific example is the process of fundamental democratisation, which means that people and groups are not passive and impotent towards power groups. In increasing measure people strive for participation in social and political control over society, thereby seeing themselves as co-responsible — and hence co-determining — in the organisation of society.

With the process of fundamental democratisation, Dekker (1982: 21) points to another aspect touching the role and function of religion in society, viz. the alteration which has come about in the content of religion. Different shifts can be found, such as the shift from orthodoxy to religious liberalism. Similarly there has been a shift from dogmatism to ethicalism. Dekker (1982, p. 22) explains this as movement from a situation which accentuated religious dogma to one which accentuates ethical opinions and active intervention. Such change is often indicated with concepts such as horisontalisation, increasing humanisation or secularisation of religion. All imply emphasis of the immanent reality of the situation here and now. Unlike in traditional theological reasoning, the accent is no longer mainly on the transcendent reality or hereafter.

Changes in the meaning of religion and religious collectivities result from these changes in the nature and character of religion in contemporary society. Dekker (1982, pp. 24-27) states that these changes hold specific implications for the individual. Man locates his own place and identity in society by means of his religion. Man decides what the meaning and order of society entails and his religion allows him a frame for experiencing his existence within this scheme meaningfully. This necessitates that the official religion as manifested in, e.g. a certain acknowledged denomination, has to adapt to its members and their situations. This leaves the official religion (the church) less independent of individual members than used to be the case. This process makes religion ever less utopian and probably more ideological. The more direct influence of religion becomes more pertinent than its conforming and pacifying functions.

The practical manifestation of religion implies, *inter alia,* that it can be seen as a mechanism following socio-economic progress or development. Man is encouraged to strive for progress on a wide scale, with religion providing one motivation for development, in the broad sense of the word. One could measure the effectiveness of religion in terms of the extent to which it helps to resist and eliminate economic, political and cultural dependency (Dussel, 1976, p. 151). Religion and development are related, because religion guides man's aspirations toward more humane life circumstances. It points out the dehumanising and conflicting aspects in economic, social and political circumstances. Together with the elimination of such dehumanisation and conflict, religion strives to promote the ongoing maintenance of meaning and significance. The functionality of religion depends on the extent to which it bestows meaning to the human lifeworld and accords with existential circumstances. This implies that man evaluates the socio-economic effectiveness of religion from within his own situation.

Research findings regarding this evaluation (Empirical data: 6) bears out this assumption to a large extent. This theme presents a calculated value representing the total responses to the following items:

- Religious movements mean little if they do not contribute in the provision of the basic needs (e.g. food and clothing) of all the people in South Africa.
- Religious movements can do little to solve general social and economic problems.

- Various religious movements should co-operate more to change South African society.
(Empirical data: 3-5)

17,9 % of Whites tend to place priority on the socio-economic effectiveness of religion, while the according percentage for Coloureds is 34,9. An obvious explanation for this discrepancy can be sought in the larger appearance of poverty among the second group. The wide range of movements attempting to escape the "poverty culture", together with the provided political channels embraced by religious leaders probably contributes to the higher percentage. With Black and Indian respondents, as with Whites, the priority of the socio-economic effectiveness of religion tends to be low (19,5 % and 21,0 % respectively).

The responses to the statement that religious movements have little use if they fail to provide basic requirements (like food and clothing) for all peoples of South Africa, highlighted the evaluation of religion's effectiveness further (Empirical data: 3). Of the White respondents 52,1 % agreed with this statement. The matching percentage for Blacks was 69,3, for Coloureds 62,2 and for Indians, 60,1. This shows that a respondent is more likely to consider the satisfaction of basic needs as an activity of a religious movement, when he or that group to which he belongs, have such needs which are not satisfied.

The accentuating of the socio-economic effectiveness of religion must however not be confused with an unconditional propagation of social change. The response to the statement that religious movements should help to limit societal change, emphasises the place allocated to traditionality (Empirical data: 7). Only one of every four White respondents (26,3 %) agreed with this statement. This tendency follows the idea of progress and concomitant change which features prominently in Western thought. By contrast every second Coloured and Indian respondent (48,5 % and 55,5 % respectively) agreed, while two thirds of the Blacks (70,1 %) agreed. This specific emphasis features again later in this addendum. Allocating functions like structural liberation, social justice, etc., to religion does not imply an unconditional rejection of traditional bonds.

With consideration of what the ongoing process of constitution of meaning and definition of the implications of being religious can have for human existence, the concept religious collectivity (church) is illuminated further. The pertinence of the process of constituting meaning regarding aspects connected with religious living, is exemplified in the custom of referring to *my church* or *our church*. This identification indicates an emotional bond with the church and also a specific relation with the concept of "church". J.H. Roberts (Eybers *et al.*, 1975, pp. 59-60) covers a wide spectrum in this regard to enumerate many examples to show that the expressions *our church* or *our beloved church* are used from ecclesiastical and political platforms, to refer to the Afrikaner. The expression *the church (the Afrikaner church) is the bastion of the nation* is often heard; Roberts considers such uses sufficient indication that to a certain group, church means the same as "national church" (volkskerk). He also argues that in the light of such typification of the church as church of the Afrikaner, a cultural legacy of the Afrikaner, etc., the "national church" character of the three so-called sister churches becomes an unquestionable fact (Eybers *et al.*, 1975, p. 60).

The tendency to associate with religious collectivities directly, indicates that members thereof clarify the place of religion in their lives to themselves consciously; in some cases even unconsciously. The role of the religious collectivity is acknowledged and allocated a certain place. The role and place thus assigned to religion combine with all the other significant institutions toward the constitution of the lifeworld, eventually to give rise to the formation of the total reference frame which guides the ordering of existence. This tendency is borne out by research conducted in the USA (Moulin, 1977, pp. 7-21) in which religion was found to play an important part in the stimulation of radical political action among Negroes. Religion becomes a basis for ethnical identity and community interests. The collective action and resentment against e.g. the "corruption of Whites" stimulates the sense of solidarity and is given further momentum by other institutions which promote community interests.

CONSTITUTION OF MEANING WITHIN A PLURAL SOCIETY

Religious differences within a particular society are by no means exclusive to the South African society. Wherever other divisions are found alongside religious differences in the South African society one finds a relatively unique situation. In our day there appears to be more involvement with the constitution of meaning, as has been indicated above. Democratisation, more liberal accentuation of human rights and the shift toward continual ethical evaluation of affairs have brought about a new vision of inequality and plurality. It is thus to be expected that in such a deeply segmented society as South Africa religious groups will be involved with wider sociopolitical contentions.

In her study of plurality with regards to religion, M.M. Meerburg (1981, pp. 283-284) shows that a differentiated and plural society results in a diversity of lifeworlds. She considers homogeneous societies as possessing a broad, encompassing sense or meaning. Religious homogeneity follows naturally and authorities would be viewed as rulers on grounds of God's grace; drastic action could be justified as being "necessary for God and fatherland". The broad society is determined collectively by transcendental origin and transcendental aim. Individual faith is taken for granted and considered largely indisputable. This results in the possibility of conceiving an institutional order or credibility structure retraceable to a homogeneous, encompassing definition of reality.

In a heterogeneous society like South Africa the situation is quite different. The acutely differentiated nature of the society induces a position and significance to religion which differs fundamentally from that of a relatively homogeneous society. Chapter 1 has already touched on the latent conflict potential of religion. Meerburg (1981, p. 287) questions the extent to which a shared perspective is conceivable within a plural and deeply segmented society. The problem resides in the different societal segments each maintaining an own orientation toward reality and set of expectations for behaviour. Any unity regarding goals or guidelines for development which would incorporate all members in more or less similar ways, is hardly possible. Instead one finds factions pursuing their own aims relatively autonomously. Their claims and ideals may differ due to the following:

- divergent orientations toward reality;
- own constitution of meaning regarding religion for their unique situation;
- different modes of expressing religious experience;
- problematic and controversial religious opinions;
- divergent approaches to ethical problems, and
- differing intentions or motivation.

This plurality and differentiation emerges from the ways respondents to the HSRC multipurpose surveys indicated to which extent it was possible for them to realise religion within the South African society. The following statement was put to respondents:

- Within the South African society I can live according to my religious principles.

(Empirical data: 8)

The majority of Whites reacted positively (91,0 %), while 80,1 % Coloureds and 79,4 % Indians considered religious realisation possible. The picture changes in the case of Black respondents, of whom less than two thirds (61,0 %) find complete religious realisation possible.

It is difficult to explain these tendencies, although the fact that the Black population group are traditionally, culturally and ideologically the most removed from the dominant White group probably plays an important role. The encompassing reality of the South African society is posited and maintained largely by the majority group (in this case, the Whites who are the dominant group, despite being one of the minority groups in terms of numbers). Dominant institutions which contribute collectively to the encompassing reality of the integrated institutional sphere of meaning, are:

- the Protestant Christian religion;
- the economy, based on the Western principle of free enterprise (capitalism);
- education, characterised by the system of Christian National teaching;
- the political system, which was based largely on the Western principle of participant democracy in South Africa until 1984 (although this has since been implemented segmentedly within each population group).

The fact that a large percentage of Blacks cannot state unconditionally that religious realisation is possible in South Africa, could possibly be ascribed to problems of adapting to a predominantly Western social structure. These adaptions seem less problematic for the Coloured and Indian population groups.

A PARADIGM OF COLLECTIVE CONSTITUTION OF MEANING

The foregoing conceptual analysis of religion pointed out that religion implies a relationship with the supernatural. Besides this religion must also be manifested practically: i.e. it must be realised within the social reality. The following elements of religion may be identified as aspects important to a paradigmatic frame of explanation of the relation between religion and social change. This provides an indication of a number of elements which emerge in the complex relationship of religion to social criticism. These elements appear in the form of statements (Greeley, 1982, pp. 15, 19, 49, 60, 84, 97, 119, 121, 123, 129 and 134).

- Every person has the characteristic of hope or expectation within himself.
- Every person seeks to confirm the hope within himself.
- Inherent to the experience of hope is the possibility of salvation or redemption — not only with regard to the hereafter but also in concrete everyday circumstances.
- People manifest their expectations through representations based on their lifeworlds.
- Religious manifestations are handed down, articulated and interpreted in the light of the "here and now" experience.
- A specific view of the world and stances toward social criticism and suffering on one hand, and prosperity and social control on the other hand, emerge from such manifestation.
- The experience of either good or bad is shared with others within the religious collectivity.
- The religious community erects a frame of interpretation for collective experiences and collective aims.
- Collective religious aims accumulate as other aims link up.
- The closer religious influencing approaches everyday existential experiences, the greater the impact thereof.
- As a result of the mutual influencing of religion and society, a religious group can assume a stance toward either social establishment or social criticism, in the light of the existential position of its members.

CONSTITUTING MEANING FROM THE EXISTENTIAL POSITION

It can be deduced from the above that a religious collectivity can be analysed in terms of its position and manifestation within the social structure, quite apart from its theological significance. This means that membership of a religious collectivity becomes a contributing factor to the broad existential base from which people organise their lifeworlds. Therefore religion plays a role in the process of social change in society, because the members of a religious collectivity continually relay its role and function back to their own existential position. If the broad lifeworld is interpreted as one in which injustice, oppression, hostility, suffering and need feature prominently, it can be assumed that the religious collectivity which finds itself in such circumstances will reveal elements thereof in its religious manifestation.

Similarly, a religious collectivity functioning from a privileged position could be tempted to continue the *status quo* and legitimate the privileged position of its members.

Research findings and investigations in the USA confirm religious involvement and constitution of meaning from a specific existential position. In this regard K.A. Roberts (1984, pp. 290-311) reports that American Negro Christians, belonging mainly to a lower socio-economic group, regularly sing songs classifiable according to a broad tendency, viz. often interpretations of a desire for redemption and escape from earthly woes. By contrast the popular songs of better off denominations reflect themes embodying high self-esteem, own value and optimism.

This tendency is confirmed from the perspective of the sociology of knowledge. One of the founders of phenomenology, Max Scheler (cited by W. Stark, 1958, p. 77), argued that people from the lower socio-economic group tend to look forward and emphasise the future as the carrier of a better regime, while those from a higher socio-economic position are more inclined toward retrospection and emphasising their descent and tradition. The examples of popular songs and themes mentioned above, could be supplemented with other aspects which have already been mentioned. The accellerating process of democratisation in society together with the increasing accent on ethical issues lead one to the assumption that people from the lower socio-economic groups will seek escape routes from their negative position by means of their religious practice and experience. Thus religion could become a mechanism toward liberation and redemption of the somewhat dire social, political or economic situation. Religion posits a frame of interpretation according to which meaning is assigned to the concrete social reality.

The findings derived from the multipurpose surveys of the HSRC confirm the assumption that a population group which sees its position as structuraly limited, will tend to ascribe to religion the role of structural liberator to a large extent. In order to examine the extent to which this role is in fact ascribed to religion, a theme on structural liberation was composed to consist of the following items (Empirical data: 16):

• Religious movements must do everything they can to eliminate discrimination in society.
• The practising of religion can never be separated from care for the poor of all population groups.
• The practising of religion can never be separated from the care of the suppressed in all population groups.
• A religious movement should take a stand against racial discrimination.
• A religious movement should always act against laws that affect the lives of its members.
• A religious movement can even condone violence when people's rights and human dignity are restricted.
• Religious movements should encourage their members to protest peacefully against injustice.

(Empirical data: 9-15)

The Black, Coloured and Indian respondents (placing a high premium on structural liberation through religion with percentages of 41,5, 36,6 and 37,4 respectively) differ markedly from the White respondents (with 10,0 % placing a high premium on structural liberation).

In terms of a specific component of structural liberation, viz. the elimination of discrimination, the following data received attention. Less than half of the White respondents (46,0 %) thought that religious movements ought to exert all possible efforts toward eliminating discrimination in society. For Black (67,4 %), Coloured (74,6 %) and Indian (73,0 %) respondents the corresponding percentages are much higher (Empirical data: 9). The most obvious explanation lies in the fact that the latter three groups are subjected to discrimination far more than Whites. It follows that they would accord a component of liberation to religious movements. Together with the liberation from spiritual and psychic needs, a high premium is also placed on social, economic and political liberation. Injustice and discrimination are not only to be pointed out, but a better regime should be implemented by active intervention.

In the South African society it is especially the Christian religious movements which plead for structural liberation. The South African Council of Churches (SACC) can be mentioned as an example:

- The Division of Inter Church Aid (a division of the SACC is involved with such community development projects with a view" . . . to establish a healthy community in a more just society, that is truly democratic and non-racial" (SACC, 1982, p. 27).
- The Dependants' Conference wish to take charge and organise the care of political prisoners, confined or banned persons and their dependants.
- The Asingeni Fund pays the legal fees of persons indicted for political crimes.
- The Division of Justice and Reconciliation acts as intelligence organisation in the distribution of critical analysis of foreign investments, forced removals, the Mixed Marriages Act and the Immorality Act, policy of apartheid, etc.
- Apartheid is formally declared to be heresy.

(SACC, 1982, 27-35)

The wide propagation of issues held up as instances of injustice and oppression inevitably effects the opinion regarding structural liberation. Within the Christian religion the argument is that the church emerged from the ranks of the oppressed: therefore it cannot but side with the oppressed (Desmond Tutu in SACC, 1982, p. 21). According to Tutu it must be added that the church occupies a unique position in the lives of people and is therefore an uncommonly appropriate organisation for helping to accomplish the process of liberation.

RELIGIOUS COHESION AS THE BASIS OF RESENTMENT

The conceptual analysis of religion and religious institutionalisation has clearly showed that religion, besides its specifically indicated manifest functions, also has some latent functions. Religion affords the opportunity of being together, social solidarity, the experience of social cohesion and the establishing of bases for emotional expression which would be hard to realise in other ways in a differentiated, secular society (B. Wilson, 1982, pp. 27-34). Religion needs therefore not only answer individual questions regarding individual formation of personality, but also gives groups the opportunity to associate collectively around certain convictions and goals. In this way religion contributes toward collective formation of identity.

While religion strives continually toward providing the individual with significance, it simultaneously has the potential for making collective constitution of meaning possible for groups. Religion has the function of constituting personal identity. Such personal identity can serve as the substructure, security foundation and establishing agent of surety. On these ground religion provides motivation for involvement in society, because the individual views *the* society increasingly as *his* society. Along the lines of this process religion attains effectiveness within society. This occurs because religious identity culminates when various people admit toward each other and toward the world, that they are assuming a certain stance toward aspects of social reality (Beckford, 1983, pp. 13-15). Individual identity culminates in group identity and provides a frame from which social criticism is delivered. The extent to which one can justifiably refer to group identity determines the collective front of action and the resultant manifestation of power (McGuire, 1983).

All forms of religious expression contribute toward the establishment of personal as well as collective forming of identity. As indicated above, the culmination of identity formation can lead to an effective form of power and assumption of a critical stance toward social reality. An important contributing factor which features prominently especially in the South African society, is the role of religious leaders in channelling social criticism. Research conducted in the USA has revealed that intense politicisation of the religious office (acute social criticism) is found among religious leaders with the following characteristics:

- mainly young clerics;
- mainly urban church leaders;
- those who are well qualified academically and otherwise;
- strong ecumenic contacts; and
- pertinent alienation from a traditional theology and traditional religious practice.

(Garrett, 1973, p. 381).

Besides the above characteristics of religious leaders who are considerably involved in social criticism, research findings (Johnson, 1966, pp. 200-208) reveal a definite correlation between the theological perspectives of religious leaders and the party political preferences of members of the religious group with which they are involved. It would thus appear that the influence of a religious leader filters through to those with whom he associates. Theological groups or religious groups often exhibit certain preferences, as groups. One could assume that the political preferences of members are influenced by officials, official mouthpieces and other opinion shapers. These research findings reveal specific similarities with what seems to be the case in South Africa. Not only is there a conspicuous similarity between the characteristics of more radical leaders in South Africa and the USA, but also between the theological views and social criticism in both cases.

OPPOSING STANCES — HERESY

This section concerns aspects of the phenomenon of religion as not only presupposing a theological frame, but the particular way in which it figures or can be made "true". The practical realisation of religion often occurs in quite divergent ways for this reason. It has been stated that religious embodiment cannot be seen apart from the existential circumstances of the people involved in the religion. The very fact that in their religious manifestation or expression, groups confront each other directly already makes this a problematical issue. A phenomenon like social change with its accompanying connotations of justice, structural limitations, liberation, etc., inevitably introduces controversial aspects. Thus it may happen that religious groups who trace their dogma and dogmatic frame to the same sources originally, differ from each other where practical application is concerned to an extent that places them in opposite sides towards each other. The divergent ways in which the consequences of dogmatic frames are brought to realisation could be so incisive that such groups react towards each other with antagonism.

An example of this phenomenon in the broad connection of Christian church groups and even specific church families is to be found in South Africa. Since 1982 church groups which defend the principle of apartheid theologically or otherwise, have been accused of heresy by various other denominations, as well as by members of their own church families. In the survey of occurrences in the sphere of church and religion in South Africa this is discussed summararily. At this stage attention is focused only on a more theoretical analysis of the assumption of opposing stances regarding religious manifestation. This analysis is limited to the verdicts and accusations regarding the supporting of apartheid as heresy.

The religious controversy surrounding apartheid as heresy originated with the dialectic categories of oppressor and oppressed; powerful and powerless, etc. E. Dussel (1976, p. 145) shows how, against a background of theological reflection of these categories, this dialectic interplay must be seen in terms of the concrete everyday life: who is the oppressed and who is the oppressor in a particular concrete situation? Oppression or domination implies that someone appoints himself as master over another. The rights, freedom and possibilities of the other person are affected. This means that the dominated or subjected person becomes reified or made instrumental toward achieving a certain aim.

In his testimony before the Eloff Investigation Committee regarding the South African Council of Churches, Peter Storey (the then president of the SACC) defined apartheid as follows: ''Elevating a person's race to the position of being the supreme criterion by which he or she is judged'' (Ecunews, March 1983, p. 3).

According to him a person's racial identity is raised to a more important indicator than his general human worthiness. Such dependence on race as the criterion determining certain opinions or decisions, can be defined as racism. Apartheid can be seen as based on racism. However it goes beyond the principle of racism, because it integrates racism into an ordered legal and accepted structure.

132

A religious group such as the Dutch Reformed Mission Church (for Coloureds) argues that the Dutch Reformed Church (for Whites) maintains the principles of apartheid in spite of the fact that it goes against the broad dogmatic frame (Bible) which it considers its foundation. Accordingly apartheid is declared heresy and "idolatry", because the oppressor places himself in the position of God, denies his fellow man freedom and maintains his own godliness. Unless a religious group (in this case allegedly the D.R. Church) distances itself and opposes apartheid pertinently, it is accessory to the action, and its religious involvement becomes heresy.

The accusation of heresy can be viewed as the most drastic and pertinent form of abhorrence and rejection that can be found among two religious movements. Heresy could be defined as a specific, articulated opinion which provides a form of institutionalised legitimation for an issue which the other party (the accuser) denounces in principle. The two parties (the accuser and the reputed heretic) should approach the particular issue of contention from the same reference frame (in this case the dogmatic framework of the Bible). A "heretic dictum or stance" reveals that the possibility of conflicting meanings or interpretations can be inherent in any ideological or religious assumption. The declaration of this stance as heresy, is based on the institutionalised support which exists for other (so-called justified) points of view. The fact that matters can go to such extremes as to arrive at different, opposing stances must be ascribed to the different ways in which followers of particular religious convictions and dogmas actualise their convictions on grounds of their existential positions.

Neither is the so-called heresy merely a difference of opinion. According to the analysis of G.V. Zito (1983, pp. 125-126) heresy is that stance which lodges an attack on or opposes the institutionalised view regarding a specific issue. Although the stance declared to be heresy may be largely verbal, it is considered a specific action and brought to bear on a specific deviation. Heresy can occur only within a specific interaction frame. It remains seen as so objectionable however, that people adhering to the principles and dogma react with hostility. Collective action against heresy is the result of collective resistance against the heretic principle. True believers are convinced that what they believe to be the truth, is distorted, despised and defiled.

Where the South African ecclesiastical sphere is concerned, the term heresy must be connected directly with opinions related to social justice. This concept (social justice) has featured most in the South African press debate since 1982, on the role and contribution of religion in society. The "popular theology" described by the media uses social justice synonymously with "love thy neighbour" to a large extent. In the South African context social justice is associated with such specific practices and particular laws as:

- Migrant labour
- Forced removals and resettlements
- Intervention at squatter camps
- Pass laws
- Influx control
- Group Areas Act
- Mixed Marriages Act and Immorality Act
- Population Registration Act.

Both in everyday parlance and in the "popular theology" social justice is used as the concept expressing that which must be instrumental in bettering the fate of the exploited members of the society. Religious movements which plead and strive for social justice wish not only to eliminate injustice, but also desire active intervention for the establishment of an alternative social structure. In this respect social justice is linked directly with the rejection of a formally legitimated apartheid, for most propagators thereof. A section of the South African Christian groups adopt a clear stance and strategy regarding social justice. In a study presented during the Conference of the Second Carnegie Inquiry into Poverty and Development in Southern Africa at the University of Cape Town (13-19 April 1984), it was stated that the church in South Africa may never ignore poverty. The church ought to monitor laws and justice and oppose oppression and impoverishment pertinently. This study group considered it obvious that a political structure which denies basic human rights to a majority of South Africans in the land of their birth and allocates power over means of production to a minority group, enabling them to create surplus value at the cost of the powerless masses, must be considered and declared sinful (Ecunews, June — July 1984, pp. 14-18).

In the light of the above it can be expected that in religious groups which feature the principle of social justice pertinently and often, its members will tend to make this issue part of the task of that group. A broad orientation regarding social justice calculated the responses of each respondent to the following four items:

- Social justice should be the most important item in the work of religious movements.
- Religious movements should always oppose all forms of suppression.
- It is acceptable that religious movements act as advocates for the rights of all people (human rights).
- Religious movements that continuously keep themselves busy with equal rights for various groups are not busy with their real task.

(Empirical data: 17-20)

As could be expected, respondents of the Black, Coloured and Indian population groups place a high premium on social justice as being the task of religious movements (Empirical data: 21). By contrast with the 10,6 % White respondents who agreed with social justice as a task, other population groups indicated that the promotion of social justice should be a part of the activities of a religious movement, to a significant extent. Percentage supporting this view were 31,1 for Blacks, 33,2 for Coloureds and 30,4 for Indians.

The responses to the individual item, ''Social justice should be the most important item in the work of religious movements'', underlined the differences between the White and other respondents still more pertinently. A minority of White respondents agreed with this statement (38,6 %), while Black (69,6 %), Coloured (62,1 %) and Indian respondents (69,5 %) found this statement quite acceptable (Empirical data: 17).

RELIGION AND SOCIAL CRITICISM

Social criticism is by no means a modern phenomenon. Questioning of or rebellion against aspects of the social reality and actions of authorities have occurred throughout human history in one way or another. What can be stated is that the intensity of, and occasion for social criticism have increased notably since the sixth decade of this age. A central common idea recurs from various regions, divergent groups and disciplines: irregularities connected with the present dispensation must be exposed at all costs. A permanently critical appraisal shapes the intellectual climate, which demands that the society cannot merely be described as it appears at any given stage, but that the focus should also fall on how this society could appear.

CRITICAL REFLECTION REGARDING THE SOCIAL REALITY

The points of departure of the modern viewpoint of man can be summarised in the idea that man can be more than he is at any specific stage. More emphasis is placed on the manifestation of a rational scope than on a traditional scope. Questions regarding the social reality generally contain the presupposition of greater participation and choice regarding the realisation of the lifeworld: How can society be made more humane? How can a more humane society still grant acknowledgement and opportunity for individuality and fraternity? How does man fulfil his responsibilities with regard to society, others and himself? How can elements resisting fraternity be eliminated without introducing more inhumane elements into society in the process?

In the first place the social reality is seen as consisting of people — people who experience this reality daily. Social thought is underpinned by a striving for a satisfactory, humane society. The social reality is a concept which cannot be used neutrally — it is our social reality, our society (Hoefnagels, 1976, pp. 19-20). In this way society is critically analysed as well as experienced, and considered opinion becomes possible, concerning societal elements which are incompatible with a truly humane society. Such analysis and experience becomes the basis for endeavouring to show how a better society can be reached (Hoefnagels, 1971: p. 7). The critical reflection related to the social reality which is being referred to here, restrains itself consciously from merely supporting the establishment. Instead the aim is to expose elements of injustice.

CRITICAL REFLECTION ARISING FROM THE PRACTICE OF THEOLOGY

South African theologians assume a similar point of view regarding the emphasis of a concrete earthly, secular and political vocation from within religion, in the Christian tradition. The practical and empirical figuring of religion often becomes the visible proof and support thereof. In this regard J.A. Heyns (Duvenhage *et al.*, 1974, p. 42) opines that a church which fails to link its message with the imperative question of modern society, is not operating with the message of the Bible. By definition theology and the practicality of being Christian should mean involvement with society. More recently Desmond Tutu (SACC, 1982, pp. 24-26) stated that love for God and love for one's fellowman are Biblical principles which represent opposite sides of the same coin, in his testimony before the Eloff Investigation Committee's investigation of the South African Council of Churches. According to this approach religion concerns the "here and now", while the conception and handling of the "here and now" simultaneously influences the hereafter. Tutu is convinced that the Christian faith opposes any form of injustice, exploitation and oppression on principle. According to him the Bible could be seen as the most revolutionary and radical book, in a particular sense.

One of the most important reasons for the absence of social criticism within a specific religious collectivity is probably to be found in the existential position of members of that collectivity within the broad society. Whereas the majority of members of a religious collectivity enjoy a position of relative prosperity and political authority in society, such members can be assumed to ascribe a specific role to the religious collectivity in society. This role will expect the religious collectivity to accompany and condone the general social situation. In such a case the maintenance of the *status quo* will probably emerge in the way the religious collectivity justifies itself regarding the fulfilling of its role. However, where the members of a religious collectivity form a cultural and especially a political minority group, religion provides the "escape" from contradictions inherent in society. It is specifically within the experience of religion that the dehumanised, alienated and deprived person discovers a place for himself. The relevance and legitimacy of religion are continually being evaluated in terms of its contribution in realising the ideal of an increasingly humane society for its members.

For groups who define their own existential position in society as one marked by injustice, religion becomes a mechanism for channeling the striving for a better dispensation. The religious collectivity takes a pertinent role in pointing out the structural characteristics of the modern society, which could threaten, complicate or hamper the process of becoming aware of the group's identity (Drehsen in Dahm *et al.*, 1975, pp. 264-265). The group is sensitised for personal experiences and social injustice. Negative experiences in society are placed within the broad connection with depersonalisation, subjection, alienation and injustice. In this way religion becomes the mechanism by means of which religious consciousness is activated for a critical attitude toward social reality.

The recent years' shifts in the theological sphere set the climate, to a large extent, in which social criticism was implemented. Increasing emphasis was placed on the functional value of religion for man's earthly existence. The sixties heralded an important turning point regarding the overt propagation and justification of the idea of liberation within religion. In adherence with the critical intellectual climate referred to above, social criticism from specifically the religious grounding was accentuated. From the ranks of the Roman Catholic Church the Second Vatican Council and especially the assembling of CELAM (Latin American Bishops Conference) at Medellín, Colombia in 1968, are of significance (Berkhof *et al.*, 1967, pp. 191-233 and Hebblethwaite, 1983, p. 599). Influences exercised from these sources via such organisations as the World Council of Churches, the World Alliance of Reformed Churches, the South African Council of Churches etc. did not leave the South African milieu quite untouched.

At the assembly in Medellín it was stated overtly that the Roman Catholic Church in Latin America adhered to the belief that Christ's incarnation relates directly to liberation from bondage and sin, as well as from the limitations of illiteracy, poverty, political suppression and injustice — a view which should again not be considered apart from the real life circumstances of the people of Latin America who remain totally dependent on larger powers in the spheres of politics, economy and culture.

The theology of liberation is a critical reflection of the practical situation as defined by those involved. It acts as the source for the focus on the transformation of structures which could lead to liberation. The critical reflection within the theology of liberation implies, according to Gutiérrez (1979, p. 11-12) firstly a reflection of man on his own situation. He examines his own needs and requirements, and from here his reflection extends to society. Social events are interpreted (also in the way they affect the individual eventually) and the injustice inherent to it is exposed. This action cannot be seen without recognition of the liberating transformation which strives for the elimination of oppression, exploitation and injustice (Gutiérrez, 1979, p. 15).

The theology of liberation views the social reality within which people find themselves in terms of certain dialectic categories. Dussel (1976, p. 145) distinguishes the first dialectic relation as that between dominator and dominated. This dialectic relation must be conceived against the backdrop of everyday concrete life: Who is the dominator and who the dominated in certain concrete situations? A further dialectic relation is that between élite and masses. In both relations the theological reflection of liberation amounts to a desire to eliminate any form of dependence which could restrain the freedom of humanness. The effectiveness of religion resides in its destruction of this dependence.

The previous cursory survey over the emergence of ideas of liberation in theological reflection provides an indication of the growing critical involvement found within religious collectivities. In South Africa a wide spectrum of Christian church associations and groups identify with the ideas of structural liberation, social justice and reconciliation. Hence the South African Council of Churches opines that a Christian church should associate with the oppressed and promote liberation. In this regard Desmond Tutu (SACC, 1982, pp. 21-22) argues that the true church should step in for the oppressed, because the future of the oppressed is the responsibility of the church. According to him the church stands to lose the social group from which it emerged when it loses the loyalty and confidence of the oppressed. Furthermore the church intervenes in structural liberation because, according to Tutu, it occupies a unique position in the lives of its members. It is in the spiritual interest of the church itself to take charge of t he social and economic interests of exploited members, because in this way the church confirms its vocation (SACC, 1982, p. 22).

A further theological foundation for social criticism is found in so-called Black Theology which is supported fairly well in South Africa. As in the case of the theology of liberation, Black Theology may be seen largely as specifically applied theology. A. Boesak (1977, p. 1) defines it as the theological reflection of Black Christians regarding the situation in which they live and in terms of their fight for liberation. The issue under question is what it means to a Black

138

person to believe in a world controlled by Whites. Hence it is a situation theology, since it represents the attempt of Blacks to cope with their situation of being Black theologically (Boesak, 1977, p. 13). It attempts to interpret the message of the Bible in a way which allows their situation to be meaningful to Blacks. One could also refer to a contextual theology. In its whole the content of Black Theology is linked inseparably with liberation.

In general it can be said that the average South African does not ascribe a role to religion which would allow impingement of the political terrain unconditionally. In this regard one could refer to the response to the statement that a religious movement should not interfere with politics (such as issues of apartheid or integration), as featured in the HSRC's multipurpose surveys. The majority of White (79,9 %) respondents endorsed this statement, while the Blacks (58,1 %), Coloureds (60,3 %) and Indians (60,8 %) were less inclined to agree as wholeheartedly. These findings appear in Empirical data: 22.

RELIGION AND LIBERATION AS INITIATORS FOR DEVELOPMENT

The ideas of liberation, as they appear in recent theology, are closely linked with the broad aim for social development. In this regard development can be defined as the direction in which human aspirations are co-ordinated in striving toward more humane life circumstances. A few criteria which accompany the satisfaction of basic needs are enumerated. These criteria for, or indications of fulfilled human well-being are found within religion through ideas of liberation, and articulated as follows:

- Opportunities for being and feeling together.
- A climate which stimulates long term relations.
- Favourable structures within which true love can be satisfied.
- Opportunities for experiencing the total reality.
- A structure which can accommodate new impulses continually.
- Opportunities for creative actualisation.
- Total welfare.
- Significance situated in life itself.

(M. Nerfin, 1977, p. 109)

Development is held up as the focus of expectation and hope. It becomes the aspect around which people guide their aspirations (Berger, 1976, p. 33). Development may be defined as a process of directed change. Its expanse includes the total social reality and thus has consequences for all social institutions. This could mean that development is manifested as a process of directed change through which occurs economic growth and political development in the direction of autonomy and social reconstruction. Ideally this process of change could be legitimated on grounds of its linking up with the convictions of those involved in the process, i.e. it would occur within the boundaries of acceptability or in terms of their definition of needs. The principles of social reconstruction, especially, are articulated by individuals and cumulated by groups (Varma, 1980, p. 15). As a result, development is the desired direction along which people decide they would like to move.

For as long as people experience existent social structures as impediments of their humanness, it can be assumed that they will identify strongly with institutions propagating and pleading for liberation from this situation. Religion is one of the most effective ways of grouping people together with solidarity in their striving for more humane life circumstances. Thus development becomes not merely synonymous with economic growth but also a process with a broadly humanistic basis. The liberation advocated via religion expresses the aspirations of the oppressed. It specifically emphasises conflicting aspects in the economy, in politics and in the social structure. Within the religious practice of the theology of liberation a special place is reserved for "liberating criticism". The effectiveness of religion is often evaluated according to the extent to which it helps dissolve all forms of dependency and oppression effectively.

RELIGION AND SOCIETAL INVOLVEMENT IN SOUTH AFRICA

It might be impossible to reconstruct the total history of the involvement of religious groups with social, economic and political events in South Africa. In one way or another religious groups have always assumed stances regarding the practical manifestation of sociopolitical events. However the altered place, meaning and nature of religion in society has resulted in various religious groups' becoming involved in social criticism in a more direct and audible way. The previous section has indicated the growing extent of horizontal constitution of meaning by religious groups during the last number of years. (Compare the section in which the shift from dogmatism to ethicalism and the process of fundamental democratisation are described).

For further illumination of the data arrived at by means of the empirical research (the multipurpose surveys conducted by the HSRC) this section examines aspects of the debate which has raged so prominently in the press since 1982. Although it would be unlikely that the members of the different religious groups would have remained fully informed about the details of the discussions, it can be expected that they are influenced by the standpoints of their religious movements. One can also assume that religious leaders sway the opinions of members regarding religion and social criticism. For this reason a number of the more prominent leaders are discussed in this survey. The media exposure given to their opinions probably has a wider influence — wider even than the circle of their own religious collectivity.

Various events in the ecclesiastical-religious fields have sequenced regularly, each generating a broad front of comment. The meeting of the World Alliance of Reformed Churches in Ottawa (Canada) as well as a series of meetings of a number of South African Christian religious collectivities (synod sessions) provoked much discussion, especially within Christian groups since 1982 (the year in which the meetings occurred). The issues arousing the most prominent media coverage were almost exclusively those concerning ideas of social justice, social change and social criticism. Not only were these themes reiterated throughout the above proceedings, but since 1982 South African society became marked by signs of relatively incisive political and social reform announcements. Amidst public declarations, reports of the then President's Council, suggestions regarding constitutional changes, new party political groups, etc., utterances from the church concerning social change, social justice, intergroup relations, etc. were made prominent. The Referendum about a new constitutional policy, elections of representative bodies for Coloureds and Indians and the growing debate on the future of urban Blacks permeated sociopolitical exchange of ideas since 1983.

The pertinent role occupied by religious leaders, collectivities and wider groups on the total political scene became conspicuous. So religious leaders sided with both the participant and the opposing factions of Coloured politics. Resistance movements against the constitutional changes from the far right ranks (including meetings of ministers from Afrikaans churches) as well as more radical left wingers (like the United Democratic Front) are lead by clergymen. Especially a resistance movement like the UDF features involvement of representative religious leaders from conspicuously divergent groups (e.g. Dr A. Boesak of the Dutch Reformed Mission Church, Father S. Mkwatsha of the Catholic Church, Bishop D. Tutu of the SACC, the Rev. Mr Frank Chikane of the Africa Apostolic Church and Sheik N. Mohammed of the Muslim Judicial Council).

CULMINATION OF RELIGIOUS RESISTANCE

One of the watersheds in the years of debate about religion in the South African society occurred towards the end of April 1982, viz. the first press discussions of a study (Racism and the World Alliance of Reformed Churches) by Dr Allan Boesak which he was to present at the WARC meeting in Canada later. This study contained stances which provoked a whole series of reactions, some indicting the opinion and attitude of some religious groups and some attacking the prevalent political ideologies in South Africa. Boesak's own opinion appears in this study as apartheid implies that White greed has appropriated 87 % of the country; Blacks are denied the right to meaningful participation in making political decisions; the most important thing about a person is his racial identity; not only is apartheid a political ideology, but its whole existence as policy is couched in theological justification by White Reformed Churches (Rapport, 2 May 1982, p. 1). Reactions to this statement ranged from acceptance and identification on one hand (Rand Daily Mail, 29 April 1982, p. 3) to disgust and rejection on the other hand (Die Transvaler, 30 April 1982, p. 8).

The sharp attack from the ranks of some religious groups has as its main gist the argument that a politico-ideology such as apartheid is declared legitimate on theological and practical grounds by pro-government religious groups (Boesak in Leadership S.A., September 1982, p. 32). The role of a group like the D.R. Church in the creation of the Immorality Act, Mixed Marriages Act, Group Areas Act, etc. featured regularly in the debate. A dictum such as "apartheid is a church policy" (appearing in the years of establishing of the policy of apartheid in e.g. Die Kerkbode, September 1948) was cited in various accusations of this group.

An Open Letter to the DRC appeared in Die Kerkbode on 9th June 1982 in answer to the accusation that the D.R. Church supported apartheid morally. The 123 subscribers made various statements about reconciliation, church unity, the prophetic mission of the church, justice, etc. As with the Boesak study, this letter became central in both popular and theological debates in the secular press and organs of various religious groups. It was soon apparent that ideas uttered in this letter were hardly representative of the officials of this group.

The divergent views on social justice, reconsiliation and the propagation of structural liberation ended the prelude to the debate on religion in South African society to some extent, with the meeting of the World Alliance of Reformed Churches (WARC) in Ottawa, Canada (17 to 27 August 1982). Although mentioned at previous meetings, the position of Afrikaans speaking White religious groups was driven to a peak at this occasion. The 400 delegates of the 149 member churches from 76 countries condemned the White D.R. Church sharply (The Sunday Times, 22 August 1982, p. 2). The D.R. Church was stripped of membership rights, and the conditions for readmission were spelled out by the WARC, as follows: Full membership would be reimplemented when

- non-Whites were freely admitted to services and Holy Communion;
- active help and service was granted all who suffered as a result of apartheid, and

● clear utterances were delivered which rejected apartheid in ecclesiastical and political spheres.

(Coetzee, 1983, p. 42)

In reacting to the decision of the WARC Dr Allan Boesak (newly elected president of the WARC) said that this was the only decision at which the Alliance could have arrived to keep its integrity intact. It was simultaneously a historical decision because of its implementing deeds to words. In South Africa where apartheid was so closely associated with the Gospel this could do much towards enhancing the credibility of the Gospel for Blacks (Beeld, 27 August 1982, p. 1). A different reaction was that of the Rev. D.T. du P. Moolman, a delegate of the D.R. Church and moderator of the Eastern Cape Synod. He felt that the decision to curtail full membership of the D.R. Church and Reformed Church was not really aimed at these churches per se, but rather represented the total onslaught proposed to isolate South African in all areas, also the ecclesiastical (Die Burger, 27 August 1982, p. 19).

ECCLESIASTICAL MEETINGS IN SOUTH AFRICA

Soon after the Ottawa meeting of the WARC a series of meetings of various religious groups occurred. The role of religion with relation to social justice, reconciliation and structural liberation featured prominently throughout. Towards the end of September and beginning of October 1982 the D.R. Mission Church (mainly a Coloured group) had a meeting at Belhar (near Bellville) during which the most important event was the acceptance of a proposed confession which derived its origin and motivation from the ''sinful structures of the South African society''. A drafter of the confession, Gustav Bam, posits that ''. . . this confession pleads for the destruction of structures of thought, church and society which had been growing for many years (Die Kerkbode, 13 October 1982, p. 3). The drawing up of a confession regarding apartheid followed the announcement of a status confessionis. Prompted by this, the religious group (D. R. Mission Church) decided to accuse the D.R. Church of theological heresy and idolatry formally (Die Burger, 2 October, 1982, p. 1). With about 15 abstentions, the 490 delegates accepted the recommended confession reading . . . ''because the secular Gospel of apartheid threatens the confession of reconciliation in Jesus Christ and the unity of the Church of Jesus Christ essentially, the D.R. Mission Church declares that it creates a status confessionis for the church of Jesus Christ.''

A further recommendation accepted with 227 votes against 174, reads: ''We declare that apartheid is a sin, that moral and theological justification thereof is a mockery of the Gospel and that its persistent disobedience to the Word of God is theological heresy''. Another recommendation accepted with about 70 dissentient votes, reads: ''The Synod (D.R. Mission Church) is convinced that the D.R. Church believes in the ideology of apartheid which is in direct opposition to the Gospel message of reconciliation and visible unity of the church''. Hence the Synod of the D.R. Mission Church ''. . . cannot but accuse the D.R. Church of heresy and idolatry, with deepest regret'' (Die Burger, 2 October 1982, p. 1).

Other signs of intensive involvement with social criticism were also rendered during the D.R. Mission Church Synod. In this regard Die Burger (28 September 1982, p. 3) reports on interviews with ministers with a view to revocation of the Group Areas Act, the Mixed Marriages Act and article 16 of the Immorality Act. The meeting also expressed condemnation of the Orderly Removal and Resettlement of Black People Act (The Argus, 29 September 1982, p. 27).

The General Synod of the D.R. Church had its meeting in Pretoria a few weeks after that of the D.R. Mission Church. The alarming articulated shift of gospel message was pointed out at this meeting and it was said that the South African Council of Churches had shelved personal salvation and conversion since 1968 in favour of involvement with social, economic and political issues (Die Kerkbode, 20 October 1982, p. 8). It can be deduced that the chosen tone and direction during the General Synod of this religious movement was one of conservatism. Comments reveal an element of disappointment about the fact that this group failed to react more specifically and incisively to ultimatums of other groups and issues of the day. Dr Allan Boesak indicates the urgent need of seeking a peacable future, and that South Africa and the Christian religious groups are not allowed the time lapse, waiting for a D.R. Church decision re apartheid (The Star, 18 October 1982, p. 3). Similarly Die Burger (15 October 1982, p. 18) states that in the light of the rapid changes in South Africa in the field of national relations, the decision to revise the standpoint of the D.R. Church (Ras, volk en nasie en volkere-verhoudinge in die lig van die Skrif — Race, people and nation and national relations in the light of the Scriptures) only within four years, was most regrettable.

Other reporters on the above two meetings underline the chasm between the intellectual climates and frames of interpretation of these two religious groups, both traceable to identical theological sources. In an article in The Sunday Times (31 October 1982, p. 39) Prof. Willie Esterhuyse referred to the accusation of practising apartheid which was levelled at the D.R. Church. He sees the unwillingness or incapability of this religious group to veer away from theological apartheid indicated in their decision to condone article 16 of the Immorality Act and the Mixed Marriages Act on grounds of practical considerations. In its retrospection of the Synod meeting The Argus (25 October 1982, p. 12) shows that this denomination confirmed the concept of institutionalised racism anew.

During the 100th annual conference of the Methodist Church of Southern Africa in October 1982, it was decided unanimously that the ideology of apartheid would be declared heresy (Ecunews, December 1983, p. 6). Subsequently this group decided, at its next conference, to reject all legal and other limitations imposed by apartheid totally (Ecunews, November 1983, p. 11).

The general meeting of the Presbyterian Church endorsed the decision of the WARC. Besides their request that the D.R. Church should render a report to them on this matter, they reconfirmed their view of civil disobedience, thus ignoring the state's curtailment of multiracial marriages (Ecunews, December 1982, p. 9).

The Anglican Church expressed the view that South Africa exhibits an irreparable racial structure, at its session of the Executive Committee held in Port Elizabeth towards the beginning of November 1982 (The Argus, 8 November 1982, p. 21). According to this meeting, South African non-Whites were legally reduced to non-persons and consequently these laws must be seen as immoral. They consider human rights within the jurisdiction of the church, which should find ways of convincing the government to terminate its policy where this affects the lives of Black South Africans significantly. At this meeting it was decided to support the D.R. Mission Church's decision to declare apartheid heresy (Ecunews, December 1982, p. 9).

Another meeting of a religious group which generated interest was that of the United Congregational Church of Southern Africa which in affiliation with other religious groups, decided that any theological justification of apartheid may be considered heresy. This group opposed the new constitutional dispensation for South Africa strongly, on grounds of the fact that it

- promotes racism and is based on racial classification;
- attempts to divide the total Black population in order to support apartheid, and
- the majority of South Africans are bereft of citizenship.

(Ecunews, October 1983, p. 20)

Besides the meetings of individual religious groups referred to above, broader associations had continuous meetings. The most important interecclesiastical group among the Christian denominations is the South African Council of Churches. The D.R. Mission Church is the only Afrikaans speaking Christian denomination included as a member of the SACC. An indication of the nature of the SACC's social involvement and socially critical stance is revealed in the resolutions accepted at the recent national conferences. During the 1983 conference the following issues led to decisions:

- Pastoral care for families of political detainees.
- Active co-operation with the World Council of Churches.
- Opposition against forced military service on grounds of the defence of an injust society.
- Specific intervention against the support of apartheid.
- Strong opposition against the new constitutional suggestions.
- Liberation of political prisoners.
- Opposition against relocation.
- Encouraging memorial services on 16 June (Soweto day).

(Ecunews, July 1983, pp. 30-44)

The theme of the 1984 conference of the SACC was "The God of the poor" and the following were the most important decisions:

- The establishment of a nationwide organisation offering sympathy, solidarity and support to "victims" of relocation.
- Opposition against the system of military chaplains.
- Rejection of the new constitutional dispensation.
- Propagation for equal and open education.
- Active involvement with the poverty issue.
- Resistance against detention without trial.

(Ecunews, June — July 1984, pp. 37-40)

From the above data it can be seen that there are divergent ways in which religious groups can operate with the phenomenon of social change and social criticism. The specific activities and characteristics of a religious group inevitably influence the way in which individual members figure toward social change and social criticism.

RELIGIOUS PLURALITY AS A PROBLEM IN SOUTH AFRICA

The preceding sections have shown that both individuals and religious groups often tend to colour the nature of their social criticism in relation to their existential positions. This causes individuals or groups who interpret their position as one of injustice or deprivation, to expect solidarity from the religious group with which they identify. Religious groups which are either ignorant or indifferent towards the existential conditions of other groups will be more likely to be ignorant or indifferent towards the social, economic or political needs and requirements of other groups. Hence religious plurality is manifested in South Africa firstly between groups which are estranged from one another ideologically-politically or socio-economically or in relation to all these aspects collectively. In the second place religious plurality may also surface within a specific religious group. This plurality springs from divergent views of reality or divergent socio-economic conditions of members of the specific group.

Among the Afrikaans church groups considerable tension is generated between internal factions regarding the role of these churches in relation to social criticism. The so-called "Open Letter" to the D.R. Church served to underline the disunity, in 1982. Similarly the new constitutional dispensation earned strong opposition from the far right flank, as well as objections that the new dispensation did not offer sufficient solutions and still carried signs of basic injustice ("Testimony of 193").

Internal strife regarding the figuration of social criticism is found also within English speaking multiracial religious groups. Thus the Anglican, Methodist, Roman Catholic and Presbyterian churches experience problems with, among others, the way in which Black members wish to demonstrate their opposition to apartheid compared to that of White members (Ecunews, May 1983, p. 14).

The alliance of the largely White Presbyterian Church of Southern Africa with the United Congregational Church of Southern Africa (consisting of nearly 80 % Black members) became involved, for instance, because four Presbyterian congregations found co-operation with the (according to them) radical Black views of the other church, unfeasible. At the occasion of his re-election as president of the South African Catholic Bishops Conference in Pretoria, archbishop Denis Hurley stated that one of the most crucial problems facing the Roman Catholic Church in South Africa was the widening communication gap between church authorities and the majority of White members (Ecunews, February 1984, p. 17). An increasing resistance on the side of White members accompanied the growing involvement of this church with social, political and economic issues and its critical stance against the South African government.

In consequence to the internal disunity in connection with stances regarding social criticism, groups accuse one another of insufficient action. Thus the Alliance of Black Reformed Churches in South Africa (ABRECSA) attacked the Black D.R. Church of Africa (member of the D.R. Church family) and the Presbyterian Church of Southern Africa anew for their failure to declare apartheid heresy (Ecunews, April 1984, p. 7).

A factor very closely connected to the phenomenon of plurality with regard to the South African society, is the ascription of a reconciliation function to religion. In order to examine the reconciliatory function of religion in a divided society, the following items connected with reconciliation were put to respondents during the HSRC multipurpose surveys:

- Organised religious movements should try to bring the different population groups closer together.
- Religious movements in South Africa should try harder to bring the various population groups with the same faith closer together.

(Empirical data, pp. 23-24)

The collective response to these two statements reveals (Empirical data: 25) that Whites place a lower premium on religion as reconciliator (46,4 %), than Blacks (84,3 %), Coloureds (79,7 %) and Indians (57,4 %). The four population groups agreed with the statement, "Organised religious movements should try to bring the different population groups closer together" (Empirical data: 23) to the following extent: Whites — 53,5 %, Blacks — 84,7 % Coloureds — 87,3 % and Indians — 77,4 %.

The presence and embodiment of plurality within and between religious groups has the most direct connection with the central thesis of this addendum, viz. that individuals and groups constitute meaning to their lifeworlds in consequence of their experience of their existential position. Religion and religious collectivities are mechanisms in terms of which this constitution of meaning is brought to the fore. In many cases this becomes an articulated outlet for deepseated aspirations or aims. As soon as certain aims have been satisfied, other emphases could start emerging.

WORKS CONSULTED

BECKFORD, J.A. 1983. The restoration of "power" to the sociology of religion. In Sociological Analysis, 44(1), pp. 11-32.

BERGER, P.L. 1976. *Pyramids of sacrifice*. London: Allen Lane.

BERKHOF, H. *et al.* 1967. *Protestantse verkenningen na Vaticanum II*. The Hague: Boekencentrum.

BOESAK, A.A. 1977. *Farewell to innocence*. New York: Orbis.

COETZEE, J.K. 1982. *Tussengroepverhoudinge binne die sosiale struktuur*. Pretoria: Human Sciences Research Council (GR-N-1).

COETZEE, J.K. 1983. *Kerk en godsdiens as begeleier van sosiale verandering. 'n Studie van twee groepe*. Bloemfontein: The University of the Orange Free State.

DAHM, K.W.; DREHSEN, V., KEHRER, G. 1975. *Godsdienst en maatschappijkritiek.* Baarn: Ambo.

DEKKER, G. 1982. *Kerk, godsdienst en samenleving.* Assen: Van Gorcum.

DURKHEIM, E. 1948. *The elementary forms of religious life.* Glencoe: The Free Press.

DUSSEL, E. 1976. *History and the theology of liberation. A Latin American perspective.* New York: Orbis.

DUVENHAGE, S.C.W. *et al.* 1974. *Reformasie en revolusie.* Potchefstroom: Institute for the Advancement of Calvinism.

DUX, G. *et al.* 1971. *International yearbook for the study of religion* (7). Oplade: Westdeutscher Verlag.

EYBERS, I.H.; KÖNIG, A., BORCHARDT, C.F.A. 1975. *Teologie en vernuwing.* Pretoria: Universiteit van Suid Afrika.

GARRETT, W.R. 1973. Politicized clergy : a sociological interpretation of the "New Breed". In *Journal for the Scientific Study of Religion,* 12, pp. 381-399.

GLOCK, C.Y. 1973. *Religion in sociological perspective : essays in the empirical study of religion.* California: Wadsworth Inc.

GOODMAN, N., MARX, G.T. 1978. *Society today.* New York: CRM/Random House.

GREELEY, A.M. 1982. *Religion : a secular theory.* New York: The Free Press.

GUTIéRREZ, G. 1979. *A theology of liberation. History, politics and salvation.* London: SCM Press.

HEBBLETHWAITE, P. 1983. Kerk en Marxisme in Latijns-Amerika. In *Streven,* April, pp. 599-605.

HOEFNAGELS, H. 1971. *Sociologie en maatschappijkritiek.* Alphen aan den Rijn: Samsom.

HOEFNAGELS, H. 1976. *Kritische sociologie.* Alphen aan den Rijn: Samsom.

JOHNSON, B. 1966. Theology and party preference among Protestant clergymen. In *American Sociological Review,* 31, pp. 200-208.

McGUIRE, M.B. 1983. Discovering religious power. In *Sociological Analysis,* 44(1), pp. 1-10.

MEERBURG, M.M. 1981. Eenheid en identiteit in een plurale kerk. In VLIJM, J.M. *Geloofsmanieren*. Kampen: J.H. Kok.

MOULIN, L. 1977. *The church and modern society*. London: Sage Publications.

NELSEN, H.M. 1981. The church and critical choices in the 1980s. In *Sociological Analysis*, 42(4), pp. 303-316.

NERFIN, M. 1977. *Another development : approaches and strategies*. Uppsala: The Dag Hammerskjöld Foundation.

ROBERTS, K.A. 1984. *Religion in sociological perspective*. Homewood: The Dorsey Press.

SMITH, D.E. 1971. *Religion, politics, and social change in the Third World*. New York: The Free Press.

STARK, W. 1958. *The sociology of knowledge*. London: Routledge and Kegan Paul.

SOUTH AFRICAN COUNCIL OF CHURCHES. n.d. *Christians and apartheid*. Braamfontein: SACC.

SOUTH AFRICAN COUNCIL OF CHURCHES. 1980. *The kingdom of God and the churches in South Africa*. Braamfontein: SACC.

SOUTH AFRICAN COUNCIL OF CHURCHES. 1982. *The divine intention*. Braamfontein: SACC.

TERZAKE IV. 1969. *Kerk buiten de kerk*. Utrecht: Ambo.

TYRIAKAN, E.A. 1963. *Sociological theory, values and socio-cultural change*. Glencoe: The Free Press.

VARMA, B.N. 1980. *The sociology and politics of development*. London: Routledge and Kegan Paul.

VLIJM, J.M. 1981. *Geloofsmanieren : studies over pluraliteit in de kerk*. Kampen: J.H. Kok.

WILSON, B. 1982. *Religion in sociological perspective*. Oxford: Oxford University Press.

WILSON, J. 1978. *Religion in American society*. Englewood Cliffs (N.J.): Prentice-Hall.

YEATTS, J.R., ASHER, W. 1982. Factor analyses of religious variables : some methodological considerations. In *Review of Religious Research*, 24(1), pp. 49-54.

ZITO, G.V. 1983. Toward a sociology of heresy. In *Sociological Analysis*, 44(2), pp. 123-130.

Newspapers and other non-academic journals

Beeld, 27 August 1982
Die Burger, 27 August 1982
Die Burger, 28 September 1982
Die Burger, 2 Oktober 1982
Die Burger, 15 Oktober 1982
Die Kerkbode, September 1948
Die Kerkbode, 13 Oktober 1982
Die Kerkbode, 20 Oktober 1982
Die Transvaler, 30 April 1982
Ecunews, December 1982
Ecunews, March 1983
Ecunews, May 1983
Ecunews, July 1983
Ecunews, Oktober 1983
Ecunews, November 1983
Ecunews, February 1984
Ecunews, April 1984
Ecunews, June — July 1984
Leadership S.A., September 1982
Rand Daily Mail, 29 April 1982
Rapport, 2 Mei 1982
The Argus, 29 September 1982
The Argus, 25 October 1982
The Argus, 8 November 1982
The Star, 18 October 1982
The Sunday Times, 22 August 1982
The Sunday Times, 31 October 1982

EMPIRICAL DATA

DATA OBTAINED BY MEANS OF THE MULTIPURPOSE SURVEYS (HSRC): MPS/OV/56-59 AND MPS/OV/71-74*

Respondents were asked to indicate how important they considered the following item. A calculated value was deduced from three items with similar gist.

The responses (expressed as percentages) are given with regard to each of the four population groups: W = Whites; C = Coloureds; B = Blacks and I = Indians.

	Group	Very import- ant	Import- ant	Neutral	Unimport- ant	Of no import- ance	N
1. The influence in	W	34,6	44,9	13,7	4,8	2,0	586
general of religious	C	34,1	41,8	15,9	6,2	2,0	742
movements on South	B	28,5	33,0	21,7	8,7	8,1	839
African society	I	28,1	42,4	21,6	5,1	2,9	877
2. Theme: The import-	W	9,2	41,2	36,9	11,1	1,5	585
ance of religion	C	16,7	51,9	26,8	4,2	0,4	742
	B	15,3	44,2	25,1	10,2	5,3	837
	I	16,4	46,2	32,4	4,9	0,1	877

In each of the following cases respondents were asked to indicate whether they agreed or disagreed with the statements presented to them. From the previous statements a theme was compiled as based on the collective response of each respondent to the particular statements.

---

* For methodological account, see:
Metodologiese oorwegings rondom meerdoelige opnames MPS/OV/56-59 en MPS/OV/71-74, H.C. Marais and J.L. Olivier (Human Sciences Research Council, Pretoria).

The responses (expressed as percentages) are given with regard to each of the four population groups: W = Whites; C = Coloureds; B = Blacks and I = Indians.

	Group	Strongly agree	Agree	Neutral	Disagree	Strongly disagree	N
3. Religious movements mean little if they do not contribute in the basic needs (e.g. food and clothing) of all the people in South Africa	W	15,4	36,7	11,8	26,8	9,3	570
	C	23,4	38,8	10,3	22,7	4,9	719
	B	35,0	34,3	10,3	13,5	6,9	802
	I	17,8	42,3	16,8	18,9	4,3	847
4. Religious movements can do little to solve general social and economic problems	W	7,5	35,0	15,4	34,1	8,0	625
	C	6,8	31,2	13,0	37,9	11,1	733
	B	21,2	42,5	13,6	14,3	8,4	932
	I	8,4	38,2	19,5	29,0	4,9	877
5. Various religious movements should co-operate more to change South African society	W	13,9	41,2	19,7	17,9	7,3	626
	C	24,3	53,1	14,0	7,0	1,6	748
	B	30,3	43,5	9,9	10,2	6,1	956
	I	17,1	50,1	21,3	9,2	2,3	864
6. Theme: Socio-economic effectiveness of religion	W	1,1	16,8	52,2	27,9	2,0	559
	C	3,1	31,8	49,6	15,0	0,4	673
	B	0,8	18,7	60,3	19,1	1,1	754
	I	0,9	20,1	60,2	18,2	0,6	771
7. A religious movement should help in limiting changes in society	W	5,4	20,9	26,6	35,4	11,8	560
	C	8,2	40,3	18,4	23,9	9,2	695
	B	24,3	45,8	14,7	9,0	6,2	790
	I	11,0	44,5	19,2	17,6	7,8	812
8. Within the South African society I can live according to my religious principles	W	51,4	39,6	4,8	2,2	2,1	584
	C	31,9	48,2	8,5	6,3	5,1	743
	B	26,6	34,4	17,5	8,9	12,7	836
	I	27,1	52,3	11,3	4,7	4,6	877
9. Religious movements must do everything they can to eliminate discrimination in society	W	11,2	34,8	17,6	27,1	9,3	569
	C	27,5	47,1	11,7	11,6	2,1	716
	B	24,5	42,9	12,9	10,4	9,4	801
	I	24,9	48,1	16,0	9,5	1,5	811
10. The practising of religion can never be separated from care for the poor of all population groups	W	18,3	56,2	12,5	11,4	1,6	630
	C	28,5	54,8	9,3	5,9	1,5	755
	B	36,8	42,9	11,3	6,5	2,5	923
	I	23,6	57,0	12,5	6,0	0,9	886

	Group	Strongly agree	Agree	Neutral	Disagree	Strongly disagree	N
11. The practising of	W	8,9	41,2	23,9	21,1	4,9	616
religion can never be	C	23,1	52,1	14,1	9,2	1,5	743
separated from the care	B	26,9	41,7	17,3	9,6	4,5	911
of the suppressed in all	I	17,6	53,0	23,5	5,3	0,6	847
population groups							
12. A religious move-	W	6,2	25,2	24,4	31,8	12,4	611
ment should take a	C	23,2	43,3	16,8	13,8	2,9	749
stand against racial dis-	B	26,4	40,5	14,8	11,5	6,8	927
crimination	I	19,2	42,6	24,7	11,6	1,9	854
13. A religious move-	W	7,6	33,4	21,6	26,8	10,6	616
ment should always act	C	24,3	41,5	16,1	14,3	3,8	745
against laws that affect	B	23,3	38,1	15,1	13,7	9,8	922
the lives of its members	I	16,6	43,1	22,7	14,7	2,9	845
14. A religious move-	W	3,3	12,8	13,8	35,5	34,6	625
ment can even condone	C	6,5	23,5	19,9	31,3	18,7	718
violence when people's	B	22,7	31,1	17,0	16,2	12,0	917
rights and human dig-	I	8,9	39,1	29,6	17,7	4,7	844
nity are restructed							
15. Religious move-	W	10,0	35,4	17,1	23,3	14,2	627
ments should encourage	C	19,9	47,9	15,6	12,6	4,0	739
their members to protest	B	23,2	37,0	13,9	14,2	11,7	939
peacefully against injus-	I	17,5	53,7	18,3	8,4	2,1	871
tice							
16. Theme: Religion	W	0,6	9,4	48,7	35,1	6,3	522
and structural liberation	C	2,6	34,0	49,8	12,8	0,8	626
	B	3,1	38,4	44,5	11,9	2,1	654
	I	1,6	35,8	55,4	7,2	0,0	693
17. Social justice should	W	8,3	30,3	19,8	28,7	12,9	567
be the most important	C	15,0	47,1	16,7	17,0	4,2	712
item in the work of	B	26,1	43,5	16,6	8,7	5,0	781
religious movements	I	14,8	54,7	20,0	8,7	1,7	824
18. Religious move-	W	11,6	40,9	20,1	21,6	5,8	621
ments should always	C	27,8	48,0	14,8	7,6	1,8	741
oppose all forms of	B	27,4	39,1	15,0	11,3	7,2	930
suppression	I	17,4	49,4	23,1	8,2	1,9	844
19. It is acceptable that	W	11,8	41,2	18,2	22,2	6,6	626
religious movements act	C	24,3	51,9	11,2	9,9	2,7	744
as advocates for the	B	20,9	35,9	16,6	14,3	12,3	914
rights of all people	I	17,1	45,6	23,9	10,3	3,1	844
(human rights)							

	Group	Strongly agree	Agree	Neutral	Disagree	Strongly disagree	N
20. Religious move- ments that continuously keep themselves busy with equal rights for various groups are not busy with their real task	W C B I	25,9 10,8 24,3 6,6	43,6 36,0 24,5 31,3	15,5 17,5 18,8 24,8	12,3 25,8 17,3 27,5	2,7 9,9 15,1 9,8	619 738 906 844
21. Theme: Religion and social justice	W C B I	0,2 3,2 2,2 1,4	10,4 30,0 28,9 29,0	44,6 53,9 46,3 59,9	37,2 11,6 18,1 9,5	7,7 1,4 4,5 0,3	549 664 691 718
22. A religious move- ment should not get itself involved in politics (e.g. apartheid or inte- gration)	W C B I	44,0 19,0 31,5 16,1	35,9 41,3 26,6 44,7	4,9 10,8 11,6 17,9	9,7 17,6 18,1 14,5	5,5 11,3 12,1 6,8	577 715 783 821
23. Organised religious movements should try to bring the different population groups closer together	W C B I	11,2 29,4 39,0 23,9	42,3 57,9 45,7 53,5	21,3 9,1 9,2 12,7	16,3 3,3 4,1 8,0	8,9 0,3 2,1 1,9	572 727 806 834
24. Religious move- ments in South Africa should try harder to bring the various popu- lation groups with the same faith closer together	W C B I	13,4 31,3 42,7 19,1	44,1 51,9 43,1 42,5	20,0 10,7 8,8 18,9	16,1 5,4 2,7 13,7	6,4 0,7 2,7 5,8	621 756 959 880
25. Theme: Religion and reconciliation	W C B I	7,5 22,5 29,1 12,9	38,9 57,2 55,2 44,5	29,7 17,9 11,4 32,9	17,8 2,1 2,5 7,8	6,2 0,3 1,8 1,8	563 719 795 811

ADDENDUM II

RELIGION, THE INTEGRATED EXPRESSION OF SOCIAL VALUES AND PROCESSES OF SOCIAL CHANGE

CUMPSTY J., HOFMEYR J., AND KRUSS G.

PART ONE: THEORY AND METHOD

INTRODUCTION

There has been a tendency in the empirical study of religion to conclude that religious group membership does not play an important role in motivating sociopolitical attitudes and actions. From the religious point of view this is a paradox, since religion has always understood itself to be fundamental in the organization of both individual and social life. This paradox we believe, is due to a failure to understand and measure religion adequately at the empirical level. Most empirical studies base their measurements of religion on an institutional definition of it. In an environment in which the institutional representatives of a religious tradition no longer fulfil the ideal functions of religion however, such measures are bound to be inadequate. In order to circumvent this problem we have based the work reported on here on what we call a "normative definition of religion". By this we intend a definition which is based on the ideal functions of religion i.e. what it ought to be; both in terms of its individual and its social function.

THE THEORETIC FRAMEWORK

The basis for our research is a typology of religion which has been connected through empirical measures to sociopolitical attitudes. The typology is based on the argument that religion is restricted to a few main types by the way it models reality. Its function is defined as connecting individuals, either singly or in groups, to that which is felt to be "ultimate" in the passing flux of experience. Thus religion is defined as "belonging". It is the demands made by the exercise of this function which result in the main components to be seen in institutional religious systems i.e. their ritual and belief dimensions. The typology therefore presents a fundamental range of the basic forms that religious systems can take. It includes three main types and a number of sub-types. The types and sub-types are named according to the way the individual relates to his overall sense of reality.

Concerning the relation of the religious system to society, we have applied an evolutionary model. Society is seen to be a complex open system in which many sub-systems exist in dynamic interrelationship. The main religious types take form as sub-systems alongside others within the social environment. In order to fulfil their function, religious sub-systems have to incorporate certain elements e.g. beliefs about the "ultimate" and how relationship to it may be achieved. In addition if they are to survive, the form and content of these elements must be matched to the environment. We see this to be a matter primarily of establishing congruence between the experience generated by individuals' participation in society on the one hand, and the way that overall experience is interpreted and given meaning in the religious group on the other. It is clear that in this view there will be a relationship between the religious function and social and political orientations.

RELIGION: THE SECULAR WORLD AFFIRMING TYPE

Of the three main types, the one focussed on in this research is the Secular World Affirming type. Some of the main features of this type are its belief in a benevolent and transcendant deity who created the world and hence also a belief in the essential "goodness" or "meaningfulness" of the world. The name of the type is based on the following features: the belief in transcendance precludes the possibility that the world be divine, hence it is secular; and its goodness reinforces a positive attitude to it, hence "world affirming". Historically it has been represented by the middle eastern religious traditions i.e. Judaism, Christianity, and Islam.

Religion of the Secular World Affirming type sub-divides into three depending on the different ways of relating to the ultimate or divine. The two main ones are the Direct and Indirect Cosmic modes. The first is a sub-type in which the adherent stands in a direct and individual relationship with God. It contrasts with the second in that in the latter, relationship is established by membership of the religious group which is understood to be related already. In Christianity, Catholicism has tended to represent the second sub-type while Protestantism the first.

From the point of view of the relation between religion and the rest of society, the most important feature of religion of the Secular World Affirming type is its insistence that the proper practice of religion relates the individual to all aspects of natural and social life. While the historical representatives of this type have not always conformed to its ideal functions, it is supposed to provide a foundation of belief and value for the development of orientations towards all the myriad sub-systems which form the social environment of which it is a part. This can be pictured in a simple way. At best, religions of the Secular World Affirming type connect the individual meaningfully to what we call "levels of aggregation" of the following sort:

Figure 1

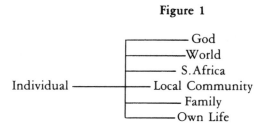

THE CONTEXT OF THE RESEARCH

Our research task was that of investigating the role of religion in motivating or inhibiting sociopolitical action at the lower end of the socio-economic spectrum. From the typology it was clear that some form of relation could be expected. We observed however that, whatever its type, religion at the "lower" ends of society tends to be non-political. This the history of religion confirms and the best known example is Pentecostal Christianity.

The Pentocostal creed of non-involvement in politics is not easily conformed to however. Whether they like it or not, people in a religious group carry influences from that group into society and in turn from society back into the group. No matter how uninvolved a religious group may try to be, there are circumstances under which it cannot avoid influencing and being influenced by its environment.

In order to focus the problem, we narrowed the task down to a field study of Christianity in the greater Athlone area of Cape Town. This is a Coloured area containing a broad spread of churches and socio-economic levels though it is poor rather than wealthy and the majority have a standard 7 education or lower. Athlone was chosen because of the wide demographic spread and the high concentration of churches to be found in it. It provided, within a manageable geographic area, a sufficient diversity of churches and social circumstances to investigate the relation between a religion of the Secular World Affirming type i.e. Christianity; and its form under different socio-economic circumstances, especially at the lower end of the socio-economic spectrum.

Implementation of the research followed a multidimensional method. We made extensive preliminary investigations in order to acquaint ourselves with the context. We participated in church services, interviewed members of the community, implemented two large scale snap surveys in order to measure the religious demographics of the area, and finally implemented an extensive questionnaire amongst a selected sample of the more significant churches representative of the area. The choice of churches was based on the results of the preparatory fieldwork while the selection of the sample for each church conformed as closely as possible to the stratified random technique. The definition of religion in terms of its ideal functions played a role in selection.

PART TWO: RESULTS AND CONCLUSIONS

INTRODUCTION

We summarise here the results found in the main questionnaire implemented among 554 members of ten different churches in the Athlone area. Two and three way tables formed the basis of analysis. The main issues analysed were:

● The assessment by respondents of the state of things at the various levels of aggregation; of the hope for improvement at each level; and of the best strategy of improvement.

● The attitude of respondents to various high profile social and political groups in South Africa representing national and regional interests.

● The willingness of respondents to be involved in various forms of social activity with either regional or national implications, this being measured on a simple scale of involvement.

● The relationship between the above issues and ethical attitudes based on religious values. Ethical attitudes formed the basis of connecting sociopolitical attitudes to the form of religion.

● Measures of religiosity and the relationship between these and the sociopolitical and ethical attitudes established in the earlier analysis.

LEVELS OF AGGREGATION AND HOPE FOR THE FUTURE

Respondents were asked to comment on "the state of things" in the world, South Africa, the local community, and their own lives. Response categories ranged from: 0 = Don't Know, 1 = Very Bad, to 5 = Very Good (See Table 1). The overwhelming majority answered that things were bad or very bad in the world and South Africa, that they were on the whole bad in the local community, but that they were on the whole good in their own lives.

A second question was asked concerning the possibility of improving things at the above four levels (See Table 2). Responses were similar, with the majority being pessimistic about the future of the world and South Africa, but reasonably optimistic about the future of their local community and extremely optimistic about their personal futures.

We interpreted these results as follows:

● With respect to the present there is a serious split between assessments of the "state of things" at the individual level and the rest. Respondents appeared relatively satisfied with their own lives.

● With respect to the future the split is between local and national levels. There is a disquieting pessimism about the future of South Africa, but an optimism about respondents' own futures.

Concerning strategies for improving things, respondents were asked to rate the effectiveness of each of the following types of organization: churches, charities, politics, and their own church. The results showed strong support for churches and especially the home church but ambivalence for politics. The majority — 35 %, answered that they thought politics could help, but a sizeable group — 23 % answered that they thought it could not. Fully 26 % answered that they did not know about politics.

The last response reported above was a consistent feature of responses to questions in the political area. For reasons which will become clear, we interpreted this, not as a lack of political sophistication, but as a preference to hide opinions on a sensitive issue.

SOCIAL AND POLITICAL ORIENTATION

In order to analyse the general social and political orientation of respondents two types of questions were asked. First, there was a question concerning the willingness of respondents to get involved in various types of organization. This is a question, not about the *effectiveness* of different social orientations, but about *degrees of involvement*. Second, a question was asked concerning the attitude of respondents to various high profile groups on the local and national scene in South Africa. This is a question about *affective allegiance* i.e. it is a question about the extent to which respondents identify emotionally with these groups.

Willingness to be involved in different forms of social organization was measured on the following scale: 0 = Don't Know, 1 = Not interested in that sort of group, 2 = Would support by donating money, 3 = Would join in with, 4 = Would help to organize. The sorts of groups for which responses were asked ranged from those with a narrow, non-political social function such as Day Care Centres, through those with a wider general social and religious function such as Church Organizations, to the overtly political such as the United Democratic Front (See Table 3).

As can be seen, there are three typical patterns of response. Most people would give money to the more narrowly functional social organization. Active involvement is reserved for the more broadly based social organizations such as church groups. Though an important minority i.e. 14 %, claimed that they would get involved in political organizations, most people claimed to be disinterested in them.

The second question asked respondents to indicate a level of sympathy for various high profile social groups in South Africa. Responses were measured on a scale from 1 = Very Sympathetic to 5 = Very Unsympathetic. Groups for which responses were elicited included: The Labour Party, the United Democratic Front, the Progressive Federal Party, the South African Council of Churches, and the government (See Table 4).

The more moderate groups e.g. the Labour Party, evoked a neutral or unsympathetic response. By contrast, there is quite a lot of sympathy for groups which are critical of the government though once again many respondents expressed no opinion or ignorance. The Progressive Federal Party, representing liberal White opinion, evoked less "sympathy" than the more radical groups such as the United Democratic Front.

We drew the following conclusions from our results:

First, the results present a picture of a community whose members relate to the world overtly quite narrowly. They are clearly positive about their own prospects, yet that does not translate into a positive attitude towards the prospects for society at large. There is then a severe hiatus between local and larger levels of aggregation for the majority of the respondents.

Second, at local community level respondents appear to believe in the greater effectiveness of religious orientations rather than political orientations as a means of improving their circumstances. This view is backed up by their expressed willingness to be involved in church based activities. As regards political orientations, significantly more people are unwilling to express an opinion or simply reply that they don't know.

Third, when asked for their feelings towards significant groups on the South African scene, most profess neutrality or ignorance. Nevertheless, where sympathies are expressed, there is a strong bias in favour of the UDF, SACC, and Trade Unions. Thus, though politics was not rated as highly as religion with regard to its effectiveness, where there is identification in political terms it is stronger with regard to the groups which represent a more "radical" approach to social change.

TYPES OF SOCIAL AND POLITICAL ORIENTATION

Response patterns to the questions discussed above suggested that there might be certain definable sociopolitical "groupings" in the sample. Taking as the first issue the question of "affective allegiance", the following "groups" appeared to be present. First, the largest, a group in which the typical response was one of neutrality or ignorance with respect to all the "high profile" social organizations in South Africa. Second, a group in which sympathy was expressed for the more "radical" organizations such as the UDF and the SACC. Third, the smallest, a group which expressed sympathy for the government and moderate organizations, but which tended to claim ignorance of or neutrality towards the "radical" groups.

The relationships between *affective allegiance* to social organizations on the one hand and judgements as to the *effectiveness* of different types of organization on the other are given in Tables 5 and 6. The results suggest that:

● On the whole, irrespective of their affective allegiances, respondents assessments of the effectiveness of religion are high.

● Those who are neutral or sympathetic to the government are significantly more negative than the rest about political possibilities.

● By contrast, those sympathetic to the UDF are significantly more positive about such possibilities.

The relationship between *degrees of involvement* in different types of social organization is given in Table 6 (See also Figure 2 below). These results suggest that:

● Overall, there is a high willingness to be actively involved in a religious organization. The proportion is about 47 % of the total.

● In addition, those who expressed a willingness to be involved politically, also expressed a significantly greater willingness to be involved with the social sort of communal organization represented by Day Care Centres than the rest.

● The result means that there is a small but important group whose willingness to be involved extends to all the forms of social activity.

● By contrast, the rest appear either to be unwilling to be involved or willing only to be involved in church activities. They would only give money to the apolitical communal sort of organization.

In sum, just as there are "groupings" as far as affective allegiance is concerned, so also there are "groupings" as far as general social and political orientation are concerned. These appear to be connected. Those who express a willingness to be socially involved tend to come from the ranks of those who express sympathy to the more "radical" groups on the South African social scene. By contrast, the rest express hesitancy or disinterest with regard to all forms of activity except those which are church-based.

RELIGION AND SOCIOPOLITICAL ORIENTATION: THE ETHICAL CONNECTION

On the basis of the above results we defined three definite "socio-political types" and used these as the basis for connecting religion and socio-political orientation. The types were isolated using the following table:

Table 1: Degrees of Organizational Support

		Church Organization				
		Nkn	NIn	Mon	Act	Ttl
Political Organization	Nkn	11	7	95	68	181
	NIn	6	28	97	119	250
	Mon	0	0	32	14	46
	Act	1	0	18	58	77
	Ttl	18	35	242	259	554

Nkn = Don't Know, NIn = No interest in that sort of group, Mon = Would give money to, Act = Would get actively involved in.

We sub-divided the table to yield three mutually exclusive groups. All those who claimed ignorance or disinterest in political organizations, except for those who were willing to be actively involved in church organizations, formed the first group. This group we called the *Neutrals*. All those who were willing to be actively involved in church organizations, except for those who also said that they would be involved in political organization, formed the second group. They were called the *Pietists*. The third group was formed by all those who said that they would be actively involved in political organizations. They were called the *Socials*.

Each group had the following features:

First, the Neutrals. At 244 or 44 % of the total they are the largest. They express disinterest in active involvement in church-based organizations. They express even less interest in political activity. They tend to be neutral or to claim ignorance on the issue of sympathy towards different high profile social groups in South Africa.

Second, the Pietists, an almost equally large group at 201 or 36 % of the total. They express no interest in political involvement, but active interest in church-based involvement. This is the main way in which they differ from the first group. Like the first they tend to express negative or neutral attitudes on politically related questions.

Third, a significant but the smallest group, the Socials. At 77 they are only 14 % of the total. They express strong interest in all forms of social activity including political activity. They are more positive in regard to the use of politics as a means to improve their circumstances. But their high degree of expressed commitment is not limited to politics, extending to non-political community and religious involvement.

The clearest connection between these types and intrinsic religiosity was found to be ethics. In order to measure the relation between sociopolitical and ethical orientations we asked the following question:

Q: The next question describes five different people. They all belong to the same church and think of themselves as Christians. However, they all have different views about what the most important virtues are for Christians in their daily life. . .

We then described five characters and asked respondents to rate them as Christians on a scale from 1 - 7. The third and the fourth on the list were described as follows:

3. He never overcharges the customers and he pays his workers well. Although he drinks a bit and flirts with women he makes arrangements for people who have bought on hire-purchase rather than reposses things.

4. He leads a rather wild private life, but he is very aware of injustice in society. He works tirelessly for social change and to expose corruption. He hates to see the rich getting richer and the poor getting poorer.

As one moved down the list of five, so each character displayed an increasingly universal social concern, but with a concomitant loss at the personal and family levels. In other words, each character represented an articulation of religious values at a different level of social aggregation. Characters 1 and 2 translated their religiosity into individual and family values, but failed to do so at national levels. Characters 3, 4 and 5, on the other hand, did so at the communal and national levels, but not at the family level.

Significant differences were found between the way that each of the sociopolitical "types" evaluated these characters as Christians. These are most clearly illustrated with respect to characters 3 and 4 mentioned above. The proportions of each type which rated the characters "okay" as Christian were as follows:

	Character 3	Character 4
Pietists	34 %	31 %
Neutrals	45 %	37 %
Socials	53 %	61 %

These percentages suggest a clear congruence between social orientation and religious ethical stance, particularly in the case of the Pietists and the Socials. For each group the results record, as it were, the religious ethical legitimation of the social orientation.

To a certain extent the results are as expected. The real significance of this question however, is more deeply embedded in the ethical tensions it embodies, for we interpret the question to be primarily a measure of the level of social aggregation at which religious values are pitched. By the way in which it forces a pay-off between the expression of ethical concern at different levels of aggregation, it forced respondents to choose between the personal, the communal, and the national level of ethical priority. The narrowest group in terms of the level of aggregation at which their religious values are pitched are the *Pietists*. Their disapproval of the "christianity" of the characters rises markedly as the personal level of ethics is neglected. This disapproval is not offset by the fact that succeding characters display a wider social concern. The *Socials*, on the other hand, express exactly the opposite tendency. Their approval increases as the level of aggregate concern rises. This does not mean that they do not approve of the family level of expression of religious values. *It does suggest however, that they would be willing to sacrifice the individual level if they felt that the national level of religious concern required it.*

To summarise: We found clear connections between the sociopolitical orientation of respondents on the one hand, and their sense of religious values, expressed in ethical terms on the other. At best religion functions to provide a basis for developing values at every level of social aggregation. It is a feature of complex societies however, that it is not always clear how to express religious values at every level. By forcing respondents to choose between levels, we achieved a clear differentiation of the ways that religious values would be articulated if a choice were ever forced.

SOCIOPOLITICAL ORIENTATION AND RELIGION: THE INSTITUTIONAL CONNECTION

Religious commitment extends beyond ethics to other forms as well. In this research four further measures of religiosity were important. All were an attempt to relate the religiosity of respondents to institutional expressions of religiosity. The first was contained in the following question:

Q: Read what each person says and then give your opinion: John says — I don't care about church, what matters is that we should help people.

In the question, John was the third of four characters. What distinguished him from the first two was his willingness to extend help to people outside the church. What distinguished him from the last was his belief that it was at all possible to help. Clear differences were apparent in the way that each of the sociopolitical types responded to this question. The results were as follows:

	Disapprove of John	Approve of John
Pietists	61 %	18 %
Neutrals	60 %	29 %
Socials	46 %	25 %

These results are consistent with what can be expected from the three groups. Once again however, the significance of the question lies in the choice it forced on respondents, for it forced respondents into a choice between ethical concern and institutional allegiance. Though the majority disapprove of John, there is a greater unwillingness on the part of the Socials to judge him, suggesting that his ethical concern makes up for his disinterest in the religious institution.

The result above might lead some to conclude that the Socials are not really religiously orientated — that they are more ''humanistic'' or ''political'' than ''religious''. Three measures of religiosity showed decisively that this is not the case. The three were: A question about the regularity of attendance at church services; a second question about the regularity with which respondents read the Bible on their own, and finally; a question about the extent to which respondents felt personally related to God (See Table 8). For all the groups degrees of commitment on all three measures was high. Even the so-called Neutrals i.e. those who expressed an unwillingness to be involved actively in religious organizations, recorded relatively high degrees of commitment on these measures. It is true that the Pietists differ significantly from the others on the institutional measures. But the measures for all the types are high. If the Pietists are to be called religious, then so must the Socials.

INTERGROUP RELATIONS, SOCIOPOLITICAL ORIENTATION, AND RELIGION

We come finally to the relevance of these results for understanding religion and intergroup relations. To begin with it is necessary to recur to the background theory of religion and the view of its role in society.

Complex societies like that of South Africa consist of a great variety of groups and sub-groups. In such societies, conflict is best avoided by the development of dynamic integration. This has to be understood against the backdrop of the hierarchical nature of social identity. This we interpret on the following framework:

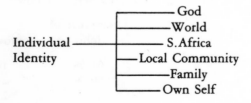

Ideally, the individual ought to be able to gain a sense of identity at all of these levels and they ought not to be in conflict. Usually, this is achieved by the emotional and intellectual bonds that are formed between the individual and the values and beliefs of groups representing each level. So, for example, someone might think of himself as a Father, Lawyer, Member of the Round Table, Afrikaans speaking South African, European, and Christian.

The key to dynamic integration is the achievement of means to integrate all the various possible identities that people in a complex society might form. At every level there exist groups in "opposition" to one another. If conflict between these groups is to be avoided, then it is essential that the "competition" between them be mediated. Such mediation is only possible if their members find ways of articulating common values and identities at the super-ordinate levels. In this process religion has a vital role to play, for, though it has often been pressed into the service of man, it is in fact the only product of our interaction with reality that provides the possibility of transcending specific human interests.

"Religion" here must be understood broadly in terms of the "normative" definition of it discussed above. The evidence of the 20th century points overwhelmingly to the failure of the existing religious traditions to transcend specific human interests. To put it crudely, all the existing religions have become no more than ideologies. Yet, it is precisely the valuative breadth and depth of religion that is needed if integrated orientations are to be achieved at every level of aggregation, from the personal to the multinational.

In South Africa, the most critical levels for intergroup relations are those of the "local community" and "national" levels. In this regard our research has produced significant and concrete findings. In the sample studied it has shown that religion is closely connected to certain definite sociopolitical orientations and that this connection is most evident in the way that religion is put to use to articulate ethics or values. The result is the emergence of distinctive attitudes to the local and national levels of aggregation. The attitudes of the different types i.e. Neutrals, Pietists, and Socials, can be pictured as follows:

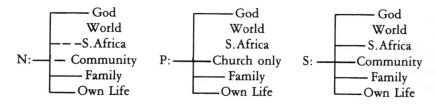

Of the three types, it is only the Socials who have articulated an identity at the mid-levels and expressed a willingness to follow that up in action. The Pietists have a weak link to community via their strong commitment to a religious organization, but by the way that it is bound to the religious organization, this link is quite narrow. The most interesting group are the Neutrals, for, while they express a developed unwillingness to be involved in any form of "mid-level" activity, they also express certain latent mid-level allegiances. These emerge in the sympathy for "radical" groups as compared to "moderate" groups on the one hand, and in the ethical evaluation of characters with a wider social concern on the other.

The most distinctive feature of the sample was its lack of mid-level aggregation. Given the history of the Coloured community this is not surprising. It has been a long history of disinheritance. If members of the Coloured community ever had a strong sense of belonging to a "South African nation" this must surely have been modified by their removal from the joint voters roll, the group areas act, and the mixed-marriages legislation. The history imposed upon them has given them nothing with which to identify. If anything, the mid-level might well have come to have a negative value for them, as a source of "common enemy" symbols.

In fact, the results of the questions relating to affective allegiance indicate that the mid-level does function as a source of "common enemy" symbols. Moderate groups such as the PFP evoked considerably less sympathy than the more "radical" groups such as the UDF. Yet, this sympathy did not translate into a general willingness to be socially involved.

The pietism of our sample must be seen in the context of the above factors. In terms of our theoretical framework we mean by pietism such an emphasis on "belonging to God" that the mid-levels play a much reduced role. By focussing "meaning" in the direct relation to God, the world is by-passed and its significance reduced. The congruence between this response and the needs of a people who have been given no positive way to identify at the mid-level is clear. Both withdrawal from social involvement on the one hand, and pietistic religious involvement on the other, can be seen as defensive moves in a situation where no choice at the mid-level appears viable.

Seen in this way, pietism is a viable religious response to a situation of severe alienation. It serves as a religious legitimation for refusing to face the consequences of what is demanded when the need for the expression of identity at the mid-level of aggregation is faced.

Though narrow, pietism is not sectarian since sectarianism usually occurs under conditions of considerable turmoil as an attempt to escape altogether an inhospitable world. Our sample, by their high degree of satisfaction with their present lives and future prospects are clearly not anomic. Theirs is not a problem

170

of finding meaning in an apparently chaotic and meaningless environment. Rather, it is a problem of integrating aggregate levels in a situation which provides no obvious means to do so.

The size of the Pietist and Neutral groups might lead one to suppose that religion might play a mediating role by default in situations of possible intergroup conflict. It might be thought that these groups, by the way that they miss out the mid-levels of aggregation, would be passive observers in any situation of intergroup conflict. Such a view would however be a mistake, particularly as regards the so-called "Neutrals". This can be seen in the context of what we call the "catalytic" event. The catalytic social event developes around any issue in which emotions run high enough to eliminate the middle-ground of opinion. The school boycotts are usually of this sort. Precisely because there is no middle-ground it is a feature of such events that, if you are not "for" a particular side, then you are "against". The significance of these events therefore is that *non-involvement* itself is not possible.

In the present state of intergroup relations in South Africa at the local and national levels, divisions appear to be so deep that the basic structure of all interaction is catalytic. The significance of this for the sample we studied is clear. It means that the sort of defensive non-involvement that our respondents have tended to express is increasingly less of an option. This brings us to a second feature of the catalytic event. Under "normal" conditions, a failure to integrate values at every level of aggregation need not be a problem since the areas of difficulty can simply be avoided. The fact that non-involvement is not an option in the catalytic event however, forces these latent tensions to the surface by forcing a choice. When this happens individuals may be confronted by extreme difficulties in the decision as to what level of aggregation is most important, for it is almost always the case that the decision to concentrate on one level is made at the expense of another. In South Africa, for example, those who choose to express their values at a national level are inevitably forced into sacrificing harmony at the local community and individual levels. This inevitability is built into the South African situation by the lack of mediating values and symbols at super-ordinate levels.

In the sample dealt with in our research, the Socials expressed just such a willingness to sacrifice the lower levels. The Pietists did not, but the Neutrals fell in-between. This is the significance of the Neutral group. If they are the equivalent of the "silent majority", then their latent emotional or affective allegiances are vital, for in the long run it is these allegiances which will play a large part in determining which way they might move when a catalytic event forces a choice. In this regard it is surely highly significant that the sample as a whole expresses far more sympathy for the "radical" groups such as the UDF than for the "moderate" groups, even those like the PFP which are in opposition to the government.

CONCLUDING REMARKS

Our research was an attempt, perhaps a little ambitious, to link religiosity to sociopolitical orientations for a specially selected sample of religious people in Athlone. Our intention was to go beyond the description of the sample in terms of multiple correlations to a more complete modeling of the relation between definite socio-political types and religiosity. The relevance of this modeling to the intergroup situation in South Africa we then derived by attempting to explicate the way that these types might be expected to behave against the backdrop of a simple hierarchical division of society into levels of aggregation.

Our results are applicable strictly only to the particular sample that we studied. Our intention in choosing the sample was to home in on people with religiosity which satisfied the "ideal" or "normative" definition of religion rather than the usual institutional one that is used in most empirical studies. Our original intention to investigate the role of religion at the lower socio-economic end of society was somewhat overridden by the strong patterns which emerged in the relation of religion and sociopolitical orientation.

If the sample we chose bears any relation to the wider community, then our findings not reflect optimistically on the future of intergroup relations in South Africa. For historical reasons it is now a feature of the South African situation that the various groups debating values at what we have called the mid-levels of aggregation, that is to say, the national level, are divided by deeply entrenched ideological differences. Quite how these might be overcome is not immediately apparent. Our research does suggest however that two conditions would have to be met. On the one hand, super-ordinate values will have to be developed as a means of regulating sub-ordinate "competition" between groups. On the other, the intensity of the debate at the sub-ordinate level has to be "cooled down" for unless this is done, no mediation is possible.

Table 1: The State of Things

Q: These are questions about how you feel about the state of things. What do you think of the situation in: The World, South Africa, Your Community, Your Life?

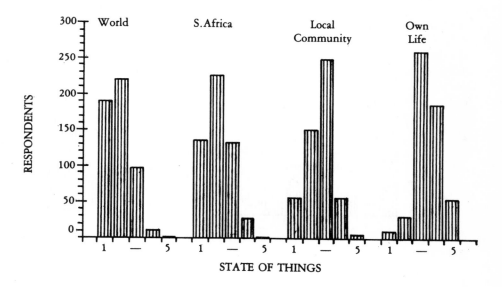

Responses: 0 = Don't Know, 1 = Very Bad, 2 = Bad, 3 = Okay, 4 = Good, 5 = Very Good

Table 2: Hope for Improvement

Q: How possible do you think it is to make the situation better in: The World, South Africa, Your Community, Your Life.

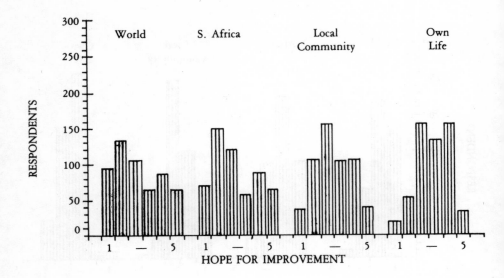

Responses: 0 = Don't Know, 1 = Very Little, 2 = Little, 3 = Perhaps a Bit, 4 = Some, 5 = A Lot

Table 3: Degrees of Support or Involvement

Q: In any community there are many different community organizations. Each person has a choice as to how involved he will get in that organization e.g. some will give money, others will help to organize. . . Please indicate how you would be prepared to get involved if you could.

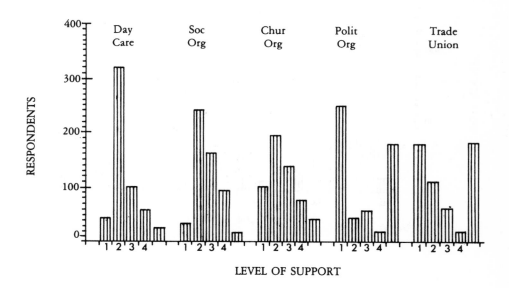

Responses: 0 = Don't Know, 1 = Not interested in that sort of group, 2 = Would support by donating money, 3 = Would join in with, 4 = Would help to organize.

Table 4: Levels of Sympathy — Affective Allegiance

Q: There are many groups that influence our daily lives. Please say, for each of the ones below, whether you feel sympathetic, neutral, or unsympathetic towards them.

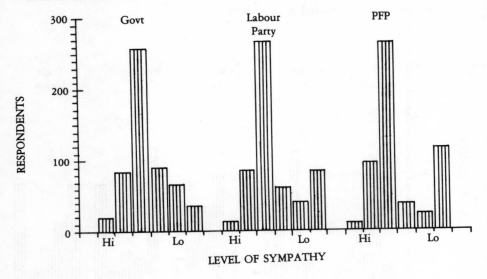

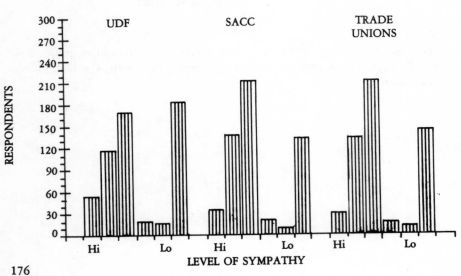

Table 5: Affective Allegiance by Judgements of Effectiveness Government and United Democratic Front Politics as against Churches

Govt		P/C	Bal	C/P	Ttl	UDF		P/C	Bal	C/P	Ttl
	Sympathetic	12	27	47	86		Sympathetic	34	56	40	130
	Neutral	22	62	81	165		Neutral	15	49	48	112
	Unsympathetic	32	62	37	131		Not Known	17	40	69	126
	Total	66	151	165	382		Total	66	145	157	368

Interpretation of the table: Rows: Levels of sympathy for the government or United Democrative Front. Columns: P/C = Politics reckoned more effective than the churches, Bal = Each reckoned equally effective, C/P = Churches reckoned more effective than Politics.

Table 6: Degrees of Involvement in types of Organization-Creche by Political Organization and Church Organization

		Pol. Org					Church Org.				
		NKn	NIn	Mon	Act	Ttl	Nkn	NIn	Mon	Act	Ttl
Creche	NKn	16	8	0	3	27	13	2	7	5	27
	NIn	3	41	0	1	45	1	22	8	14	45
	Mon	122	136	38	25	321	2	9	210	100	321
	Act	40	65	8	48	161	2	2	17	140	161
	Ttl	181	250	46	77	554	18	35	242	259	554

df = 9; Xsq = 101,2; P < ,005

Table 7: Religiosity — Attendance at Church, Bible Reading and Experience of God — for each of the types

	Services				Bible				Experience			
	We	Mo	Yr	Ttl	Oft	Som	Sel	Ttl	Reg	Mem	Nev	Ttl
Neutrals	154	48	42	244	138	47	59	244	122	86	33	241
Pietists	160	25	16	201	127	48	26	201	103	63	28	194
Socials	56	13	8	77	37	22	16	77	34	30	13	77
Totals	370	86	66	522	302	117	101	520	259	179	75	512

$$df = 4, \ Xsq = 15,19 \quad df = 4, \ Xsq = 11,97 \quad df = 4, \ Xsq = 2,4$$

$$p < ,005 \qquad p < ,025 \qquad p < ,9$$

Responses:

We = At least once a week, Mo = About once a month, Yr = Less than once a month.

Oft = Often, Som = Sometimes, Sel = Seldom or never.

Reg = Regularly, Mem = On a memorable occassion, Nev = Never.

NOTES

Based on the report: *The Role of Religion in Motivating or Inhibiting Socio-political action in the Lower Socio-economic Group and Ensuing Counter Influences upon the Group,* Cumpsty, J.S. Hofmeyr, J.H. and Kruss, G. (HSRC Investigation into Intergroup Relations, 1984).

ADDENDUM III

SUMMARY OF THE REPORT: RELIGION AND INTERGROUP RELATIONS IN METROPOLITAN DURBAN*

G.C. OOSTHUIZEN AND J.H. HOFMEYR

PART ONE: THEORY AND METHOD

INTRODUCTION

South Africa is a country in which many religions are represented. This variety is well-reflected in metropolitan Durban. The 1980 census puts the population of this city at 1,8 million of whom 50,7 % are Black, 25 % Indian, 22,3 % White and 3 % Coloured. Among the religious represented are: Christianity of various kinds, Hinduism, Islam, Judaism, African Indigenous religion, and Buddhism. All of the major racial groups include members of more than one religion though the majority in most groups are Christian.

---

* THE FOLLOWING PERSONS PARTICIPATED IN THE PROJECT:
HINDUISM: Dr T. Naidoo, Mrs N. Singh, Mr A. Sooklal: Department of Science of Religion (DSR); University of Durban-Westville (UDW).
BUDDHISM: Mr L. van Loon (DSR, UDW)
JUDAISM: Rabbi I. Richards, Durban. Part-time Lecturer (DSR, UDW)
PARSEES (ZOROASTRIANISM): Dr N. Randeria, Durban.
ISLAM: Prof. S.S. Nadri, Mr S.E. Dangar: Department of Islamic Studies, UDW.
CHRISTIANITY: Blacks: Prof. G.C. Oosthuizen (DSR, UDW; presently University of Zululand) Afrikaans churches: Prof. W.A. Krige, Faculty of Theology, UDW. English language churches (Whites): Rev. A. Pitchers, Fact. of Theol., UDW. Indian Christians: Dr G. Pillay and Rev. A. Pitchers, Fact. of Theol, UDW. Coloured Christians: Rev. A. Pitchers. Greeks: Dr E.A. Mantzaris (Member, Greek Orth. Church) Dept of Sociology, UDW. Portuguese: Dr E.A. Mantzaris. Chinese: Rev. A. Song, Dept of Oriental Studies, UDW.

Very little has been done on the role of religion in intergroup relations in South Africa. With its multi-religious and multi-ethnic society, metropolitan Durban offers an ideal microcosm in which to research this question. Accordingly, in 1983 a team was assembled by Oosthuizen at the University of Durban-Westville to do such research. The purpose of the survey was to measure the influence of religion on intergroup attitudes and relations.

THE RESEARCH PROCEDURE

The research was based on a questionnaire designed to measure a range of attitudes and opinions dealing with religious and racial issues. A survey was carried out among a wide variety of groups: Indian Christians, Black Churches, Portuguese Christians, Buddhists (Indian and White), Muslims (mostly Indian), Hindus (again Indian), Afrikaans Christians, White English-speaking Christians, Coloureds, Greek Christians and Jews. In view of this variety, the survey is best described as multi-ethnic.

Interviewing and interpretation of the results for each group were carried out by designated members of a research team on the basis of their knowledge of that group. Each member was left to determine the procedure for implementing the survey best suited to his group. As a result, sampling and interviewing procedures varied from group to group, some being mail-based for example, while others were conducted in person. Field-workers took care to record comments made by respondents as an aid to interpretation. Irrespective of the procedure adopted, the broad requirements of empirical survey method were adhered to.

Completed questionnaires were coded and the results for each group analysed and written-up in independent reports. The reports were then blended into one whole consisting of eleven parts. The basis of analysis was simple univariate statistics. Coherence was maintained between reports by structuring them all in the same way. While there was therefore no cross-comparison of the results for each group, the fact that each report has a uniform structure makes cross-comparison possible. Uniformity of structure between reports was gained by basing the structure of each report on that of the questionnaire.

STRUCTURE AND CONTENT OF THE QUESTIONNAIRE

The questionnaire had a fundamentally simple structure. The attitude of respondents to multi-religious and multi-racial interaction of various sorts was its focus. For example, respondents were questioned on their attitudes to multi-religious and multi-racial worship, marriage, and schooling. In this way the questionnaire provided a basis for measuring which of the two sorts of division, religion or race, had the strongest influence on respondent attitudes.

Further questions included standard demographic questions e.g. age, sex, and a range of questions to measure respondents opinions on the effects of religion. Respondents were asked whether religion caused friction in the family, whether it influenced their own intergroup attitudes and in what way, and whether it might be effective in helping the intergroup situation in South Africa.

Finally, there were questions with relevance to the present political dispensation in South Africa. For example, respondents were asked whether they agreed with racial segregation as implemented by the government and whether ethnic identity should be protected by law. Further, they were asked whether the preservation of ethnic identity mattered to them. The laws enforcing racial segregation in this country were the background to these questions.

Some difficulties were experienced with the phrasing of some of the questions. In some groups this lead to a high proportion of non-responses, notably the Indian Christian group.

SCOPE OF THE RESEARCH

In its attempt to cover the widest possible range of groups, the project was an ambitious one. In total over 1200 interviews were conducted. However, sample sizes varied greatly between groups — while 298 Blacks were interviewed for example, only 30 Jews and 29 Portuguese were. This variation was unavoidable within the constraints of time and the research budget. It is therefore not possible to use the findings of the survey as a basis for generalizing beyond the sample. Sample sizes in many groups were too small. The real significance of the research lies elsewhere. It provides a general illustration of the complexity of the relation between religious and racial factors in the make-up of group identity. In this way, the metropolitan project offers a profound insight into the potential dynamics of intergroup interaction under conditions of social change. As an indication of how particular ethnic groups in South Africa might think, it can only be used as a guide.

PART TWO: FINDINGS OF THE SURVEY

In what follows below, we have selected what we believe to be the most important findings of the survey. The range of issues dealt with in the questionnaire was broad, but fortunately there was some redundancy thus making summary possible without too much loss of information. The tables used below all report group proportions i.e. percentages — the numbers interviewed in each group are given in brackets after its name.

MULTI-RELIGIOUS AND MULTI-RACIAL WORSHIP

The fundamental group divisions which informed the research were those of religion and race. An initial question in this regard asked respondents whether they objected to worshipping with members of another race group but belonging to their religion. A second question asked for the attitude of respondents to having a service lead by a member of another race group but of the same religion. Response categories ranged from approval through indifference and uncertainty to disapproval. The results for all the groups are reported in Tables 1 and 2.

As can be seen, large majorities in most of the groups approved of multi-racial worship. Similarly, they approved of having a service lead by a member of a race group different to themselves. The exceptions were the Indian Christian, Portuguese and Afrikaans groups. In the case of the last, about half had no objections while in the case of the second, only about 25 % had no objections. The number of non-responses is rather high in both of the first two groups. Taking all the groups together however, the results suggest that for most of those interviewed, religion was a binding factor capable of transcending race in inter-group relations. In the area of religious worship, racial differences were perceived by most to be less important than religious differences.

These results are re-inforced by those obtained for another question. Respondents were asked for their attitude to having a member of the same race but of a different denomination (if Christian) or religion leading their services. In this case, the majority in most groups objected (See Table 3). The only exceptions were the Buddhists and Hindus, results which could have been anticipated given the known "religious universalism" of these groups. This result suggests that religious differences are potentially more divisive than racial differences.

A final question provides an overview of the attitude of many of the groups to multi-group religious interaction. Respondents were asked for their attitude to having religious worship structured on linguistic, racial, and denominational or religious lines. As the results in Table 4 indicate, by far the majority rejected the structuring of religious worship on racial lines. The only exception was the Afrikaans Christian group.

MULTI-RELIGIOUS AND MULTI-RACIAL MARRIAGE AND SCHOOLING

If a preference for multi-racial interaction was generally expressed in the area of religious worship, then the trend was somewhat reversed in the areas of marriage and schooling. With regard to the first, respondents were asked whether or not they objected to multi-religious and multi-racial marriage. The results are shown in Tables 5 and 6. There is much less uniformity in the way that each group responded to these questions. With some interesting exceptions, large proportions in most of the groups disagreed with multi-religious marriage. The exceptions were the English Christians, Coloureds, Jews, Buddhists, and Hindus. Regarding multi-racial marriage, the results are less clear cut. Blacks are divided on the issue while the majority of the Indian, Portuguese, Afrikaans, and English Christians are against it. The majority of Buddhists, Muslims, Hindus, and Jews have no objections.

When contrasted with the questions on multi-group worship, the questions on multi-group marriage indicate some interesting tendencies. For one, religion emerges by implication as a potential binding factor in that most respondents in most of the groups appear to have felt that a multi-religious marriage had less chance of success than a multi-racial one. Yet, the far higher proportions within each group who objected to multi-racial marriage by comparison with multi-racial worship indicates the ethnic sensitivity of a close relation like marriage. Some groups, notably the Blacks, were polarized by the issue. Clearly, while religious identity was seen by many to be capable of transcending racial differences in respect of worship, it was not seen to be capable of doing so in respect of marriage. We shall return to the significance of this result later.

Further interesting observations can be made with respect to the response patterns of particular groups. The Indians, for example, provide a clear illustration of the way that religious affiliation may play a role in determining intergroup attitudes. The Indian Christians, Hindus, and Muslims differ consistently from each other on the various questions on intergroup interaction in a way which could be predicted from the character of their religion. Thus, while Indian Christians and Muslims object on the whole to multi-religious marriage, the Hindus do not. On the other hand, Hindus and Muslims approve of multi-racial marriage whereas Indian Christians are quite polarized.

Results for the question on multi-racial schooling are shown in Table 7. With one exception, these reflect the pattern of responses on multi-racial worship. By far the majority in most of the groups have no objection to multi-racial schooling. A predictable exception as usual are the Afrikaans group. A further interesting exception however are the Blacks. In their case the majority are against multi-racial schooling. As the researchers point out, this result indicates that multi-group interaction in the educational sphere might be seen by many Blacks as a threat to their identity. This also is a result to which we shall return.

LEGALLY ENFORCED SEGREGATION AND ETHNIC IDENTITY

In South Africa, intergroup interaction is most overtly regulated by legally enforced segregation on racial lines. That is to say, the law treats race as the most important factor in the control of multi-ethnic interaction. We have seen that the majority of those interviewed in metropolitan Durban are not in favour of such segregation in many areas such as schooling and worship. According to the survey, religion has emerged as a factor capable of transcending racial differences in many areas of intergroup interaction. Marriage was a significant exception.

A further set of questions makes it possible for us to caste these results into an overall framework of significance. Respondents were asked a range of questions concerning their attitude to legally enforced racial segregation. They were asked whether or not they agreed with racial segregation as implemented by the government. Secondly, they were asked whether or not they agreed with the preservation of ethnic identity by law. Finally, they were asked whether the maintenance of ethnic identity was important to them or not. Results for these questions are given in Tables 8, 9, and 10.

As Table 8 indicates, large majorities in most of the groups were against racial segregation as implemented by the government. Exceptions were the Afrikaans, Portuguese, and English groups. In the case of the last two, while many respondents did not object to the government, only a minority expressed approval. The only group in which a majority expressed approval was the Afrikaans one.

With regard to the protection of ethnic identity by law, the results as indicated in Table 9 are more complex. For those groups who were against law-enforced racial segregation, the proportions varied. In most cases they were large, but the English Christian proportion was notable in being only just more then 50 %. On the basis of these results, there are those in all the groups who object to the way that the government has attempted to protect ethnic identity, yet would not be against a different legal system whose objective was the same. Still, the majority in most of the groups appear willing to put their identity at risk in processes of multi-group interaction.

Table 10 indicates the results of the question as to whether or not ethnic identity was important to respondents. Given the general inclination of most respondents against group seperation, the results of this question are significant. Very large majorities in all the groups who responded, are in favour of maintaining their ethnic identity. Of all the questions dealt with so far this was the only one for which there was a virtually uniform response between all the groups.

ETHNIC, RELIGIOUS AND RACIAL IDENTITY

When we put the results of these questions together, a pattern emerges. In general it can be summarised as follows: Most respondents had a sense of group identity which was important to them and for which the best term used in the questionnaire appears to have been the word "ethnic". Religious and racial identity were also important, but only as contributing parts in the larger sense of ethnic identity. The pattern of responses to the range of questions on multi-religious and multi-racial interaction provides a means of measuring the relative importance of the religious and racial components in group identity. In this regard, the pattern for particular groups becomes explicable. Thus, the Muslim group exhibits a clear pattern in which religious identity is overwhelmingly more important than racial identity in group identity. They are the only group for whom ethnic identity and religious identity are virtually one and the same.

By contrast with the Muslim group, the English-speaking Christians are at the other end of the spectrum. For them religion appears to play a very muted role in the general sense of identity. On the other hand, race appears to be a stronger factor given their responses to the question on multi-racial marriage. Yet, they are a group which appears on the whole not to assign too much importance to either religion or race in the general sense of identity. Their apparently neutral stance therefore belies their very strong concern to maintain ethnic identity.

The Black pattern of responses is interesting as an indication of the areas of potential multi-group interaction in which they feel threatened. Thus, while the majority were prepared to have multi-racial worship, large proportions were against multi-racial marriage and schooling. These results make sense given the importance to Blacks of the maintenance of ethnic identity. In multi-group marriage and schooling many of them clearly perceive a threat to their identity. For this reason many Blacks, as also many respondents in the other groups adversely affected by segregation, expressed a preference for the *status quo*. They appeared to be wary of the chaos that might follow any changes.

Finally, the Afrikaans group — this group was outstanding in a sense in being the only group which was consistently out of step with all the rest. In this group both religious and racial factors clearly contributed largely to the general sense of identity and multi-group interaction of both kinds appeared to constitute a threat. The Afrikaans and Portuguese groups were the only two in whom a majority did not judge racial segregation to be unethical, unfair, unjust, or inhuman. Yet, in the case of the former there was a willingness to tolerate multiracial worship which suggests that the "rank and file" in the church are "ahead" of their leadership.

FURTHER TRENDS AND TENDENCIES

Since the term "multi-ethnic" best describes the metropolitan survey, a further range of interesting tendencies emerged in the responses of all the groups to various questions. Most of those interviewed, for example, indicated that religion was important to them and that it influenced their attitude to the members of other religious and racial groups in a positive way. In other words, most repondents rated themselves as tolerant of others, believing that their religion played a role in making them tolerant. Moreover, most respondents also rated religion as having an important role to play in meliorating intergroup tension. Yet, when asked whether they felt that another group was hostile towards them, many respondents replied in the positive. The hostility that one group perceived to emanate from another often involved a situation in which the two groups could be seen to be "competing" for the same "social space". Thus, while the members in most of the groups perceive themselves to be tolerant, they are perceived to be hostile by others with whom they interact closely. Their self-evaluation does not coincide with the way they are perceived by other groups.

A final result is important here. Large majorities in all the groups were in favour of spreading information about themselves and other groups through the media. Superficially, this can be taken as a natural curiosity about the life-styles and values of others. However, we interpret this as an indication of something deeper i.e. a perception by each group that it needs to know and understand the other better. One of the tragic consequences of segregation in South Africa is that it has cut the lines of intergroup communication which are needed so badly if misunderstanding between groups is to be avoided. Large numbers in all the groups indicated that they had seldom entertained or mixed with people of a different race group in casual social circumstances. This is a practical issue to which attention should be given.

PART THREE: CONCLUDING REMARKS

The results of the metropolitan project cannot be generalized beyond the sample, and yet they illustrate a clear pattern in the relation between religious and racial identity which we believe is of general significance. The lesson which emerges with respect to all the groups is two-fold: First, it is clear that they have a strong sense of identity and that there is a concern that this identity should be preserved. But second, the sense of identity that they have is complex and delicate and many factors play a role in it. Both religion and race are components in the identity of most of the groups, yet the force of these two factors varies from group to group. *As a result, there is no simple way to organize and structure social interaction along religious or racial lines which would not cause a reaction from some or other group.*

The significance of the complexity of group identity is compounded by the fact that many respondents are themselves not aware of how complex that identity is. In many respondents, for example, there is a latent tension between the religious and racial components of group identity. Thus, whereas the Blacks would accept multi-racial worship so long as religion was a unifying factor, many of them would not accept multi-racial marriage. The importance of these latent tensions is that they tend to lie unrecognized within the heart of the individual until changing social circumstances bring them to the surface. Then, processes of multi-group interaction are released, whether violent or non-violent, which usually have painful consequences for all involved as they attempt to sort through their priorities under the new conditions.

TABLES

Table 1: Multi-racial Worship

Q: Do you object to worshipping with members of your religion, but who belong to another race?

	Yes	Uncertain	No	Other
Black Christians (298)	9	–	89	2
Indian Christians (150)	–	–	48	52
Coloureds (80)	–	–	95	5
Afrikaans Christians (78)	25	–	50	25
English Christians (140)	12	–	70	18
Hindus (240)	5	5	68	22
Muslims (158)	1	–	92	7
Buddhists (20)	–	–	100	–
Jews (30)	–	–	75	25
Greek Orthodox (35)	8	6	71	15
Portuguese (29)	28	17	31	34

Table 2: Multi-racial Leadership in Worship

Q: Would you have any objections if a leader of your religion, but of another race group, performed religious ceremonies in your place of worship?

	Yes	Uncertain	No	Other
Black Christians (298)	12	13	75	–
Indian Christians (150)	4	–	34	62
Coloureds (80)	–	–	93	7
Afrikaans Christians (78)	31	–	56	–
English Christians (140)	9	–	80	11
Hindus (240)	–	–	80	20
Muslims (158)	2	–	97	1
Buddhists (20)	–	–	100	–
Jews (30)	–	–	82	18
Greek Orthodox (35)	6	–	66	28
Portuguese (29)	20	7	20	53

Table 3: Multi-religious Leadership in Worship

Q: Would you have objections if a leader of another religion, but of the same race group as yours, performed ceremonies in your place of worship?

	Yes	Uncertain	No	Other
Black Christians (298)	58	25	18	10
Indian Christians (150)	37	1	7	56
Coloureds (80)	–	–	–	–
Afrikaans Christians (78)	81	–	8	11
English Christians (140)	66	–	11	23
Hindus (240)	21	–	54	25
Muslims (158)	90	3	4	3
Buddhists (20)	70		30	
Jews (30)	46	–	28	24
Greek Orthodox (35)	28	26	28	18
Portuguese (29)	41	18	41	–

Table 4: Structure of Worship — Positive Responses

Q: Do you think worship should be structured in terms of:

	Race	Language
Black Christians (298)	30	–
Indian Christians (150)	2	39
Coloureds (80)	6	38
Afrikaans Christians (78)	57	74
English Christians (140)	19	Even
Hindus (240)	Minority	Minority
Muslims (158)	2	6
Buddhists (20)	–	30
Jews (30)	7	21
Greek Orthodox (35)	3	3
Portuguese (29)	21	41

Table 5: Multi-religious Marriage

Q: Would you agree to marriages between people from different religions?

	Yes	Uncertain	No	Other
Black Christians (298)	–	–	21	70
Indian Christians (150)	9	1	85	5
Coloureds (80)	56	–	11	33
Afrikaans Christians (78)	10	–	82	8
English Christians (140)	50	–	40	10
Hindus (240)	61	–	19	20
Muslims (158)	12	–	85	3
Buddhists (20)	85	–	–	15
Jews (30)	40	10	50	–
Greek Orthodox (35)	14	28	26	32
Portuguese (29)	7	17	62	14

Table 6: Multi-racial Marriage

Q: Would you agree to mixed racial marriage within the same religion?

	Yes	Uncertain	No	Other
Black Christians (298)	47	6	40	7
Indian Christians (150)	32	8	56	4
Coloureds (80)	89	–	3	8
Afrikaans Christians (78)	1	4	90	5
English Christians (140)	23	17	53	17
Hindus (240)	67	–	15	18
Muslims (158)	92	–	·4	4
Buddhists (20)	–	–	100	–
Jews (30)	57	10	28	3
Greek Orthodox (35)	11	40	17	32
Portuguese (29)	–	34	59	7

Table 7: Multi-racial Schooling

Q: Would you mind having children of other racial groups attending the same school as your children?

	Yes	Indifferent	No
Black Christians (298)	54	13	33
Indian Christians (150)	1	–	99
Coloureds (80)		No figures	
Afrikaans Christians (78)	60	28	13
English Christians (140)	21	17	62
Hindus (240)	14	9	77
Muslims (158)	5	10	85
Buddhists (20)	–	–	100
Jews (30)	7	21	72
Greek Orthodox (35)	17	31	46
Portuguese (29)	72	21	7

Table 8: Racial Segregation by the Government

Q: Do you believe the government should segregate people on the grounds of race?

	Yes	Uncertain	No	Other
Black Christians (298)	14	6	76	4
Indian Christians (150)	9	6	84	1
Coloureds (80)	1	–	93	6
Afrikaans Christians (78)	69	–	20	11
English Christians (140)	26	–	53	21
Hindus (240)	–	7	76	14
Muslims (158)	6	–	90	4
Buddhists (20)		No figures		
Jews (30)	3	12	85	-
Greek Orthodox (35)	–	3	94	3
Portuguese (29)	27	34	21	17

Table 9: Protection of Ethnic Identity by Law

Q: Is there to your thinking any justification for racial segregation by legislation to protect ethnic identities?

	Yes	Uncertain	No
Black Christians (298)	20	16	64
Indian Christians (150)		No figures	
Coloureds (80)	6	26	68
Afrikaans Christians (78)	76	18	6
English Christians (140)	34	22	34
Hindus (240)	19	15	66
Muslims (158)	15	8	77
Buddhists (20)	35	(Indian)	65
Jews (30)		Not reported	87
Greek Orthodox (35)	11	11	78
Portuguese (29)	52	21	28

Table 10: Desire to Maintain Ethnic Identity

Q: Do you believe in maintaining your ethnic identity?

	Yes	No
Black Christians (298)	83	15
Indian Christians (150)	No figures	
Coloureds (80)	61	35
Afrikaans Christians (78)	78	3
English Christians (140)	5	15
Hindus (240)	75	25
Muslims (158)	72	28
Buddhists (20)	No figures	
Jews (30)	87	7
Greek Orthodox (35)	100	–
Portuguese (29)	96	4

Note
Based on the report: *Religion and inter- and intragroup relations in a pluralistic religious context of a South African city*. Oosthuizen, G.C. (HSRC Investigation into Intergroup Relations)

SELECTED BIBLIOGRAPHY OF SOUTH AFRICAN PUBLICATIONS ON INTERGROUP RELATIONS

The following selected bibliography was compiled by the Institute for Theological Research at Unisa and commissioned by the Work Committee: Religion. The bibliography covers the period 1900-1984. A list of abbreviations appears at the end of the bibliography.

ALANT, C.J. *'n Sosiologiese studie van die wyse van Sondagviering in die Nederduits Gereformeerde Kerk van Transvaal.* D.Phil. thesis, UNISA. 1966.

ALBERTYN, J.R. *Die twee volkspilare: die funksie van staat en kerk in die volkslewe.* Kaapstad: N.G. Kerk-uitgewers, 1951. 119 p. (Kerk en volk-reeks; nr. 6).

ALDERSON, C.W., TOWNSEND, H.G. & MEW, K. *Christianity and separate development: a series of three lectures delivered at Ranche House College in October 1967.* Salisbury: Mambo Press, in association with the Salisbury Council of Churches, 1967. 55p.

ALEXANDER, D.S. Future African: catholic or marxist? *SACR 4* (4, 1952), 171-181.

ANGER, T.O. *State and church in Southern Rhodesia, 1919-1939.* Salisbury: Historical Association of Rhodesia and Nyasaland, 1961. 28p. (Central Africa Historical Association. Local series; no. 4).

ANONYMOUS. South African consultation postponed (S.A. churches and W.C.C. concerning the program to combat racism). *Min* 11(2/3, 1971), 73-87.

BADENHORST, F.G. *Die rassevraagstuk, veral betreffende Suid-Afrika, in die lig van die Gereformeerde etiek.* Amsterdam: Noord-Hollandsche uitgevers, 1939. 224p. Th.D. thesis, Vrije Universiteit, Amsterdam.

BADENHORST, L.H. *'n Histories-sosiologiese ondersoek van die invloed van verstedeliking op die godsdiens en die kerk, met besondere verwysing na die Nederduitse Gereformeerde Kerk in Suid-Afrika.* D.Phil. thesis, UOFS, 1971. 2v.

BANDEY, D.W. Ethics and governments. *JTSA* (16, 1976), 19-23.

BANDEY, D.W. A positive evaluation of conflict. *JTSA* (31, 1980), 18-22.

BAPTIST UNION OF SOUTH AFRICA. A statement of attitude and faith on matters affecting the people of South Africa. *Cr* 16(2, 1969), 9-11.

BARNARD, L.D. Die verspreiding van kernwapens en internasionale orde. *TGW* 19(3, 1979), 215-224.

BAUMANN, J. *Mission und Okumene in Südwestafrika; dargestellt am Lebenswerk von Hermann Heinrich Vedder.* Leiden: Brill, 1965. 168p. (Oekumenische Studien; VII).

BAVINCK, J.H. *Een geheel andere waardemeter;* J. van den Berg [redakteur]. Amsterdam: Bekkin [1961?]. 132p. "Beschouwingen van prof. dr. J.H. Bavinck over het rassenvraagstuk en over Zuid-Afrika."

BAX, D.S. *A different gospel: a critique of the theology behind apartheid.* Johannesburg: Presbyterian Church of S.A., [1979]. 46p.

BERG, C.L. van der. Kerk en owerheid, en die rassevraagstuk in S.A. *HTS* 16(3, 1960), 201-231.

BERGH, G.N. van den. *Die posisie van die politieke partye in die Afrikaanse volkslewe: 'n histories-prinsipiële beskouing.* IBC F1(52, nd), 15pp.

BERRY, S.M. *Christian unity; a realistic view.* Grahamstown: Rhodes University College, 1950. 13p. (Peter Ainslie memorial lecture; no. 2).

BESTER, M.J. de B. *Die betrekkinge tussen die Kaapse N.G. Kerksending en die Suid-Rhodesiese regering, (1891-1937).* M.A. thesis, UNISA, 1969.

BLANK, W.J. Considerations and theses regarding problems of the church and its public role in South Africa. *Cr* 6(4, 1969), 6-11.

BLAXALL, A.W. *Between two mill stones: the Coloured people of South Africa.* London: Society for the Propagation of the Gospel in Foreign Parts, 1932. 23p. (Problems of the mission field).

BOESAK, A. Civil religion and the black community. *JTSA* (19, 1977) 35-44.

BOOYENS, B. *Kerk en staat, 1795-1843.* D.Phil. thesis, US, 1963. Published in *Archives Year Book for South African History,* 1965, vol. 2.

BOOYENS, B. *Die verhouding tussen kerk en staat aan die Kaap in die tyd van die Kompanjie, 1652-1795.* M.A. thesis, US, 1946.

BOSCH, D.J. Geestelike opbou en ekumeniese betrekkinge by die Ned. Geref. dogterkerke. *NGTT* 13(3, 1972), 129-139.

BOSHOFF, C.W.H. Die gemeente in die lig van die Skrif. *LM* 4(1972), 9-28.

BOSHOFF, C.W.H. *Kerklike verhoudinge in die Nederduitse Gereformeerde Kerk*. Pretoria: N.G. Kerkboekhandel, 1976. 27p.

BOTHA, D.P. *Die Kleurlinge en ons Kleurlingbeleid*. IBC F1 (110, 1977), 13pp.

BOTHA, J.C. Kerklike eenheid. *GV* 10(1, 1942), 9-10.

BOTHA, J.C. Mag die Christen deelneem aan "politiek"? *GV* 10(12, 1942) 286-287.

BOTHA, L.J. Reaksie op prof. J.C. Coetzee se inleiding oor: Die profetiese roeping van die kerk volgens die Skrif t.o.v. ons volkereverhoudings. *Cf.* 2230. Ids 11(44, 1977), 22-27.

BOUCHER, M. *The frontier and religion: a comparative study of the United States of America and South Africa in the first half of the nineteenth century*. M.A. thesis, UNISA, 1967. Published in *Archives Year Book for South African History*, 1968, v.2.

BRADSHAW, J. A biblical approach to the race issue. *CM* 2(8, 1966), 17.

BRAND, C. *Religious bases of group cohesion among Dutch Calvinists*. Cape Town: Abe Bailey Institute of Inter-racial Studies, [197-?]. 21p.

BRAUN, M. The structures of the congregation in an urban setting. *LM* 4(1972), 124-135.

BREEDT, L.A. Die kerk binne die industriële gebied. *HKA* 1977, 15-18.

BRINK, C.B. *Die kerk en die rassevraagstuk*. Kaapstad: N.G. Kerk-uitgewers, 1957. 15p.

BRITISH COUNCIL OF CHURCHES. Department of International Affairs & CONFERENCE OF BRITISH MISSIONARY SOCIETIES. *Violence in Southern Africa: a Christian assessment; report of a working party*. London: SCM Press, 1970. 118p. Chairman of working party: Philip Mason. (Also in German).

BROUWER, P. Reg en menseregte. *TCW* 13(3/4, 1977), 152-166.

BROWN, S.I. *A sociological study of the influence of the Christian religion on the Bantu community at Rwarwa*. M.A. thesis, UNISA, 1969. (Rwarwa is a small village in the Ciskei).

BRUWER, J.P. van S. Indiwiduele vryheid en gebondenheid in die patroon van rasseverhoudings. *Ko* 32(1964) 61-70.

BRUYN, P.J. de. *Kerk en industrie.* IBC F1(106, 1976), 16pp.

BRYANT, R.H. Toward a contextualist theology in S.A. *JTSA* (11, 1975), 11-19.

BUIS, R.P.D. *Religious beliefs and ethnic attitudes: empirical research into the attitudes of three congregations in Somerset-West.* M.A. thesis, US, 1973.

BUIS, R.P.D. *Religious beliefs and White prejudice.* Johannesburg: Ravan Press, 1975. 71p. (Based on research for M.A. thesis).

BUTHELEZI, M. The Christian presence in today's South Africa. *JTSA* (16, 1976), 5-8.

BUTHELEZI, M. Daring to live for Christ. *JTSA* (11, 1975), 7-10.

BUTHELEZI, M. Towards a biblical faith in South African society. *JTSA* (19, 1977), 55-58.

BUTHELEZI, M. Violence and the cross in South Africa today. *JTSA* (29, 1979), 51-55.

BUTI, S. Die taak van die kerk ten opsigte van geregtigheid in die Suid-Afrikaanse samelewing. *Geregtigheid in die Suid-Afrikaanse samelewing.* IBC F3(7, 1977) 98-103.

CATHOLIC CHURCH. Rhodesia Catholic Bishops' Conference. *The Land Tenure Act and the church.* Gwelo: Mambo Press on behalf of the Conference, 1970. 56p.

CATHOLIC CHURCH. Southern African Catholic Bishops' Conference. *Statement on apartheid.* [Pretoria: The Conference, 1957]. 4p. (English and Afrikaans).

CAWOOD, L. *The churches and race relations in South Africa.* Johannesburg: South African Institute of Race Relations, 1964. 140p.

CHICHESTER, Bp. The problem of race relations. *SACR* 3(4, 1951), 92-100; 4(2, 1951), 49-54; 4(3, 1951), 97-102.

CHRISTIAN COUNCIL OF RHODESIA. *The church and human relations: a consultation held at the University College of Rhodesia and Nyasaland, 25th - 29th August 1965.* [Salisbury: the Council, 1965]. 39p.

CHRISTIAN COUNCIL OF SOUTH AFRICA. *A challenge to the churches/ 'n Uitdaging aan die kerke.* Pretoria: the Council, [1940?]. 19p. (Contributions in English and Afrikaans).

CHRISTIAN COUNCIL OF SOUTH AFRICA. General Missionary Conference (1940: Pretoria). *"African family life": Report and papers read at the General Missionary Conference held at Pretoria 26th and 27th June, 1940/"Naturelle familielewe": Verslag en gelewerde referate van die Algemene Sendingkonferensie gehou in Pretoria 26 en 27 Junie 1940.* Pretoria: the Christian Council, [1940]. 66p.

CHRISTIAN COUNCIL OF SOUTH AFRICA. *Christian handbook of South Africa/Die Suid-Afrikaanse Kristen-handboek.* Lovedale: Lovedale Press, 1938. 288p. (Compiled by K.G. Grubb). (Text in English and Afrikaans).

CHRISTIAN COUNCIL OF SOUTH AFRICA. *The last bastion; documents of the Christian Council of South Africa, 1964-1965.* Cape Town: Griffiths, printer, [1965]. 11p.

THE CHRISTIAN COUNCIL OF SOUTH AFRICA. A declaration of church principles. *CM* 2(8, 1966), 32.

CHRISTIAN COUNCIL OF SOUTH AFRICA. Conference (1968: Johannesburg). *Pseudo gospels in church and society: Papers and reports from a national conference held under the auspices of the Christian Council of South Africa, Johannesburg, May 1968.* Johannesburg: South African Council of Churches, 1968, 58p. (Includes lectures by the Rev. John Davies and Dr B. Engelbrecht).

CHRISTIAN INSTITUTE OF SOUTHERN AFRICA. *Summary of actions taken against the Christian Institute and Spro-Cas between August 1973 and January 1974.* Johannesburg: Program for Social Change, 1974, 8p.

CHURCH LEADERS. A message and appeal from church leaders to Christian people of Rhodesia — 5th June 1969. *Min* 9(4, 1969), 175-178.

CHURCH OF THE PROVINCE OF SOUTH AFRICA. Diocese of Cape Town. *Cape Town diocesan mission to Moslems: commissioning of the Rev. G.A. Swartz as Director of the Mission, 1 Feb. 1962.* Cape Town: Griffiths, 1962. [5]p.

CHURCH OF THE PROVINCE OF SOUTH AFRICA. *That they may be one; a contribution to the movement towards unity between the Church of the Province of South Africa (the Anglican Church), the Presbyterian Church of Southern Africa and the Bantu Presbyterian Church of South Africa.* Cape Town: C.P.S.A., [1964]. 23p.

CHURCH OF THE PROVINCE OF SOUTH AFRICA & METHODIST CHURCH OF SOUTH AFRICA. *The Church which is His body: a report of conversations and discussions by a group of Anglican and Methodist clergymen in the Transvaal on the subject of Church union.* Cape Town: the Churches, [1964]. 8p.

CHURCH UNITY COMMISSION. *A draft plan of union.* Johannesburg: the Commission, 1972. 41p. (Published on behalf of the Church of the Province of South Africa, the Methodist Church of South Africa, the Bantu Presbyterian Church, the Presbyterian Church of Southern Africa, the Tsonga Presbyterian Church, the United Congregational Church of Southern Africa).

CILLIERS, W.J.C.., LOMBARD, J.A., and others. A second open letter to ministers of the Dutch Reformed Church in South Africa. *CM* 2(8, 1966), 27.

CLARK, W. Christian journalism: an ethical influence on secular politics. *Min* 7(4, 1967), 187-189.

CLAYTON, G.H. *Christian unity: an Anglican view.* Grahamstown: Rhodes University College, 1949. 10p. (Peter Ainslie memorial lecture; no. 1).

COERTZE, P.J. Feitelike toestande en prinsipiële siening van die rasseverhoudingspatroon in S.A. *HTS* 16(3, 1960), 179-200.

COERTZE, P.J. & BRUWER, J.P. D.P. Botha: die opkoms van ons derde stand: twee beskouinge. *Sta* 14(2, 1960), 48-60.

COERTZE, R.D. Ontwikkelingstempo binne bantoegebiede by afsonderlike ontwikkeling. *HTS* 16(3, 1960), 163-178.

COETZEE, J.C. Die profetiese roeping van die kerk volgens die Skrif — ten opsigte van ons volkereverhoudinge. *Cf.* 2220. *IdS* 11(44, 1977), 4-21.

COETZEE, J.C. Rasse-verhoudinge in Suid-Afrika *Ko* 19(4, 1952), 188-193.

COETZEE, J.H. Bevolkingsvraagstukke: oorsig en perspektief. *Die atoomeeu — 'in U lig'.* IBC F3(1, 1969), 152-170.

COETZEE, J.H. *Blanke volksontwikkeling in die lig van die Calvinisme.* Potchefstroom: Instituut vir die Bevordering van Calvinisme. [1968]. 30p. (Brosjurereeks; no. 4).

COETZEE, J.H. *Die calvinis en volkereverhoudinge.* IBC F1(46, nd), 21pp.

COETZEE, J.H. Evaluering van ons volkereverhoudingsituasie in die huidige tydsgewrig. *Ids* 11(44, 1977), 28-33.

COETZEE, J.H. Geregtigheid en liefde in ons volkereverhoudinge. *Ids* 7(27, 1973), 12-22.

COETZEE, J.H. Die kleurkrisis en die weste (die boek van B.J. Marais), *Ko* 20(4, 1952), 145-149.

COETZEE, J.H. Rasseverhoudings in Suid-Afrika: 1652-1952. *Ko* 19(4, 1952), 188-193.

COETZEE, P.C. Ras, geskiedenis en ideologie: rondom vier boeke oor die rassevraagstukke. *Sta* 18(2, 1964), 46-53.

COHEN, P. *The Hebrew Christian and his national continuity.* London: Marshall, [1909]. 147p.

COLEMAN, F.L. *Marxism, the church and South Africa.* Pretoria: Christian League of Southern Africa & South African Catholic Defence League, 1978. 13p. (Encounter information booklet). A paper presented to a round table Conference of anti-Communist organisations, convened by the Christian League of Southern Africa, Pretoria, April 1978.

CONFERENCE ON CHURCH UNION (1909: Bloemfontein). *Union of churches; the draft constitution adopted and recommended as a possible basis of union by the Conference at Bloemfontein (March 24th to 26th, 1909), comprising delegates from the Wesleyan Methodist, Presbyterian, Congregational, and Baptist Churches of South Africa.* (Preface by the Rev. John Smith, D.D. of Pietermaritzburg). [s.l.: the Conference, 1909]. 12p.

CONFERENCE ON CHURCH UNION (1910: Kimberley). *Union of churches; the draft constitution adopted and recommended as a basis of union by the Conference at Kimberley, March 16th to 18th, 1910, comprising delegates from the Presbyterian, Congregational, and Baptist Churches of South Africa.* [Cape Town]: T.T. and S., printers, [1910]. 16p.

CONVOCATION OF PASTORS OF THE FELCSA, CAPE. Comment by the convocation of pastors of the Evangelical Lutheran Church in Southern Africa (Cape church) regarding the "message" (of the S.A.C.C.). *Cr* 16(3, 1969), 6-10.

COTTESLOE CONSULTATION (1960: Johannesburg). *The report of the consultation among South African member churches of the World Council of Churches, 7-14 December 1960 at Cottesloe, Johannesburg.* Johannesburg: The Consultation, [1961]. 100p.

COTTON, W.A. *Peasantry or proletariat? Missions, governments and Native welfare from a South African point of view.* London: Society for the Propagation of the Gospel in Foreign Parts, 1929. 24p. (Problems of the Mission field).

COTTON, W.A. *Racial segregation in South Africa: an appeal.* London: Sheldon Press, 1931. 158p.

COULSON, C.A. *The church in the world.* Grahamstown: Rhodes University, 1962. 24p. (Peter Ainslie memorial lecture; no. 13).

COUPRIE, P. The 1964 Institute for Theological College Staffs in Southern Africa (official report). *Min* 4(3, 1964), 128-130.

CRAGG, D.G.L. *The relations of the Amapondo and the Colonial authorities (1830-1886) with special reference to the role of the Wesleyan missionaries.* D.Phil. thesis; University of Oxford, 1959.

CRAGG, D.G.L. The role of the Wesleyan missionaries in relations between the Mpondo and the Colonial authorities. In: Saunders, C.C. & Derricourt, R. eds. *Beyond the Cape frontier: Studies in the history of the Transkei and Ciskei.* London: Longman, 1974, pp.145-162.

CRAIG, R. *The Church: unity in integrity:* Grahamstown: Rhodes University, 1966. 16p. (Peter Anslie memorial lecture; no. 16).

CRAIG, R. *Politics and religion: a Christian view.* Salisbury: University of Rhodesia. 1972. 23p.

CRONJÉ, C.P. Onreg, nasionalisme en politieke taakstelling. *Ko* 44(5, 1979), 328-338.

CRONJE, G., NICOL, W. & GROENEWALD, E.P. *Regverdige rasse-apartheid.* Stellenbosch: Christen-Studenteverenigingsmaatskappy van Suid-Afrika, 1947. 207p.

DANNHAUSER, J.A. Politieke geweld: bevryding of terrorisme? *TCW* 16(1/2, 1980) 124-128.

DE BLANK, J. *The church in South Africa; warning: time is not on our side.* Oxford: Church Army Press, printer, 1962. 7p. (Reprinted from: *Church Times,* 20 July 1962).

DE FLEURIOT, G. *Church and industry: introduction to the teachings of the church on labour and related matters.* Durban: Thrust Publications, 1979. 196p.

DELAYED *action: an ecumenical witness from the Afrikaans speaking church,* by A.S. Geyser . . . [et. al.]. Pretoria: N.G. Kerk-boekhandel, [1960]. 168p. (Also in Afrikaans).

DENGERINK, J.D. Onze maatschappelijke en politieke verantwoordelijkheid. *BCW* 11(45, 1975), 32-41.

DEVENTER, B. van. Eiendom en sosiale heropbou: 'n Christelike siening. *Ko* 25(1, 1957), 38-45.

DOCUMENTATION. The Koinonia Declaration (Nov. 1977). *JTSA* (24, 1978), 58-64.

DREYER, A. Die opheffing van slawerny in Suid-Afrika. *NKGJ* 1935, 66-70.

DREYER, A.J.G. Die boodskap van bevryding. Oor die verhouding van die volke in die kerk. *HTS vRded,* 7-18.

DREYER, P.S. Die mens in die industriële samelewing. *HKA* 1977, 11-14.

DREYER, T.F.J. Eerbied (vir ouers en heilige dinge). *HKA* 1929, 85-89.

DUBB, A.A. *The role of the church in an urban African society.* M.A. thesis, RUC, 1961. (Investigation undertaken in East London).

DUMONT, C. *On the road to unity: pastoral guidance on ecumenism.* Pretoria: Department of Ecumenical Affairs of S.A.C.B.C., [1965]. 11, 11p. (Unitas series; no. 3). (Afrikaans and English).

DU PREEZ, A.B. *Eiesoortige ontwikkeling tot volksdiens: die hoop van Suid-Afrika.* Kaapstad: H.A.U.M., 1959, 280p. (Chapters on Church and State). (Also in English).

DU PREEZ, A.B. *Die Skriftuurlike grondslag vir rasseverhoudinge.* Kaapstad: N.G. Kerk-uitgewers, 1955. 52p.

DURAND, J.J.F. Beginselverskille of meningsverskille? *NGTT* 6 (2, 1965), 89-93.

DURAND, J.J.F. *Swartman, stad en toekoms.* Kaapstad: Tafelberg, 1970. 170 p. (Includes chapters on the role of the church in Black urban society).

DURRIN, T.E.V. *The Indian in Durban: an exploratory study of the Roman Catholic Indian minority, with special emphasis on the sociological aspects of conversion.* M. Soc. Sc. thesis, UN, 1963.

DUVENHAGE, B. *Beroepsarbeid in the lig van die Christelike etiek.* Th.D.thesis., PU for CHE, 1957.

DUVENHAGE, B. Is the nuwe moraal rewolusionêr? *BCW* 4(15, 1968), 191-197.

EISELEN, W. Gedagtes oor die beplanning van ons toekoms (rasseaange-leenthede). *Ko* 20(5, 1953), 156-167.

EKUMENE: *'n besinning oor interkerklike verhoudinge, W.A. Land-man.* . . [et al.] ; onder redaksie van A.J. van Wijk. Stellenbosch: Kosmo-uitgewery, 1964.

ELFERS, A. *Das sich Mensch zum Menschen finde: Tatsachen und Tragik im Rassenproblem Südafrikas.* Hermannsburg: Missionshandlung, 1954. 32p.

ELOFF, G. Drie gedagtes oor rasbiologie veral met betrekking tot Suid-Afrika. *Ko* 5(5, 1938), 18-26.

ELOFF, G. Rasverbetering deur uitskakeling. *Ko* 1(3, 1933), 30-34.

EMMEN, E. *Het Christelyk Instituut in Zuid-Afrika.* Amsterdam: Bekking, 1971. (Zuid-Afrikareeks).

ENGELBRECHT, B.J. & VERHOEF, P.A. Vertraagde aksie: twee reaksies. *Sta* 14(2, 1960), 33-47.

ENGELBRECHT, J.J. Geregtigheid as agtergrond van die verbinding tussen geregtigheid en revolusie. *HTS vRded,* 26-35.

ENGELBRECHT, S.P. Niks nuuts onder die son — Pred. 1:10. *HTS* 16(4, 1961), 287-300.

ESTERHUYSE, W.P. 'n Grondslag vir maatskappykritiek? *NGTT* 14 (3, 1973), 169-184.

ESTERHUYSE, W.P. 'n Grondslag vir maatskappy-kritiek? *Reformasie en revolusie.* IBC F3(2, 1974), 267-279.

ESTERHUYSE, W.P. Moraliteit en ekonomie. *TGW* 19(3, 1979), 190-207.

ESTERHUYSE, W.P. Die nuwe staatsbestel vir die toekoms. *TGW* 18 (2, 1978), 87-96.

EWBANK, R.A.B. *State and church.* Bulawayo: Diocese of Matabeleland, 1966, 16p.

FLOOR, L. Reformasie versus revolusie: 'n prinsipiële oriëntering. *Reformasie en revolusie.* IBC F3(2, 1974), 11-22.

FOSSEUS, H. The unity for which we strive. *Cr* 13(1, 1966), 12-16.

FREELAND, S.P. *The Christian gospel and the doctrine of separate development.* [s.l.]: Christian Citizenship Department of the Methodist Church of South Africa, 1961. 52p.

FREND, W.H.C. *Liberty and unity: (some historical barriers to Christian unity).* Grahamstown: Rhodes University, 1965. 19p. (Peter Ainslie memorial lecture; no. 15).

GARRISON, W.E. *Liberty and unity.* Grahamstown: Rhodes University, 1961. 29p. (Peter Ainslie memorial lectures; no. 12).

GASSICK, M.C. *The Griqua, the Sotho-Tswana, and the missionaries, 1780-1840: the politics of a frontier zone.* Ph.D. thesis, Univ. of California, Los Angeles, 1969.

GEERTSEMA, P.G. *Die Christelik-etiese implikasies van die sewende gebod met betrekking tot die sending in Suid-Afrika.* D.D. thesis., UP, 1961.

GEMSER, B. Eerbied vir die owerheid as eis van Gods Woord. *HKA* 1942, 33-56.

GERDENER, G.B.A. *Onder de Slamsen in de Kaapstad: afval en strijd.* Kaapstad: [s.n.], 1914. 7p.

GERDENER, G.B.A. *Verslag van werk onder de Slamsen in het Kaapse Schiereiland: VI — De voortgang van het werk.* Kaapstad: De Schrijver, 1915. 8p.

GEREFORMEERDE *Kerke en geregtigheid in volkereverhoudings; 'n woordelikse weergawe van die radiogesprek wat op 30 April 1970 in die Afrikaanse Diens van die Suid-Afrikaanse Uitsaaikorporasie uitgesaai is.* [Johannesburg]: Suid-Afrikaanse Uitsaaikorporasie, [1970], 25p.

GEYSER, A.S. Christelike godsdiens en eiesoortige volksdiens. *HTS* 16(1, 1960), 1-30.

GLASSER, A.F. Reconciliation between ecumenical and evangelical theologies and theologians of mission. *Mis* 7(3, 1979), 99-114.

GOBA, B. The role of the Black church in the process of healing human brokenness. *JTSA* (28, 1979), 7-13.

GOLDEN, S.G.A. Prediking, politiek en die "Politisches Nachtgebet in Köln" van Dorothee Sölle en Fulbert Steffensky. *HTS vRded,* 36-44.

GOOSEN, G.C. Justice not charity. *JTSA* (13, 1975), 51-56.

GOOSEN, G.C. *A theology of racial equality.* Ph.D.thesis, UN, 1975.

GOVENDER, S. Reconciling mission in the contemporary South African situation of cultural pluralism and identity. *Mis* 7(1979), 78-89.

GQUBULE, T.S.N. A distinctive Christian political witness? *Min* 7 (4, 1967), 160-162.

GRAGG, E.L. Segregation and integration. *CM* 2(8, 1966), 9.

GROENEWALD, E.P. *Die kerk en die ekumeniese bewegings.* Pretoria: Nasionale Raad vir Sosiale Navorsing, [1953?]. 25p. (Nasionale Raad vir Sosiale Navorsing. Toekennings vir oorsese reise; Verslag no. 4). (Mimeographed).

GRUCHY, J.W. de. *The church in our cities.* Johannesburg: South African Council of Churches and the Church Unity Commission, [1970?]. 47p. (South African Council of Churches. In focus pamphlets; no. 1).

GRUCHY, J.W. de. The civil religion debate. *JTSA* (19, 1977), 2-4.

GRUCHY, J.W. de. Consultations on publications of the South African Council of Churches, Johannesburg, 24-25 June 1969. *Min* 9(3, 1969), 130-133.

GRUCHY, J.W. de. English-speaking South Africans and civil religion. *JTSA* (19, 1977), 45-54.

GRUCHY, J.W. de. The identity of the church in South Africa: with special reference to the sanctam ecclesiam. *JTSA* (8, 1974), 38-51.

GRUCHY, J.W. de. Reflections on dialogue between the Afrikaans and English-speaking churches. *NGTT* 15(2, 1974), 120-128.

GRUCHY, J. de. The unity of the Church in future perspective. *Mis* 2(1974), 131-134.

GRUCHY, J.W. de. & DE VILLIERS, W.B. eds. *The message in perspective: a book about "A message to the people of South Africa."* Johannesburg: South African Council of Churches, [1969]. 71p.

HADFIELD, F.L. *Christ and the colour bar in Southern Africa.* Cape Town: Central News Agency, 1953. 97p.

HALTON, D.J. The psychology of race prejudice. *SACR* 8(4, 1956), 145-151.

HAMPSON, A.R. *The mission to Moslems in Cape Town.* Cape Town: [s.n.], [1934]. 16p.

HANEKOM, T.N. *Kerk en volk: die verhouding tussen Afrikaanse lewenskringe.* Kaapstad: N.G. Kerkuitgewers. [1953]. 143p. (Kerk- en Volksreeks; nr. 10).

HASELBARTH, H. Family problems of the Federation of Lutheran Churches in Southern Africa. *Cr* 13(3, 1966), 20-24.

HELBERG, J.L. *Gemengde huwelike.* IBC F1(125, 1978), 19pp.

HEXHAM, I. Christianity and apartheid: an introductory bibliography. *JTSA* (32, 1980), 39-59.

HEYNS, J.A. Enkele opmerkinge oor die Bybelse beskouing van geregtigheid. *Geregtigheid in die Suid-Afrikaanse samelewing.* IBC F3(7, 1977), 1-10.

HEYNS, J.A. Geregtigheid in 'n Suid-Afrikaanse samelewing. *NGTT* 16(1, 1975), 37-45.

HEYNS, J.A. Kerk en samelewing. *Reformasie en revolusie.* IBC F3(2, 1974), 37-46.

HEYNS, J.A. *Teologie van die revolusie.* IBC F1(128, 1978), 15pp.

HOFMEYR, J.H. *Christian principles and race problems.* Johannesburg: S.A. Institute of Race Relations, 1945. 31p. (Hoernlé memorial lecture, 1945).

HOFMEYR, J.M. Black students and the Afrikaans churches. *Mis* 2 (1974), 172-179.

HOFMEYR, J.W. & VORSTER, W.S. eds. *New faces of Africa.* Pretoria: Unisa, 1984, 249p.

HOMDROM, T. *The problem of Lutheran unity in South Africa.* M.Th. thesis, Luther Theological Seminary, St. Paul, Minnesota, 1959.

HOWE, M.S. *The story of Moriah Hall, Cape Town.* [Cape Town]: Darter, 1907, 8p. (The Hall at this time belonged to the South African Mission to the Jews. The leaflet contains an appeal for financial support).

HUDDLESTON, T. *Naught for your comfort.* London: Collins, 1956. 256p. (Experiences of an Anglican priest in the Black townships of Johannesburg).

HUDSON, C.W. *Maatskaplike vorms aan die Kaap in die tydperk 1652 tot omstreeks 1795.* Ph.D.thesis, UW, 1952.

HUGO, G.F. de V. *Die huidige boodskap van die Calvinisme op staatkundige en politieke terrein in Suid-Afrika.* Bloemfontein: Calvinistiese Studiekring, 1946k. 42p.

HUNT, E.A. *The social application of the Gospel being a paper read to the Synod of the Diocese of Southern Rhodesia.* Bulawayo: Printing and Publishing Co., 1943. 7p.

HURLEY, D.E. *Apartheid: a crisis of the Christian conscience.* [Johannesburg]: South African Institute of Race Relations, 1964. 22p. (Hoernlé memorial lecture, 1964).

HURLEY, D.E. *Catholics and ecumenism: prospects and problems.* Grahamstown: Rhodes University, 1966. 20p. (Peter Ainslie memorial lecture; no. 17).

HUYSER, J.D. *Die naturelle politiek van die Suid-Afrikaanse Republiek.* D.Litt.thesis, UP, 1937.

INMAN, T.G.V. Living together in the church. *Min* 4(2, 1964), 68-70.

INMAN, T.G.V. & GEYSER, A.S. *Living together:* [*addresses given at C.U.S.A. Assembly, Durban, October 1963*]; ed. for publication by C. Kemp. [Claremont]: Congregational Union of South Africa, 1964, 16p.

JAARSVELD, F.A. van. The Afrikaner's idea of his calling and mission in South African history. *JTSA* (19, 1977), 16-28.

JABAVU, D.D.T. *Native unrest: its cause and cure; a paper read at the Natal Missionary Conference, Durban, July, 1920; revised by the author.* Durban: Jones, printer, [1920]. 8p.

JACKMAN, S.B. *The numbered days.* London: SCM Press, 1954. 100p. (Essays on the church and racial and social problems in South Africa).

JOHANSON, B. *Church and state in South Africa.* Johannesburg: South African Council of Churches, 1973. 14p.

JOHANSON, B. ed. *The church in South Africa today and tomorrow.* Johannesburg: South African Council of Churches, 1975. 80p.

JOHANSON, B. Race, mission and ecumenism: reflections on the Landman report. *JTSA* (10, 1975), 51-61.

JONKER, W.D. Die aktualiteit van die sosiale etiek. *SI,* 78-107.

JOOSTE, J.P. *Die verhouding tussen kerk en staat aan die Kaap tot die helfte van die 19e eeu.* Bloemfontein: SACUM, 1946. 285p. D.D. thesis, UNISA, 1940.

JORDAAN, P.J. *Die sosiale probleme en taak van die Kerk in die industriële gebied.* Kaapstad: Tafelberg, 1972. 110p.

JUBBER, K. The Roman Catholic Church and apartheid. *JTSA* (15, 1976), 25-38.

KEET, B.B. *Suid-Afrika — waarheen? 'n Bydrae tot die bespreking van ons rasseprobleem.* Stellenbosch: Universiteits-uitgewers, 1955. 96p.

KEKANA, L.J. Kerk en arbeid: werkloosheid. *TV* 6(2, 1978), 58-60.

KEMP-BLAIR, H.J. *The problems of racial tensions in South Africa and the challenge they present to Protestants in the United States.* Th.M.-thesis, Southern California School of Theology, 1957.

KERK en industrie: Referate en besluite van landswye kongres, 22-24 April 1969, Universiteit van die Witwatersrand. Pretoria: N.G. Kerk Boekhandel, 1969, 128p.

KERKLIKE KONGRES VAN DIE GEFEDEREERDE NEDERDUITSE GEREFORMEERDE KERKE. INSAKE MAATSKAPLIKE EUWELS. (1949: Johannesburg). *Referate en besluite.* Pretoria: Federale Raad vir Bestryding van Maatskaplike Euwels [1949?]. 221p. Bandtitel: *Om hulle ontwil.*

KIKILLUS, G. Ware en valse demokrasie. *GV* 14(7, 1946), 13-14.

KILEFF, C. & PENDLETON, W.C. eds. *Urban man in Southern Africa.* Gwelo: Mambo Press, 1975, 254p.

KISTNER, W. *Beweerde slawerny en slawehandel in Tvl. 1852-1868.* M.A.thesis, UP, 1945.

KLERK, P.J.S. de. Die rassevraagstuk en die kwessie van nasionaliteit in Amerika. *Ko* 14(4, 1947), 152-155.

KOCK, P. de B. Die kerk en die staatkunde. *GV* 10(7, 1942), 167-168; 10(8, 1942), 207-208.

KOLBE ASSOCIATION OF SOUTH AFRICA. *The Church and ecumenism: papers delivered during the Christian Unity Week, May - June 1965/Die kerk en die ekumene: referate gelewer by geleentheid van die Week vir Christelike Eenheid, Mei - Junie 1965.* Pretoria: The Association, 1966. 107p.

KÖNIG, A. Apostolisiteit — toekoms — Afrika. *TE* 7(3, 1974), 151-158; (English translation: *Mis* 2(1974), 153-159).

KÖNIG, A. The church and politics. *TE* 12(1, 1979), 23-34.

KÖNIG, A. Reformatoriese sekerheid teenoor Roomse onfeilbaarheid. *TeV,* 128-159.

KÖNIG, A. Die roeping van die kerk in die heersende politieke en ekonomiese probleme in Suid-Afrika. *TV* 6(1, 1978), 43-57.

KÖNIG, A. Die "stiefkind" onder die eienskappe van die kerk — opmerkings oor die apostolisiteit. *TE* 7(1, 1974), 33-40.

KOTZÉ, C.S. *Die Ned. Geref. Kerk en die ekumene: 1780-1910: 'n kerk-historiese oorsig van interkerklike kontak en onderlinge verhoudinge.* D.Th. thesis, US, 1978.

KOTZÉ, J.C.G. *Ons eenheid in Christus.* Stellenbosch: Christen-Studenteverenigingmaatskappy, 1955, 32p.

KOTZÉ, J.C.G. *Ras, volk en nasie in terme van die Skrif:* Stellenbosch: Christen-Studenteverenigingmaatskappy van Suid-Afrika, 1961. 158p.

KRIEL, A. *Die spore van vertroue: die Christen se roeping in Suid-Afrika.* Stellenbosch: Kosmo-uitgewery, 1968. 109p.

KRIEL, J.D. *Die verhouding tussen kerk en staat in die Republiek van die O.V.S. (1854-1902).* M.A. thesis, UCOFS, 1944.

KRIEL, L.M. *Het ontstaan van de besturen der Ned. Geref. Kerk in Zuid-Afrika en hunne botsingen met den staat.* [s.l.: s.n., 1916]. 23p.

KRIGE, W.A. *Die Christelike sending as ontstammingsfaktor in Basoetoland.* M.A. thesis, US, 1951.

KRÜGER, J.C. *Kerkvereniging in die lig van uitverkiesing en bekering.* Pretoria: N.G. Kerkboekhandel, 1980. 186p.

KRÜGER, J.S. Eén vaderland. *NGTT* 13(4, 1972), 241-251.

KRÜGER, J.S. Rassevooroordeel en seksualiteit — 'n herwaardering van ons moraal. *TE* 6(2, 1973), 114-126.

KRUGER, J.S. 'n Sosiologiese studie van arbeidslegitimering. *TE* 9(2/3, 1976), 161-170.

KRÜGER, J.S. Theology as response to social change. *TE* 11(2/3, 1978), 1-12. (Also in *Mis* 7(1979), 17-30).

KUPER, L. *An African bourgeoisie: race, class and politics in South Africa.* New Haven: Yale University Press, 1965. 452p. (Includes scattered references to churches and missions).

LAMPRECHT, J.A. Commending Christ in a multi-racial society. *JTSA* (11, 1975), 20-31.

LANDMAN, W.A. *A plea for understanding: a reply to the Reformed Church in America.* Cape Town: N.G. Kerkuitgewers, 1968. 144p.

LATEGAN, D. Die krisis in die sendingkerk. *GV* 7(4, 1939), 106-108.

LAVIS, S.W. *Christian ideals and the social order: (South Africa's tragic contrasts of gold and poverty; a sun-kissed land and disease-breeding hovals); address at the National Conference on the Poor White problem at Kimberley, October, 1934.* Cape Town: Cape Times, printer, 1934. 12p. (Reprinted from the *Cape Times,* October 16th, 17th and 18th).

LAVIS, S.W. Christianity in industry: the reality of the brotherhood: a charter for human society. Cape Town: *Cape Times,* printer, 1941. 8p.

LEDERLE, H.I. Regverdiging en sosiale geregtigheid. *TE* 11(1, 1978), 43-61.

LEE, A.W. *Christianity and the Bantu: failure or success? An address at the Natal Missionary Conference, Durban, 1932.* 32p.

LEE, A.W. & DUBE, J.L. *The clash of colour; papers read before the Natal Missionary Conference, on the subject: "The relations between the White and Black races of South Africa, and means for their improvement,"* Durban, 7 July 1926. 11p.

LE FEUVRE, P. *Cultural and theological factors affecting relationships between the Nederduitse-Geref. Kerk and the Anglican Church (of the Province of South Africa) in the Cape Colony, 1806-1910.* Ph.D.thesis, UCT. 1980.

LEKGATHA, S.M. Ecumenical movements in an urban area. *Cr* 13(3, 1966), 14-19.

LELLO, G.A. Selections from articles for an "in between" point of view (concerning race relations in South Africa). *CM* 2(8, 1966), 18.

LELLO, G.A. Selections from other articles "against segregation". *CM* 2(8, 1966), 10.

LELLO, G.A. Selections from other articles "for segregation". *CM* 2(8, 1966), 14.

LELLO, G.A. A statement on race relations in South Africa by the Dutch Reformed Church. *CM* 2(8, 1966), 23.

LEVINE, E.D. *The second Eden: myth and religion in the Afrikaner political community.* M.A. thesis, University of Chicago, 1962.

LINDE, F.J. *'n Sosiologiese studie van pluralisme in die Nederduitse Gereformeerde Kerk. M.A. thesis,* Unisa, 1974.

LOADER, J.A. Die kerk in ekumeniese perspektief. *HTS* 24(1969), 1-11.

LOGGERENBERG, N.J.H. van. 'n Kritiese bespreking van Roskam se siening van apartheid as grondslag van die Suid-Afrikaanse samelewing. *Ko* 30(1963), 441-454.

LOMBARD, J.A. Die Christelike kerk en die liefde vir die vaderland. *TE* 3(1, 1970), 41-48.

LOMBARD, R.T.J. *Die Nederduitse Gereformeerde Kerke en rassepolitiek, met spesiale verwysing na die jare 1948-1961.* D.Litt. et Phil.thesis, Unisa, 1974.

LOOTS, P.J. *Pluralisme in staat en kerk, met spesiale verwysing in die tydperk 1559-1824.* Ph.D. thesis, UCT, 1962. 2v.

LOUW, A.F. Die Christen Raad. *HZ* 14(10, 1936), 292.

LOWRY, D. Economics and the mystical body of Christ. *SACR* 6(3, 1953), 97-108.

LÜCKHOFF, A.H. *Cottesloe.* Kaapstad: Tafelberg, 1978. 197p.

LÜCKHOFF, A.H. *Die Cottesloe kerkeberaad.* Ph.D.thesis, UW, 1976.

LÜDEMA, E.A. A Lutheran compares the resolutions of Lunteren with the Message (S.A. Council of Churches). *Cr* 16(3, 1969), 15-24.

MACLEOD, G.F. *Church union and social concern.* Grahamstown: Rhodes University, 1952. 14p. (Peter Ainslie memorial lecture; no. 4).

MACMILLAN, W.M. *Bantu, Boer, and Briton: the making of the South African Native problem.* London: Faber & Gwyer, 1929. 328p.

MALAN, D.J. Gelykheid, eenheid, verskeidenheid. *HZ* 14(8, 1936), 218.

MALAN, D.J. New wine in old bottles. *GV* 26(3, 1957), 31-38.

MALAN, D.J. *Rassehaat.* M.A.thesis, US, 1941.

MALAN, F.S. The biblical notions of justice and mercy in the process of development. *TV* 2(2, 1974), 82-92.

MALAN, J.H. Teologie, politiek en volkereproblematiek. *TCW* 14(1/2, 1978), 74-79.

MANGOPE, L.M. *Address to the Missiological Institute, Lutheran Theological College, Umpumulo, on the role of the church in independent homelands, 11.9.74.* Mapumulo: the Institute, 1974. 10p.

MANGOPE, L.M. Die taak van die kerk ten opsigte van geregtigheid in die Suid-Afrikaanse samelewing: besien as politieke leier. *Geregtigheid in die Suid-Afrikaanse samelewing.* IBC F3(7, 1977), 92-97.

MANS, C.J. Enkele kritiese opmerkings oor die teologiese grondslae van menseregte en 'n teologie van bevryding. *HTS* 29(4, 1973), 129-145.

MANS, C.J. Kerk en rewolusie. *HKA* 1969, 82-86.

MARAIS, B.J. A historical flashback. The Christian church and race (colour). *TE* 10(2/3, 1977), 60-72.

MARAIS, B.J. *Human diversity and Christian unity.* Grahamstown: Rhodes University, 1957. 21p. (Peter Ainslie memorial lecture; no. 9).

MARAIS, B.J. *Rondom die eenheid van die kerk van Christus en die ekumeniese beweging.* Kaapstad: N.G. Kerk-uitgewers, [1958]. 15p.

MARAIS, B.J. Die Skrif en rasse-apartheid. *GV* 18(1, 1950), 14-25.

MARKS, S. *Reluctant rebellion: The 1906-8 disturbance in Natal.* Oxford: Clarendon Press, 1970. 404p. (Oxford studies in African affairs).

MARTIN, M.L. The Christian and his work. *Min* 9(3, 1969), 108-111.

MAURY, P. *Christian witness among intellectuals.* Grahamstown: Rhodes University, 1954. 19p. (Peter Ainslie memorial lecture; no. 6).

MEIRING, A.M. *Christian unity: a Dutch Reformed view.* Grahamstown: Rhodes University, 1953. 18p. (Peter Ainslie memorial lecture; no. 5).

MEIRING, P.G.J. *Die kerk op pad na 2000; twaalf gesprekke oor die rol van die kerk in die laaste kwart van die 20ste eeu.* Kaapstad: Tafelberg, 1977. 156p.

MEIRING, P.G.J. & LEDERLE, H.I. *Die eenheid van die Kerk: opstelle byeengebring.* Kaapstad: Tafelberg, 1979. 198p. (Includes articles on relations within the family of Dutch Reformed churches; and on SACLA (South African Christian Leadership Assembly)).

MENTZ, J.F. Kerklike pluriformiteit. *GV* 9(11, 1941), 329-333.

MENTZ, J.F. Die rassevraagstuk. *GV* 13(10, 1945), 11-12.

MERWE, A. van der. Apostolisiteit en koninkryksgerigtheid. *TV* 2 (1, 1974), 35-45.

MERWE, D.C.S. van der. Etiese beskouing oor geregtigheid in die Suid-Afrikaanse samelewing. *Geregtigheid in die Suid-Afrikaanse samelewing.* IBC F3(7, 1977), 11-35.

MERWE, H.P. van der. Blanke en Zwarte rassen in Zuid-Afrika. *HZ* 3(10, 1925), 293.

MERWE, P. van der. Die kerk se invloed op die parlementêre stelsel. *HKA* 1969, 78-81.

MERWE, W.J. van der. Ekumeniese sendingaksie in N.G. kring. *NGTT* 16(1, 1975), 88-98.

MERWE, W.J. van der. A federative affiliation between Dutch Reformed mother and daughter churches. *NGTT* 10(2, 1969), 65-71.

MERWE, W.J. van der. Gesamentlike besinning en verbondenheid binne die kring van die N.G. kerke. *NGTT* 3(4, 1962), 469-480.

MERWE, W.J. van der. Samewerking tussen die Ned. Geref. Kerk en ander kerke in Suid-Afrika in belang van die Sending. *NGTT* 4 (4, 1963), 197-203.

MERWE, W.J. van der. Die verband tussen ouer en jongere kerke in Suidelike Afrika. *NGTT* 2(2, 1961), 65-79.

METHODIST CHURCH OF SOUTHERN AFRICA. Conference (1979: Cape Town). *A critique of the WCC programme to combat racism: as adopted by the Conference.* Cape Town: Methodist Publishing House, [1979]. 7p.

METHODIST CHURCH OF SOUTHERN AFRICA. Post-war Development Commission. *Towards a Christian South Africa: the Union for Christ.* Durban: Provincial Printing Co., [1945?]. 36p.

MEYER, R. *Poverty in abundance, or abundance in poverty?* Johannesburg: Christian Institute of Southern Africa, [1973]. 65p. (Christian Institute studies).

MILK, L.O. Commentary on "A message to the people of South Africa" (S.A.C.C.) at FELCSA Conference, Stellenbosch, Feb. 1969. *Cr* 16(2, 1969), 14-18.

MISSIOLOGICAL INSTITUTE AT LUTHERAN THEOLOGICAL COLLEGE (Mapumulo). *Church and nationalism in South Africa.* (editor T. Sundermeier). Johannesburg: Ravan Press, 1975. 152p.

MISSIOLOGICAL INSTITUTE AT LUTHERAN THEOLOGICAL COLLEGE (Mapumulo). *Church and state.* Mapumulo: the Institute, 1968. 225p.

MISSIOLOGICAL INSTITUTE AT LUTHERAN THEOLOGICAL COLLEGE (Mapumulo). *Migrant labour and church involvement: a consultation held in Umpumulo (Natal).* Mapumulo: the Institute, 1970. 209p.

MONTANYANE, A. Peace: its biblical and contemporary significance. *Min* 11(1, 1971), 21-23.

MOODIE, T.D. *Power, apartheid and the Afrikaner civil religion.* Ph.D. thesis, Harvard University, 1972.

MOODIE, T.D. *The rise of Afrikanerdom: power, apartheid and the Afrikaner civil religion.* Berkeley: University of California Press, 1975. 328p. (Perspectives on Southern Africa; 11).

MOSS, R.P. Pollution. *Reformasie en revolusie.* IBC F3(2, 1974), 329-345.

MOULDER, J. Conscientious objection in South Africa. *NGTT* 20(3, 1979), 243-253.

MOULDER, J. A response to "Theology and politics in South Africa". *JTSA* (18, 1977), 11-16.

MOULDER, J. Romans 13 and conscientious disobedience. *JTSA* (21, 1977), 13-23.

MULDER, C.P. *Watter uitwerking het die noue omgang met die Bybel gehad op die ontstaan van die Afrikaanse volkskarakter?* Ph.D.thesis, UW, 1956.

MÜLLER, J.J. Kerklike veelvormigheid of sonde. *GV* 12(7, 1944), 8-9.

NASH, M.A. *Ecumenical movement in the 1960s.* Johannesburg: Ravan Press, 1975. 430p.

NAÚDE, C.F.B. & STRAUSS, W. de W. *Kerk en jeug in die buiteland en Suid-Afrika*. Kaapstad: N.G. Kerk-uitgewers, 1955. 284p.

NEDERDUITS GEREFORMEERDE KERK. Ministers of the Dutch Reformed Church. A report on migratory labour in South Africa. *CM* 2(8, 1966), 33.

NEDERDUITS GEREFORMEERDE KERK. Algemene Sinode. *Ras, volk en nasie en volkeverhoudinge in die lig van die Skrif:* [rapport] *goedgekeur en aanvaar deur die Algemene Sinode van die Nederduitse Gereformeerde Kerk, Oktober 1974*. Kaapstad: N.G. Kerkuitgewers, 1975. 102p. (English translation: *Human relations and the South African scene in the light of Scripture,* 1976).

NEILL, S. *Rome and the ecumenical movement*. Grahamstown: Rhodes University, 1967. 29p. (Peter Ainslie memorial lecture; no. 18).

NEL, J.J.A. *Die verhouding tussen staat en kerk. (Kaapkolonie, 1652-1910)*. M.A. thesis, UNISA, 1935.

NEWBIGIN, J.E.L. *The mission and unity of the church*. Grahamstown: Rhodes University, 1960. 20p. (Peter Ainslie memorial lecture; no. 11).

NICOL, W. Kantiene vir naturelle. *HZ* 10(5, 1932), 151.

NIEKERK, A.S. van. The church and contemporary society. *TV* 6(2, 1978), 55-57.

NIEKERK, F.N. van. Kerk en owerheid. *GV* 14(3, 1946), 9-10.

NIEKERK, F.N. van. *Die Wêreldraad van Kerke (Babelse Spraakverwarring); waarheen?* Potgietersrust: Morester Drukkery, [1957?]. 73p.

NIELSEN, S. The aim of Christian unity. *NGTT* 10(3, 1969), 166-177.

NORVAL, E.J.G. *Arbeid; prinsipiële ondersoek van arbeid met 'n kritiese toespitsing op enkele aktuele hoofprobleme van die arbeidsetiek*. D.Phil.thesis, PU, 1966.

NÜRNBERGER, K.B. Christian witness and economic discrepancies. *JTSA* (29, 1979), 72-77.

NÜRNBERGER, K. *Socio-economic ideologies in a Christian perspective*. Durban: Lutheran Publishing House for the Missiological Institute at Lutheran Theological College, Mapumulo, 1979. 65p.

NÜRNBERGER, K.B. Reconciliation in a situation of severe economic discrepancies. *Mis* 7(1979), 47-64.

OBERHOLZER, J.P. Die interkerklike konferensie oor die kerk en sosiale geregtigheid, 1979, *HKA* 1980, 1-13.

ODENDAAL, B.J. *Die kerklike betrekkinge tusen Suid-Afrika en Nederland (1652-1952) veral met betrekking tot die Ned. Geref. Kerk.* Franeker: Wever, 1957. 96p.

OELOFSE, J.C. *Die Nederduitsch Hervormde Kerk en die Afrikaner-Broederbond.* Krugersdorp: N.H.W.-pers, printer, [1964]. 63p.

OOSTHUIZEN, A.J.G. Die kerk en visie op die resente gebeure in S.A. *HTS* 16(3, 1960), 243-248.

ORR, R. & AMOORE, F.A. *Anglicans and Presbyterians meet; study papers on church unity.* Cape Town: Griffiths, printer, 1965. 25p.

PAGE, C.A. *Black America in White South Africa; church and state reaction to the African Methodist Episcopal Church in Cape Colony and Transvaal, 1896-1910.* Ph.D. thesis, University of Edinburgh, 1978.

PAKENDORF, P.G. The relation of FELCSA member churches to each other. *Cr* 16(3, 1969), 10-14.

PATON, A.S. *Christian unity; a South African view.* Grahamstown: Rhodes University, 1951. 12p. (Peter Ainslie memorial lecture; no. 3).

PEACEY, B. Christianity and race relations in South Africa. *CM* 2(8, 1966), 13.

PEACEY, B.W. *"When He separated the children of men . . .": a Christian approach to the problem of colour in South Africa.* Pretoria: State Information Office, 1955. 20p.

PERQUIN, B.A. The repercussions of industrialisation on the Catholic Church in South Africa. *SACR* 1(1, 1948), 25-32.

PHELPS, F.R. *The reunion of Christendom; a sermon preached in the Baptist Church, Alice on Sunday March 15, 1925.* Grahamstown: Grocott & Sherry, 1925. 11p.

PHILLIPS, R.E. *The Bantu are coming: phases of South Africa's race problem.* London: Student Christian Movement Press, 1930. 283p.

PIENAAR, H.J. Christendom en politiek. *HZ* 1(4, 1923), 124.

PISTORIUS, P.V. Ons apartheidsbeleid en die Skrif. *GV* 18(1, 1950), 26-33.

PLESSIS, H. du. Assimilasie of algehele segregasie: die enigste alternatiewe vir oplossing van die naturelleprobleem. *Ko* 2(6, 1935), 32-41.

PLESSIS, J. du. Wat is de revolutiegeest? *HZ* 2(9, 1924), 279-285.

PLESSIS, L.J. du. Calvinistiese perspektief: 'n konstruktief bedoelde benadering van ons rassevraagstuk. *Ko* 28(2, 1960), 98-103.

PLESSIS, L.J. du. Die naturellevraagstuk in Suid-Afrika. *Ko* 8(1, 1940), 2-10.

PLESSIS, L.J. du. Rasverhoudinge. *Ko* 1(2, 1933), 10-15.

PLESSIS, L.J. du. 'n Valse dilemma. *Ko* 23(5, 1956), 262-267.

PLESSIS, L.M. du. Menseregte en konfliksituasies. *Ko* 44(5, 1979), 339-353.

PLESSIS, P.G.W. du. Sosiale etiek en H.G. Stoker se stryd om die ordes. *Ko* 43(4, 1978), 351-362.

PONT, A.D. Die Afrikaner en sy kerk. *HKA* 1968, 84-90.

POTGIETER, F.J. & MUNNIK, J.P. *Militêre diensplig en diensweiering.* IBC F1(78, 1974), 16pp.

POTGIETER, F.J.M. Die apartheidsvraagstuk. *GV* 18(1, 1950), 2-4.

POTGIETER, F.J.M. Teologiese fundering van menseregte. *TCW* 13(3/4, 1977), 167-171. (Also in *NGTT* 19(1, 1978), 69-74).

POTGIETER, F.J.M. *Veelvormige ontwikkeling: die wil van God; rede gelewer by geleentheid van die sluiting van die Teologiese Kweekskool te Stellenbosch, Des. 1956.* Bloemfontein: Sacum, [1956?]. 12p.

POTGIETER, F.J.M. Veelvormige ontwikkeling: die wil van God. *GV* 26(1, 1958), 5-15.

POTGIETER, P.J.J.S. Pigment en proletariaat: die Kleurvraagstuk in Skrifbeligting. *Reformasie en revolusie.* IBC F3(2, 1974), 346-361.

PREEZ, A.B. du. Die afsonderlike ontwikkeling van Bantoegebiede en die eis wat dit aan ons sendingwerk stel. *NGTT* 1(2, 1960), 46-53.

RANDALL, P. ed. *Anatomy of apartheid.* Johannesburg: Study Project on Christianity in Apartheid Society,1970. 88p. (Spro-Cas. Occasional publications; no. 1).

RANDALL, P. ed. *Apartheid and the church; report of the Church Commission of the Study Project.* Johannesburg: Study Project on Christianity in Apartheid Society, 1972. 92p. (Spro-Cas. Publications; no. 8).

RANDALL, P. ed. *Directions of change in South African politics.* Johannesburg: Study Project on Christianity in Apartheid Society, 1971. 85p. (Spro-Cas. Occasional publications; no. 3).

RANDALL, P. ed. *Law, justice and society: report of the Legal Commission of the Study Project.* Johannesburg: Study Project on Christianity in Apartheid Society, 1972. 100p. (Spro-Cas. Publications; no. 9).

RANDALL, P. ed. *Power, privilege and poverty: report of the Economics Commission of the Study Project.* Johannesburg: Study Project on Christianity in Apartheid Society, 1972. 127p. (Spro-Cas. Publications; no. 7).

RANDALL, P. ed. *South Africa's minorities.* Johannesburg: Study Project on Christianity in Apartheid Society, 1971. 77p. (Spro-Cas. Occasional publications; no. 2).

RANDALL, P. *A taste of power: the final, co-ordinated Spro-Cas report.* Johannesburg: Study Project on Christianity in Apartheid Society, 1973. 225p. (Spro-Cas. Publications; no. 11).

RANDOLPH, R.H. *Church and state in Rhodesia 1969-1971: a Catholic view.* Gwelo: Mambo Press for the Rhodesia Catholic Bishops' Conference, 1971. 148p.

RAUTENBACH, C.H. Die toekoms van die kerk in die samelewing: kollig veral op die sosiaal-etiese, insluitende politieke afmetings van Christelike kerkbly in Suid-Afrika. *C&S,* 68-97.

REA, W.F. *The missions as an economic factor on the Zambezi, 1580-1759.* Ph.D. thesis, University of London, 1974.

REEVES, R.A. *The church in relation to the state.* Johannesburg: St. Benedict's House, 1953. 16p. (St. Benedict's booklets; no. 4).

REFORMED ECUMENICAL SYNOD. *A report of the RES Interpretative Commission to the South African churches of the RES.* [s.l.]: Reformed Ecumenical Synod, 1978. 29p.

REFORMED ECUMENICAL SYNOD. (1958: Potchefstroom). *Acts of the fourth Reformed Ecumenical Synod of Potchefstroom, South Africa, August 6-13, 1958.* Potchefstroom: [the Synod], 1958. 168p.

RENNIE, J.K. *Christianity, colonialism and the origins of nationalism among the Ndau of Southern Rhodesia, 1890-1935.* Ph.D. thesis, Northwestern University, 1973.

RENSBURG, S.P.J.J. van. Die kerk, die eenheid en die grens van die kerk. *HTS* 21(2/3, nd), 31-38.

RETIEF, G.J. Die verheerliking van God op staatsterrein. *GV* 6(9, 1938), 283-284; 6(10, 1938), 319-320; 6(12, 1938), 375-376.

RIESSEN, H. van. Christen-overheid-krijgsmacht-moderne bewapening. *BCW* 7(28, 1971), 35-45; 7(29, 1971), 43-53.

ROBINSON, P.J. *Die verhouding van die N.G. Kerk tot sy Bantoedogterkerke.* B.D.thesis, US, 1959.

ROMAN CATHOLIC CHURCH IN S.A., THE BISHOPS OF THE. The official Roman Catholic position on race relations in South Africa. *CM* 2 (8, 1966), 30.

ROOYEN, E.E. van. Die apartheid van die nasies en hul roeping teenoor mekaar. *GV* 16(4, 1948), 6-7.

ROOYEN, E.E. van. Interessante besonderhede oor sendingaangeleenthede en naturellebeleid. *GV* 11(4, 1943), 85-86.

ROOYEN, E.E. van. Twee redevoeringe in Europa deur 'n Suid-Afrikaanse staatsman — Genl. J.C. Smuts. *GV* 16(8, 1948), 7-9.

ROSSLEE, D.D. Kerk en stad: 'n religieuse benadering. *TCW* 9(2, 1973), 83-92.

ROSSLEE, D.D. Die naturelle-probleem gesien by die lig van die wysbegeerte van die wetsidee. *GV* 16(3, 1948), 13-14.

ROSSLEE, D.D. *Sabbatsontheiliging as kerk-staat-vraagstuk in S.A. by die lig van die wysbegeerte van die wetsidee.* M.A.thesis, UV, 1949.

ROUX, L.A.D. Die rassevraagstuk. *GV* 15(4, 1947), 14-15.

ROUX, C. du P. le. *Vooroordele en stereotipes in die rassehoudings van Kleurlinge.* M.A.thesis, US, 1959.

SACHS, B. *The road to Sharpeville.* Johannesburg: Dial Press, 1961. 218 p. (Chapter V: The religio-political front).

SADIE, M.M. *Apartheid voor die regerstoel: 'n ondersoek van die Wêreldraad van Kerke se aanklagte teen die Suid-Afrikaanse rassebeleid.* Durban: ESP-Instituut, 1970. 134p.

SALES, W. The ethical task of the church in South Africa. *Min* 9(3, 1969), 105-107.

SAUNDERS, C.C. *Tile and the Thembu Church; politics and independency on the Cape Eastern Frontier in the late nineteenth century.* Cape Town: Abe Bailey Institute of Interracial Studies, 1971. 17p. (Abe Bailey Institute of Interracial Studies. Reprint; no. 3).

SCHALKWYK, A. van. Apartheid en die kerklik-godsdienstige lewe van die Bantoe. *GV* 18(1, 1950), 34-41.

SCHEEPERS, D.J.J. *Die beginsel van soewereiniteit in eie kring as waarborg vir burgervryheid in die Christelike staat.* M.A.thesis, UV, 1952.

SCHOLTZ, G.J.L. *Perspektiewe oor sport, politiek en menseverhoudinge.* IBC F1(88, 1975), 24pp.

SCHÖNE, J. The gospel and political structures. *Cr* 17(2, 1970), 5-15.

SCHULZE, L.F. Die filosofiese agtergrond van die huidige sosiopolitieke struktuurbeskouinge. *IdS* 12(47, 1978), 8-21.

SETILOANE, G.M. Christian citizens of the future. *Min* 3(3, 1963), 110-113.

SIMPSON, T. Politics and salvation. *JTSA* (8, 1974), 5-15.

SMITH, G.A. & JOLSON, A. eds. *The role of the church in rural development: report on the proceedings and recommendations of the Working Conference on the role of the church in rural development held at the University of Rhodesia, Salisbury 27th - 30th August, 1972.* Salisbury: Agricultural Missions of New York in association with the Rhodesian churches, 1972. 118p.

SMOLJAR, P. *The Messiah and His followers; an appeal to the Jewish people.* [3rd ed.]. Cape Town: Mildmay Mission to the Jews, South African Branch, 1948. 16p.

SNYMAN, D.R. Die Bybelse voorstelling van die verhouding tussen kerk en staat. *OP* 6(5, 1932), 456.

SNYMAN, W.J. Rasseverhoudinge in die Skrif (in besonder in die Nuwe Testament). *Ko* 25(3, 1957), 159-174.

SOUTH AFRICAN COUNCIL OF CHURCHES. A message to the people of South Africa. *Cr* 16(2, 1969), 5-8. (Also published in *Min* 9(1, 1969), 27-30)

SOUTH AFRICAN COUNCIL OF CHURCHES. National Conference (8th: 1976: Hammanskraal). *Liberation: the papers and resolutions of the Eighth Conference, held at St. Peter's Conference Centre, Hammanskraal, July 27-29, 1976.* [Edited by] D. Thomas. Johannesburg: the Council, 1976. 85 p.

SOUTH AFRICA. Commission of inquiry into certain organisations. *Interim and final reports.* Pretoria: Government Printer, 1975.

SOUTH AFRICAN VIGILANCE COMMITTEE. *The voice of the Churches of South Africa on the imperial policy in South Africa.* Cape Town: South African Vigilance Committee, 1900. 8 p. (Vigilance papers, no. 1) (Cover title: The voice of the Churches).

SPOELSTRA, B. *The Afrikaner's nation-state policy: in the light of the Bible.* Pretoria: S.A. Bureau of Racial Affairs, 1979. 18p.

SPOELSTRA, B. Die Bybel en ons Afrikaanse volkerebeleid. *IdS* 4 (15, 1970), 34-45.

SPOELSTRA, B. Kerklike standpunte ten opsigte van trekarbeid. *IdS* 10(38, 1976), 27-46.

STADSKERKKONFERENSIE (1963: Pretoria). *Die kerk in aksie in die moderne stad: stadskerkkonferensie, Pretoria, 19 Maart 1963, gehou deur die Sin. Ev. Kom. van die N.G. Kerk.* [s.l.: s.n., 1963?]. 371.

STEENKAMP, C.S. *Beskouinge van 'n groep predikante van die Nederduitsch Hervormde Kerk oor die relevantheid van sekere aangeleenthede met betrekking tot godsdienstigheid; 'n godsdienssosiologiese ondersoek.* M.A. thesis, UP, 1973.

STOKER, H.G. Die beginsel: eenheid en differensiasie. *Ko* 30(1/2, 1962), 20-45.

STOKER, H.G. Die samehangende verskeidenheid van menslike vryheid veral in samelewingsverband. *Ko* 31(1964), 469-505.

STRASSBERGER, E.J.C. *Ecumenism in South Africa, 1936-1960, with special reference to the mission of the church.* D.Th.thesis, US, 1971. Publ. Johannesburg, S.A. Council of Churches, 1974.

STRAUSS, H.J. Beskawing, staatsvorm en stemreg in S.A. *GV* 20(3, 1952), 136-141.

STRAUSS, H.J. Partypolitieke beginselrigtings. *GV* 28(2, 1959), 13-17.

STRAUSS, H.J. Religieuse koers en burgervryheid. *GV* 23(2, 1954), 17-25.

STRYDOM, J.G. Segregasie of gelykstelling. *GV* 6(10, 1938), 306-308.

STUBBS, A. *The planting of the Federal Theological Seminary of Southern Africa.* Lovedale: Lovedale press, 1973. 18p.

SUNDKLER, B.G.M. *The Christian ministry in Africa.* London: SCM Press, 1960. 346p. (World mission studies).

SWANEPOEL, H.L. Die verhouding owerheid-onderdaan in die atoomeeu. *Die atoomeeu — 'in U lig'*. IBC F3(1, 1969), 198-203.

SWANEPOEL, J. Bestaansnood of bestaansgeleenthede vir al die kinders van die Republiek van Suid-Afrika. *TV* 6(1, 1978), 21-29.

SWART, G.J. *God's een kerk en ons baie kerke*. Brits: die Skrywer, 1957. 16p.

SWART, G.J. *Die vraagstuk van die eenheid, verskeidenheid en verdeeldheid van die kerk; 'n ekumenies-ekklesiologiese ondersoek*. D.D.thesis, UP, 1960.

SYNNOTT, F. *Justice and reconciliation in South Africa: Report by the Justice and Reconciliation Department of the Southern African Catholic Bishops' Conference, together with basic social teaching from the Gospels and Church authority*. Pretoria: Southern African Catholic Bishops' Conference, [197-?]. 36p. (Pastoral action; no. 5).

TALJAARD, J.A.L. 'n Prinsipiële begronding van die apartheidsbeleid. *Ko* 32(1964), 342-354.

TEMPLIN, J.A. *Permutations of the idea of the elect people in South Africa*. Ph.D. thesis, Harvard University, 1966.

THERON, E. Geregtigheid in die Suid-Afrikaanse samelewing: sosiale beskouing. *Geregtigheid in die Suid-Afrikaanse samelewing*. IBC F3(7, 1977), 36-43.

THERON, P.F. *Die ekklesia as kosmies-eskatologiese teken; die eenheid van die kerk as "profesie" van die eskatalogiese vrede*. D.D.thesis, UP, 1976.

THOMAS, D.G. *Councils in the ecumenical movement, South Africa, 1904-1975*. Johannesburg: S.A. Council of Churches, 1979. 123p.

THOMAS, N.E. *Christianity, politics and the Manyika: a study of the influence of religious attitudes and loyalties on political values and activities of Africans in Rhodesia*. Ph.D. thesis, Boston University, 1968.

TODD, R.S.G. *Christian unity: Christ's prayer*. Grahamstown: Rhodes University, 1955. 15p. (Peter Ainslie memorial lecture; no. 7).

TOIT, A.B. du. Enkele gesigspunte in verband met die Woord van God en die heersende politieke en ekonomiese problematiek in Suid-Afrika. *TV* 6(1, 1978), 1-11.

TOIT, D.A. du. Geregtigheid en mensbeskouing. *TGW* 18(3/4, 1978), 258-267.

TOIT, J.D. du. & TOIT, S. du. *Die Afrikaanse rassebeleid en die Skrif.* Potchefstroom: Pro Rege-pers, 1955. 34p.

TOIT, K.W. du. Work: the state and labour relations. *TV* 6(2, 1978), 1-9.

TOIT, S. du. Openbaringslig op die apartheidsvraagstuk. *Ko* 17(1, 1949), 13-24.

TOWNSEND, H.G. *As we are one: the Christian in a plural society.* Gwelo: Catholic Mission Press, 1962. 120p.

TREURNICHT, A.P. *Die praktiese belewing van die Calvinisme in Suid-Afrika.* Potchefstroom: Instituut vir Bevordering van Calvinisme, P.U. vir C.H.O., 1969. 14p. (Studiestukke no. 032).

TRIAL of Beyers Naude: *Christian witness and the rule of law; edited* by the International Commission of Jurists, Geneva; introduction by Sir. R. Birley; legal background by A.N. Allott. London: Search Press in conjunction with Ravan Press, 1975. 188p.

UNITED SOCIETY FOR THE PROPAGATION OF THE GOSPEL. *Ecumenical involvement: views from South Africa, Zambia, etc.* London: the Society, 1968. 15p. (Observation posts, 5).

UNIVERSITY OF SOUTH AFRICA. Institute for Theological Research. Symposium. (1st: 1977: Pretoria). *Church and society; proceedings of the first Symposium held at the University of South Africa in Pretoria on the 20th and 21st of September 1977.* W.S. Vorster, editor. Pretoria: University of South Africa, 1978. 97p. (Miscellanea Congregalia, 6).

UNIVERSITY OF SOUTH AFRICA. Institute for Theological Research. Symposium. (3rd: 1979: Pretoria). *Church unity and diversity in the Southern African context; proceedings of the third Symposium heldd at the University of South·Africa in Pretoria on the 12th and 13th September 1979.* W.S. Vorster, Editor. Pretoria: University of South Africa, 1980. 146p. (Miscellanea Congregalia, 17).

VENTER, E.A. Gedagtes oor 'n Christelike staatsleer. *GV* 9(12, 1941), 358-360.

VENTER, E.A. Die Heilige Skrif en die apartheidsvraagstuk. *GV* 18 (1, 1950), 5-13.

VENTER, F. *Die "rule of law".* IBC F1(112, 1977), 8pp.

VENTER, I.S.J. *Die Anglikaanse Kerk en sy stryd om staatsondersteuning in die Oranje-Vrystaatse Republiek.* Pretoria: Universiteit van Suid-Afrika, 1958. 64p. (Mededelings van die Universiteit van Suid-Afrika. Reeks C; no. 4).

VENTER, W.J. Die ekonomiese orde in die branding. *Reformasie en revolusie.* IBC F3(2, 1974), 309-328.

VENTER, W.J. Die uitdaging van die tegnologiese eeu aan die Christen in die industrie. *Die atoomeeu — 'in U lig'.* IBC F3(1, 1969), 368-378.

VERHOEF, P.A. Matrimonium mixtum. *NGTT* 2(2, 1961), 153-168.

VERHOEF, P.A. Volkereverhoudinge in die lig van die Skrif. *NGTT* 21(1, 1980), 106-117.

VERRYN, T.D. *The vanishing clergyman: a sociological study of the priestly role in South Africa.* Johannesburg: South African Council of Churches, [1971]. 208p.

VILJOEN, A.C. ed. *Ekumene onder die Suiderkruis.* Pretoria: Unisa, [1979]. 208p.

VILJOEN, S.P. *Die voortbestaan van die Blanke ras.* UP, Publikasiereeks IV 7, 1937, 19pp.

VILJOEN, S.P. du T. Politieke en ekonomiese desentralisasie in Suid-Afrika *Geregtigheid in die Suid-Afrikaanse samelewing.* IBC F3(7, 1977), 44-57.

VILLA-VICENCIO, C. South African civil religion: an introduction. *JTSA* (19, 1977), 5-15.

VILLA-VICENCIO, C. Theology and politics in South Africa. *JTSA* (17, 1976), 25-34.

VILLA-VICENCIO, C.M.L. Christian social ethics as a deabsolutizing discipline. *JTSA* (31, 1980), 7-17.

VILLA-VICENCIO, C.M.L. *The theology of apartheid.* Cape Town: Methodist Publishing House, [1977]. 38p.

VORSTER, J.D. Die duur van die skeiding. *NGTT* 20(4, 1979), 372-374.

VORSTER, J.D. Is die beleid van eiesoortige ontwikkeling sedelik te regverdig? *NGTT* 20(4, 1979), 374-376.

VORSTER, J.D. Is hierdie beleid Christelik? *NGTT* 20(4, 1979), 366-372.

VORSTER, J.D. Kan 'n Christen-Afrikaner die beleid van eiesoortige ontwikkeling regverdig? *NGTT* 20(4, 1979), 360-366.

VORSTER, J.D. Die Kleurlyn en Kleureerbiediging. *Ko* 6(4, 1939), 11-17.

VORSTER, J.D. Die rassevraagstuk volgens die Skrifte. *GV* 15(8, 1947), 4-5.

VORSTER, J.D. *Veelvormigheid en eenheid.* Kaapstad: N.G. Kerkuitgewers, 1978. 119p.

VORSTER, J.M. *Die Kerk en die Kleurvraagstuk vandag: die hantering van die Kleurvraagstuk deur die Wêreldraad van Kerke en die Gereformeerde Kerke in Nederland teen die agtergrond van die kontemporêre kultuur.* D.Phil.thesis, PU, 1978.

VORSTER, J.M. Knelpunte tussen Christene in Suid-Afrika t.o.v. die politieke betrokkenheid van die kerk. *IdS* 13(52, 1979), 3-12.

VORSTER, J.M. *Die roeping van die Kerk ten opsigte van die Kleurvraagstuk vandag.* IBC F1(131, 1978), 17pp.

VORSTER, W.S. In gesprek met die Landmankommissie: oor Skrifgebruik. *EkS*, 182-208.

VYVER, J.D. van der. The future prospects for the protection of human rights in South Africa. *Ko* 42(6, 1977), 473-497.

VYVER, J.D. van der. Die juridiese faset van geregtigheid in die Suid-Afrikaanse samelewing. *Geregtigheid in die Suid-Afrikaanse samelewing.* IBC F3(7, 1977), 58-82.

VYVER, J.D. van der. *Menseregte.* IBC F2(6, 1974), 74pp.

WADLOW, R.V.L. *African churches and social development.* Bulawayo: Daystar Communications, 1973. 8p.

WALSH, P. *Church versus state in South Africa; the Christian Institute and the resurgence of African nationalism.* Waltham: African Studies Association, 1976. 19p.

WALT, B.J. van der. *Reformasie of revolusie.* IBC F1(154, 1980), 31pp.

WALT, I.J. van der. *Die pluraliteit van die kerk.* Th.M.thesis, PU, 1957.

WALT, N. van der. Eenheid of eensaamheid: oor die gemeenskap van die gelowiges. *Venster op die kerk.* IBC F3(12,1980), 20-28.

WALT, N.G.S. van der. Behandel ons die Naturel Christelik? *GV* 16 (8, 1948), 10-11.

WALT, P.J. van der. Menslike verhoudinge onder die soeklig. *Ko* 25(1, 1957), 45-53.

WALT, S.J. van der. *Die segregasiebeleid in wese en in werking gedurende die regime van die Suid-Afrikaanse Republiek 1849-1899.* M.A.-thesis, Unisa, 1936.

WALT, S.P. van der. Indrukke van die Amerikaanse Kleurbeleid in vergelyking met ons beleid van apartheid. *Ko* 17(5, 1950), 187-191.

WALT, T. van der. Kerk-geregtigheid-samelewing. *Geregtigheid in die Suid-Afrikaanse samelewing.* IBC F3(7, 1977), 83-91.

WARK, D. *Church and the war: Has Christianity failed? New moderator's remarkable speech.* [Pietermaritzburg: Times of Natal, 1916]. 13p.

WEISSE, W. *Südafrika und das Antirassismusprogram: Kirchen im Spannungsfeld einer Rassengesellschaft.* Bern: Lang, 1975. 465 p. (Studien zur interkulturellen Geschichte des Christentums; Bd.1).

WESSELS, F.J.H. Die probleem van tussenstaatlike verhoudinge — humanisties en Christelik. *GV* 27(2, 1958), 8-17.

WESTHUIZEN, H.G. van der. Die bybelse basis vir menseregte. *HTS* 34(1/2, 1978), 88-96.

WET, J.I. de. Organisatoriese kerkverband en avondmaalgemeenskap. *HTS* 18(3, 1962), 116-126.

WHISSON, M.G. & WEST, M. eds. *Religion and social change in Southern Africa; anthropological essays in honour of Monica Wilson.* Cape Town: Philip; London: Collings, 1975. 223p.

WILCOCKS, D. Die nuwe wêreldorde. *HZ* 11(1, 1933), 8-15.

WILLIAMS, D. *The missionary as government agent on the eastern frontier, 1818-1931.* M.A. thesis, VW, 1954.

WILSON, M. & MAFEJE, A. *Langa: a study of social groups in an African township.* Cape Town: Oxford University Press, 1963. 190p.

WITWATERSRAND CHURCH COUNCIL. *Gold chains: a record of fifty years of Christian co-operative service through the Witwatersrand Church Council on the world's greatest goldfields, 1898-1948;* by B. Holt, *et al.* Johannesburg: Programme Committee, Witwatersrand Church Council, 1949. 18p.

WOLMARANS, H.P. Die Christelike plig van die Blankes teenoor die Nie-blankes in S.A. *HKA* 1953, 100-112.

WOLMARANS, H.P. Menswaardigheid en menslike regte na aanleiding van die Skrif, *HTS* 18(3, 1962), 83-89.

WORLD COUNCIL OF CHURCHES. A message to Christians in South Africa. Cr 8(1, 1962), 10-11.

WORLD COUNCIL OF CHURCHES. *Mission in South Africa, April-December 1960; report prepared by the WCC elegation to the Consultation in December, 1960:* F.C. Fry, Chairman. Geneva: the Council, 1961. 36p.

WYK, F.J. van. The church and race. *Min* 3(2, 1963), 61-63.

WYK, J.A. van. Latente motiewe in die verklaring van die N.G. Kerk oor: Ras, volk en nasie en volkeverhoudinge in die lig van die Skrif. *NGTT* 17(2, 1976), 98-109.

WYK, J.A. van. Skeiding en verskeidenheid. 'n semantiese studie. *Sta* 26(2, 1972), 38-44.

WYK, J.A. van. Some considerations on the basics of human rights. *TV* 3(2, 1975), 137-141.

WYK, J.A. van. Staatswetgewing en kerklike vryheid. *Stk* 2(3, 1952), 14-24.

WYK, J.A. van. Stellings oor die mens in die arbeid in christelike perspektief. *TV* 8(1, 1980), 44-54.

WYK, J.A. van. *Vernuwing of rewolusie: het die Kerk daar iets oor te sê?* Pretoria: N.G. Kerkboekhandel, [1973]. 50p.

WYK, J.H. van. Kerklike kontak tussen die Afrikaanse en Engelse kerkegroepe in Suid-Afrika. *IdS* 6(24, 1972), 11-44.

WYK, J.H. Van. Nuanses in pasifisme en militarisme. *BCW* 5(20, 1969), 42-55.

WYK, J.H. van. *Die oorlogsvraagstuk: 'n oriëntasie.* IBC F1(49, nd), 21pp.

WYK, J.H. van. Vrede onder bedreiging van oorlog. *Reformasie en revolusie.* IBC F3(2, 1974), 99-118.

YOUNG, E.W.D. Theological reflection on church/state relations in South Africa today. *JTSA* (1, 1972), 37-44.

YOUNG, S.E. Die vyfde gebod. *HKA* 1951, 83-87.

ZULU, A.H. *The dilemma of the Black South African.* Cape Town: University of Cape Town, 1972. 14p. (T.B. Davie memorial lecture; no. 12).

LIST OF ABBREVIATIONS

BCW   *Bulletin van die Suid-Afrikaanse vereniging vir die bevordering van Christelike Wetenskap.*

CM   *Christian Minister*

Cr   *Credo*

C.P.S.A.   Church of the Province of South Africa

C & S   *Church and Society*

EkS   *Ekumene onder die Suiderkruis*

GV   *Die Gereformeerde Vaandel*

HKA   *Almanak*, Nederduitsch Hervormde Kerk

HTS   *Hervormde Teologiese Studies*

HTSvRded   Hervormde Teologiese Studies Studia Theologica Varia, S.P.J.J. van Rensburg dedicata.

HZ   *Het Zoeklicht*/Die Soeklig

IBC   Instituut vir die Bevordering van Calvinisme

IBC F1   Studiestukke/Pamphlets
F3   Versamelwerke/Collections

Ids   *In die Skriflig*

JTSA   *Journal of Theology for Southern Africa*

Ko   *Koers 1*

LM	*Lux Mundi*
Min	*Ministry*
Mis	*Missionalia*
NGKJ	Ned. Geref. *Kerkjaarboek*
NGTT	*Ned. Geref. Teologiese Tydskrif*
OP	*Die Ou Paaie*
PU	Potchefstroom Universiteit
RUC	Rhodes University College
S.A.C.C.	South African Council of Churches
SACR	*South African Clergy Review*
SACUM	Suid Afrikaanse Christelike Uitgewers Maatskappy
SI	*Sol Iustitiae.* Erebundel opgedra aan proff. B B Keet, J C G Kotzé, J J Muller, W J van der Merwe e.a. onder redaksie van P A Verhoef, D W de Villiers en J L de Villiers
Sta	*Standpunte*
Stk	*Die Studiekring*
TCW	*Tydskrif vir Christelike Wetenskap*
TE	*Theologia Evangelica*
TeV	*Teologie en vernuwing,* onder redaksie van I H Eybers, A König en C F A Borchardt. Pretoria: Unisa
TGW	*Tydskrif vir Geesteswetenskappe*

TV	*Theologia Viatorum*
UCOFS	University College of the Orange Free State
UK	University of Cape Town/Kaapstad
UN	University of Natal
UNISA	University of South Africa
UP	University of Pretoria
US	University of Stellenbosch
UV	University of the Orange Free State
UW	University of the Witwatersrand